Activist Identity Development of Transgender Social Justice Activists and Educators

# International Issues in Adult Education

*Series Editor*

Peter Mayo (*University of Malta, Msida, Malta*)

*Editorial Advisory Board*

Stephen Brookfield (*University of St Thomas, Minnesota, USA*)
Waguida El Bakary (*American University in Cairo, Egypt*)
Budd L. Hall (*University of Victoria, BC, Canada*)
Astrid von Kotze (*University of Western Cape, South Africa*)
Alberto Melo (*University of the Algarve, Portugal*)
Lidia Puigvert-Mallart (*CREA-University of Barcelona, Spain*)
Daniel Schugurensky (*Arizona State University, USA*)
Joyce Stalker (*University of Waikato, Hamilton, New Zealand/Aotearoa*)
Juha Suoranta (*University of Tampere, Finland*)

VOLUME 31

The titles published in this series are listed at *brill.com/adul*

# Activist Identity Development of Transgender Social Justice Activists and Educators

*By*

Ksenija Joksimović

BRILL
SENSE

LEIDEN | BOSTON

All chapters in this book have undergone peer review.

The Library of Congress Cataloging-in-Publication Data is available online at http://catalog.loc.gov

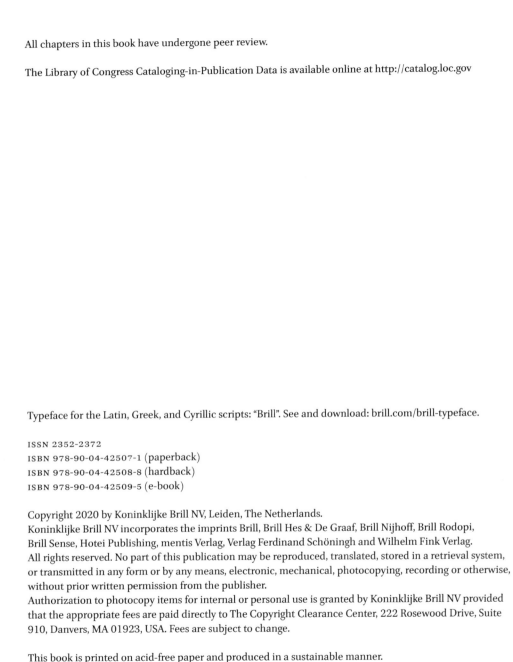

Typeface for the Latin, Greek, and Cyrillic scripts: "Brill". See and download: brill.com/brill-typeface.

ISSN 2352-2372
ISBN 978-90-04-42507-1 (paperback)
ISBN 978-90-04-42508-8 (hardback)
ISBN 978-90-04-42509-5 (e-book)

Copyright 2020 by Koninklijke Brill NV, Leiden, The Netherlands.
Koninklijke Brill NV incorporates the imprints Brill, Brill Hes & De Graaf, Brill Nijhoff, Brill Rodopi, Brill Sense, Hotei Publishing, mentis Verlag, Verlag Ferdinand Schöningh and Wilhelm Fink Verlag.
All rights reserved. No part of this publication may be reproduced, translated, stored in a retrieval system, or transmitted in any form or by any means, electronic, mechanical, photocopying, recording or otherwise, without prior written permission from the publisher.
Authorization to photocopy items for internal or personal use is granted by Koninklijke Brill NV provided that the appropriate fees are paid directly to The Copyright Clearance Center, 222 Rosewood Drive, Suite 910, Danvers, MA 01923, USA. Fees are subject to change.

This book is printed on acid-free paper and produced in a sustainable manner.

# Contents

Acknowledgments  VII

1 Introduction  1
   1  Setting the Framework  9
   2  Key Concepts and Terms  18
   3  Conclusion  22

2 The Research  24
   1  Review of the Existing Research  24
   2  The Research on TGNC Activist Identity Development  31
   3  Research Findings  46
   4  Discussion and Conclusions  69

3 Experiences of Transgender and Gender Non-Conforming People  78
   1  Experiences of Trans and GNC Students  78
   2  Visibility of Trans and GNC Students in Education  81
   3  Psychological Consequences of the Experienced Discrimination  81
   4  Experiences with Mental Health Professionals  84
   5  The Spectrum of Privilege within Trans and GNC Community  87
   6  Discrimination and Microaggressions  89

4 Legal and Policy Framework: Examples of Good Practice  94
   1  Introduction to Legal and Policy Framework  94
   2  General Overview: International Mechanisms and Gender Recognition Laws  98
   3  Examples of Relevant International Mechanisms  101
   4  Legal Gender Recognition: Examples of Good Practice  109
   5  LGBTQI Affirming Education Laws, Policies and Practices  113
   6  Conclusion  121

5 Issues in Trans Community Organizing and Activism  126
   1  History of Transgender Community Organizing  126
   2  Summary of the Issues Trans People Face in Their Daily Life  133
   3  Current Issues in Trans Community Organizing and Activism  138
   4  Contribution of Social Justice Education to Trans Activism  147

**6 Recommendations** 153
1. Recommendations for Education Practice 153
2. Recommendations for Further Research 159

**References** 163

# Acknowledgments

I would like to express my gratitude to Professor Peter Mayo from the University of Malta, for his great encouragement and belief in my work during the process of conducting my Master thesis research, which is presented in this book. Furthermore, I would like to thank my friends: Loren Scott for his valuable feedback on my book, Judith Velasco Rodriguez for her encouragement and belief in me, Ivana Živković for holding a space for me throughout the book writing process, and Radoš Keravica for his moral and financial support in the months that I took off from work, to be able to write this book. Without support from all of you, this book wouldn't have come into life.

Moreover, I would like to thank the participants of my research for their openness, trust, courage, and readiness to be vulnerable and exposed, sharing some of their most challenging life experiences with me. You enriched my life with your life stories of resilience, persistence, radical vulnerability and courage. I hope to represent your voices in the most authentic way.

Finally, I would like to thank to Brill | Sense for recognizing the value of this book, and for offering me a publishing agreement, which I signed on TDOR – International Transgender Day of Remembrance, dedicated to remembrance of trans and gender diverse people who lost their lives due to transphobia. My deepest gratitude goes to Jolanda Karada, Brill | Sense Production Editor, for her professionalism, kindness, and support in the book's production process.

I dedicate this book to the heroes of our queer movement, who have been erased from the history of trans activism and queer activism in general: Marsha P. Johnson and Sylvia Rivera. This book was submitted to the publisher in June 2019, a month that marked the 50 years anniversary of the Stonewall Uprising. They shall not be forgotten.

CHAPTER 1

# Introduction

The book *Activist Identity Development of Transgender Social Justice Activists and Educators* introduces a new area to education, specifically social justice education and adult education for social change. The book draws from my Master thesis research on the same topic conducted with eight trans[1] activists from different European countries, who were at the time the research was conducted, in the leadership positions in organizations working on LGBTQI[2] human rights. The book provides an overview of the issues trans people face in their daily life, such as: discrimination in education and employment; microaggressions in everyday life and from mental health professionals; spectrum of privilege within the trans community; psychological effects of the experienced discrimination and oppression; societal oppression reflected in the history of pathologization and medicalization of trans identities, and other social, human and epistemic injustices that trans people face throughout the world and especially in the European context. Throughout the book, I address how different domains of power, such as hegemonic, structural, disciplinary, and interpersonal, influence the experiences of trans people, and consequently their activist identity development. The book contains chapters on the research on activist identity development among transgender and gender non-conforming (TGNC) social justice activists and educators I have conducted; international legal and policy frameworks relevant for trans-affirming education provision; current issues in trans community organizing and activism; and recommendations for educational theory, practice, and research. The book advocates for trans-affirming, intersectional approach to educational provision, theory, and research. Activist identity development is understood in this book from an intersectional perspective, understanding the multiplicity of identities (both oppressed and privileged) that trans people can have, which exist within the context of connected systems and structures of power (laws, policies, state governments, political and economic unions, religious institutions, media, etc.), and determine trans people's social situatedness, and agency, including the epistemic agency.

The book introduces an anti-oppressive, critical and intersectional approach to social justice activism and education, and adult education for social change. Throughout the book, I use "social justice education" and "adult education for social change" as synonyms for the same type of work on progressive social change.

This book is written for social justice educators and activists, education researchers, especially in the field of anti-oppressive education; educators working in formal education settings, academics and anyone who is interested to learn more on the subject. The book seeks not only to understand and interpret power structures, power relations and inequalities in society which determine social positionality of trans activists and influence the formation and development of their activist identity, but also to challenge them by raising critical consciousness, questioning dominant cultural, political, and social domains.

The Master thesis research titled *Queering the Environment: The Development of the Identity of Adult Educator and Activist for Social Change among Transgender and Gender Non-Conforming People,* presented and elaborated in detail in Chapter 2 of this book, was conducted between February and June 2018, during the last semester of my Master studies – International Master in Adult Education for Social Change. I was a holder of the full Erasmus Mundus scholarship of the European Commission for this program. The program was coordinated by the University of Glasgow, UK, and delivered in cooperation with the University of Malta, Tallinn University, and the Open University of Cyprus. This 2 years long Master program included spending one semester at each partner university.[3] The 4th semester was dedicated to research design, implementation, analysis and writing the Master thesis. I spent this semester at Tallinn University, while traveling to different European countries to conduct face-to-face in depth interviews (Life Story interviews) with participants of my research. My qualitative narrative study was grounded in critical educational research paradigm and intersectionality theory. It explored how transgender and GNC people experience and describe the development of the identity of adult educator and activist for social change, taking into account the intersections between their gender and other identities and material realities (e.g., race, ethnicity, socio-economic status, bodily diversity/sex characteristics, sexual orientation, religion, geographical location). The research sought to understand how activist identity development is mediated through one's intersecting identities, and the role this other identities and experiences of social injustices, played in that intersection. In my research, I used data from conducted Life Story interviews to identify main common themes in adult educator and activist for social change identity development among interviewed trans participants, as described in more detail in Chapter 2. The research I conducted was limited by time and financial factors. As I didn't have a research travel grant, I had to rely only on my monthly scholarship when traveling to interview participants (which impacted the choice of my participants), during the time frame for conducting this research (one semester). Another limiting factor was time availability of my potential interviewees, as all my participants are very busy and are engaged in social justice work not just in the countries they live and work in, but also on the international level. Had I had more time and resources, I would invite more trans activists to participate in my research and of more diverse identities (especially in terms of race, disability, religious affiliation and variations in sex characteristics).

My interest in this specific research topic came from my personal, as well as from my social justice activist experience. I identify as a gender non-conforming person, or more precisely gender non-binary person, and I often use the label queer when talking about my identity and sexuality. Throughout this book, I use the term queer also as an umbrella term, when referring to LGBTQI communities, which will be elaborated further. Moreover, my academic interest in the activist identity development of TGNC people came from my experience of social justice activism on the European level, through my past role of a member of the Executive Board (in 2016) and later a Co-Chair (in 2017) of the world's biggest LGBTQI Youth and Student Network – IGLYO. IGLYO is a pan-European network of over 90 member organizations from more than 40 countries, and is based in Brussels, Belgium.[4] Throughout my work with IGLYO, working on the capacity building of IGLYO member organizations, and participating in numerous international advocacy and networking events, I met with many trans and gender non-conforming (TGNC) activists. I could not avoid noticing that there is a lack of visibility of efforts that trans activists are putting into their social justice work, and the lack of representation of trans activists in the positions of power, influence, and agency even within LGBTQI organizations and queer movement at the European level. Moreover, many TGNC activists I met, often talked about systemic oppression they were experiencing in their countries. At the beginning, I had an assumption that trans activists from the countries which are usually considered to be safe for LGBTQI people and affirmative of their human rights, such as Western European and Nordic countries, are not facing many issues and challenges, as activists coming from the Central and Eastern Europe (as I am) are. But my work experience on the international level from 2015 onward proved that assumption to be wrong. I realized that trans activists, especially those of multiple minority identities, for example, trans activists of color, or living with disabilities, or who belong to an ethnic minority group, face a myriad of issues, regardless of the country they are coming from. These issues are related, but not limited to: lack of access to accessible legal gender recognition procedures, and therefore hindered access to education and employment; access to trans-affirming rather than pathologizing healthcare; overt violence and discrimination because of being trans; homelessness because of difficulties with getting a job due to inaccessible or non-existing legal gender recognition procedures and social stigma, and resulting poverty; engagement in sex work to be able to survive and earn money to cover gender-affirming surgeries, especially in countries where gender affirming surgeries are not funded by the national, public health insurance; criminalization of sex work, and resulting incarceration, etc. During numerous external representations I did on the behalf of IGLYO, participating in and/or moderating panel discussions at the conferences of international organizations, bodies, and institutions (such as the World Health Organization), I noticed a pattern. Apart from the lack of representation of trans people (present at these events), in the positions of power and decision-making, the representatives of the countries present at these events, such as ministers, often believed their country is doing enough for the LGBTQI communities, if it has achieved marriage equality and has adopted anti-discrimination laws. In reality, trans people's human rights have been neglected for decades, until recently. For example, only recently, on May 25, 2019, the World Health Organization has adopted the 11th revision of the International Classification of Diseases, which has removed trans identities from the mental health disorders chapter. Being trans is not considered a mental illness anymore. Moreover, trans people's lived realities, issues they are facing in their daily life, have been invisible not just on the legal and policy level, but in every sphere of life, such as education, employment, healthcare, which is reflected in trans erasure from education theory, research and practice (education provision). Trans issues have been historically neglected within the queer (LGBTQI) communities as well, and have been gaining more attention in the last decade. That is why I have decided to tackle human rights, social, educational and epistemic injustices that trans people face, by using my research as a platform to raise the visibility of the issues concerning trans communities, and to give that platform to trans activists so their voices can be heard. Therefore, I see my Master thesis research and this book as a step towards reparative justice[5] when it comes to trans and gender non-conforming people and their lived realities and epistemologies.

Chapter 1 is dedicated to setting the framework both for the book and my research presented. I discuss the anti-oppressive education, critical perspectives, intersectionality theory and concept of epistemic injustice to ground this book in the field of adult education for social change and social justice activism.

Chapter 2 elaborates my research in more detail, and provides direct quotations of my participants' narratives in relation to the common themes in their activist identity development I identified. However, I decided to include in this book additional chapters, that I haven't written in my thesis. Therefore,

Chapter 3, "Experiences of Trans and Gender Non-Conforming People", is focused on trans people's experiences of discrimination in everyday life, in education, from mental health professionals, and psychological effects of the experienced discrimination on trans people's mental health and well-being; as well as on the spectrum of privilege within TGNC communities, and visibility of trans and GNC identities. Chapter 4, "Legal and Policy Framework", focuses on existing international laws and policies related to trans issues, and provides examples of good practice of trans-affirming laws, policies, and practices that have direct or indirect, but relevant and significant, impact on trans peoples' access to education and the existence of LGBTQI affirming educational provisions. The examples of good practices in the field of education in different countries are provided, specifically in Malta, Norway and the Netherlands. I hope this will be of use to educators working in formal education settings, to become aware of what can be done in relation to LGBTQI affirming education provision. Chapter 5, "Current Issues in Trans Community Organizing and Activism" discusses the issue of trans erasure from the history of queer movements, using as an example trans erasure from the Stonewall Uprising in 1969, an event, or a series of events, which has a historic significance for the LGBTQI communities. Furthermore, this chapter elaborates on the current issues in trans community organizing and activism, and provides an overview of the organizational and funding needs, experiences of trans activists, their groups, and issues they are facing in their daily work (such as lack of funding opportunities for trans organizations and their projects, lack of paid staff in trans specific organizations, and capacity building needs of trans activist groups). This chapter additionally highlights the impact of growing facism in Europe on LGBTQI activism and community organizing, and issues in trans organizing in totalitarian contexts, such as Russia, where currently queer people face persecution. Finally, this chapter discusses the contribution of social justice education to trans activism. Chapter 6, "Recommendations", provides recommentadions for trans inclusive and affirming educational theory, practice and research.

This book is focused mostly on the European context of trans activism and community organizing, as the participants of my resarch are curently living and working in the European context. However, chapters on Legal and Policy Framework and Issues in Trans Community Organizing and Activism, provide examples of good practice and data from across the world.

I hope this book will inspire academics, educators working in formal education settings, social justice and adult education for social change educators and activists, and genderal public reading this book, to reflect on their own social situatedness and positionality, and resulting priviledges, blind-spots, and triggers related to them, as well as on their agency in society and ways in which they can use it to support the trans movement. They can support the trans movement by advocating for trans people's rights, on the local, community, regional, national and international level; advocating for trans-affirming laws, policies, and practices, including those related to education and cross-curricular implementation of LGBTQI affirming education. My hope is that this book will invite the readers to reflect upon the critical questions: Whose history gets remembered and whose history gets erased? Whose living experiences are considered valid, trustworthy, a norm? Whose living experiences are Othered? Who is invited at the decision-making table when important organizational/institutional decisions are being made, and who is left out and why? Who is making important decisions in the name of trans people and about trans people? Who is (over)represented in the positions of power and agency in society and who is underrepresented and why? Who participates in knowledge production in the field of education theory, practice and research and who doesn't and why? How accessible that knowledge production is to persons who are marginally situated in the society on the bais of their multiple minority identitities? All these questions are relevant to anti-oppressive education, as is discussed in the following subchapters of this Introduction chapter.

Finally, I would like to invite the readers to reflect on the mechanisms, means, and tools we have today at our disposal when initiating progressive social change and facilitating social justice activism and adult education for social change. In which ways our means of the fight for human rights are different today from those used during the Stonewall Uprising? I believe we are indebted to the generations of social justice activists and educators who came before us. They deserve to be acknowledged, known, mentioned, discussed, learned about, remembered, and honored. Especially the heroes of our queer movement Marsha P. Johnson and Sylvia Rivera, who played an instrumental role in Stonewall Uprising. They were transgender women, drag queens, persons of color and sex workers, stuggling with homelessness and incarceration (because of homelessness and their gender identity). Their role in the Stonewall Uprising was crucial for the development of queer movements we know today.

I would like to end this Introduction with the quote from the account of Jemiah, a participant of my research. Jemiah is a trans and gender non-binary person of color, social justice activist and educator, currently living and working in Sweden. They moved to Sweden after immigrating from Colombia during their childhod, thanks to their grandmother who immigrated first and invited Jemiah and their mother to join her. Jemiah vividly reflects upon different means of the fight for social justice in different contexts and periods of time, as well as on the importance of understanding how interlocking power structures operate, creating our points of oppression and privilege:

> My grandma used to work as a nurse in Colombia. She left Colombia before I was born. She had also been organized as a sindicalist in Colombia, protecting her sugar cane plantations from the state, paramilitary groups, and private owners. From everyone who wanted to steal her land. The history of my conutry, which is very specific and has a lot of conflicts within, has always lived in me through my DNA. Even though I haven't lived the violence per se, and I haven't been hurt because of the war, I feel it. The legacy of my grandma, the sindicalist legacy is still with me. She is completely apolitical now, but she fought for collective agreements in Colombia. She is the reason why people have salaries, vacations and the right to organize unions in Colombia. And all of her life she has been cleaning white people's toilets, after we moved here. She is the Che Guevara of Colombia and no one knows it. She is completely anonymous, because of racism and everything. But I know. My mom doesnt really care much about activism. She has seen my grandma doing these activist stuff, but she doesn't understand what it feels like to devote your life to a cause. I know what it is like. I can see and acknowledge what my grandma has done. She doesn't speak much about her life as a syndicalist and an activist. She is not identifying as a feminist, but I think she is a feminist. She used to talk to me what it's like to fight patriarchy within the syndicalist movement in Colombia, the men in Colombia. And how they would always make women's voices less heard within their movement, because they thought that class fight is going to solve everything. And the same stuff that she had been fighting for in the 70s in Colombia, I am fighting in 2018 in Sweden.
>
> My grandma had a weapon when she was protecting her sugar cane plantations in Colombia. She is a bit more radical than I am. My goal is not to get into the power of the state and climb to the top. That was the wish of my grandma. She wanted to reach the constitutional mechanisms in Colombia. That's not my goal. But she would ask me: "What have you done in the last couple of months?" And I would say: "Well, I organized this huge event, I did this demonstration, I organized this conference". And she would say: "Yes, but what's the outcome? What's the difference?" And I would say: "Well, there hasn't been a difference in the legislation yet, but we are changing attitudes and norms ...". And she would say: "You have to arm yourself. You have to get a weapon. That's the only way you can fight". I'm like: "No grandma, it doesn't work like that. You cannot just

get a weapon in Sweden and fight. Its a different context. You could hide in a jungle in Colombia, but where am I gonna hide to create a guerrilla?" (laughs).

When it comes to transgenerational trauma, that issue is deffinitelly influential in my case. My mom is so loyal to the Swedish people. There is a Swedish word for immigrants which is "blatte". It's a slur and it means a cockroach. So if you'd want to describe black people owned as slaves in the 1700s and 1800s in the States, you would categorize them in 2 groups: those who worked in the field and those who worked inside the house. The second group, would work in better conditions, compared to those in the field, and they would be called "house N word". When black people, who were working in the field, started the revolution against their white owners, the black people working in the house would protect their owners. They wanted a status quo to remain. In Sweden, we use the word "house" and "field" to describe two different kinds of brown people or immigrants: the ones who want to protect the white person in power and the ones who want to fight white supremacy. My mom is "the house one" because she is so grateful to Swedes for accepting her, giving her asylum and the opportunity to live and work there. She feels we should never complain against white supremacy, and that racism doesn't exist and all that stuff. But I am completely different. And my grandma, who has been oppressed in Sweden for so many years, she knows how capitalism works, she is aware that she is being oppressed. She was a great fighter for people's movement in Colombia, and now in Sweden, she couldn't even retire, because she cannot afford to retire. She is still cleaning white people's toilets. So that transgenerational trauma impacts the way I see Sweden as a society. On the other side, I have a lot of privilege in Sweden, as opposed to my grandma and my mom. I know the language, I have an education, access to opportunities. But with that privilege, I had to learn about oppression, so that I can understand power structures in society, my place in it, and my agency. Because at the end of the day, it is always the woman who is going to do all the house work, its always the brown person who is going to talk about anti-racism and post-colonialism; the black person who is going to raise the voice about afro-phobia. Its always the poor person to talk about what is like to be a from the working class, and the disabled person is gonna talk and advocate for the disability rights movement. And that is not the way it should be. We should advocate for each other's rights. That is also a matter of class: access to information and knodledge about your rights and institutionalized suport you can have access to.

As we can see from Jemiah's account, learning about the development of the identity of social justice educator and activist for social change among transgender and GNC people, from the critical, intersectional perspective is important, because of the lack of trans epistemologies in education, and from the critical, intersectional perspective. This book and the research presented aim towards reparative justice in the field of education, especially adult education for social change and social justice theory, research and practice when it comes to trans epistemologies.

## 1     Setting the Framework

### 1.1     *Anti-Oppressive Education and Critical Perspectives*

This book, the research I have conducted, and my practical social justice education work are grounded in and informed by anti-oppressive education. Johnson (2017, p. 4) highlights that anti-oppression theories: a) acknowledge that we learn oppression through our daily experiences of social and political life and b) we can transform our experiences of oppression through anti-oppressive education aiming at fostering critical consciousness, and collectively transforming oppressive social systems. I would agree with Kumashiro (2002) in understanding oppression as: "a dynamic in which certain ways of being (e.g., having certain identities) are privileged in the society, while others are marginalized" (p. 25). Like Kumashiro, I use in this book the term "Other" to refer to those social groups that are marginaly positioned in the society, and are perceived, treated and understood as *other* than what is considered to be the norm (often cisgender,[6] heterosexual, White, able-bodied, middle-class man). Therefore, I use the word privilege to refer to social situatedness, which doesn't expose the person occupying it to specific forms of oppression. For example, a cisgender, heterosexual, White, able-bodied, middle-class, Christian man living in a predominately Christian, patriarchal society, doesn't experience personally transphobia, sexism, homophobia, racism, disability erasure, islamophobia, poverty and lack of access to social services and opportunities as a result of it. Therefore, he is privileged. He might suffer other life injustices, and discrimination on other grounds, for example, body size, but on the basis of the mentioned identities and material realities resulting in his social situatedness, he is considered to be privileged. Because what we personally don't experience we often think it doesn't exist, McIntosh (1999) spoke about the failure of many men to acknowledge the degree of privilege they have in a society and which they often take for granted in their interactions with others, particularly with women. If we do not critically reflect on our social positionality, and the amount of privilege we hold by the virtue of being, for example, White in a predominantly white society, therefore considered a "norm", we are unaware of the amount of power that racism allows us to have, in our everyday interactions and experiences with others, when looking for a job, etc. If we, however, critically reflect on our social situatedness and take ownership of the social power assigned to us (just because we are born with certain identities), we can use the privilege of having what is perceived as "trustworthy" identities, to speak out about social injustice and act in solidarity with people of marginally situated identities.

Anti-oppressive education, wether it is in the field of social justice education or adult education for social change, is not a settled body of theories and practices, but it rather includes various approaches and frameworks, such as feminist, critical, multicultural, postcolonial, queer[7] (Kumashiro, 2000). Kumashiro (ibid.) understands the anti-oppressive approach as any aducational approach aiming at challenging multiple forms of oppression, which includes asking the difficult and challenging questions. That process of asking difficult questions might make us, educators, uncomfortable, as well as learners (some of the questions are outlined in the above paragraph). But without critically reflecting on what is normalized in one society, what is considered to be the norm, and better said who, and whose lives are considered to be a deviation from the norm, we cannnot understand how knowledge production and what is considered to be a "comonsense" is created (ibid.).

Critical pedagogy is one of the most influential forms of anti-oppressive education. Freire (2000) believed that education is not neutral, and that it can either serve to perpetuate social inequity and oppression, or it can use the curriculum to support learners to critically reflect on their positions in the society and agency they have to initiate social change. Freire acknowledged that social, political and cultural realities are created by us, people, and that they can be changed by people who engage in critical reflection about the systems of power that perpetuate social inequity, and who engage in action to change them. Therefore, social transformation is possible, it is everyone's responsibility, and any curriculum that ignores to tackle the oppression actually supports the status quo. This book, and the research presented in it, are anchored on these premises. Therefore, the aim of this book is to foster critical consciousness among the readers, understood as the capacity of a person to critically reflect on their own lived experience in an opresive society, and to act toward social transformation (Freire, 2000).

Likewise, the research I conducted (presented in Chapter 2) is grounded in Critical theory and intersectionality theory. Critical theory is a framework, a way of thinking and a way of problematizing, and can be understood as an umbrella for a range of other theories: critical race theory, critical pedagogy, critical disability theory (Cohen et al., 2011), and of relevance for this book, intersectionality theory. The critical theory allows us to understand the power structures within systems of oppression experienced by TGNC individuals, and also to recognize the multiple realities within the various s systems of power and oppression for TGNC persons (Prasad, 2005). The critical research paradigm originated from the criticism that educational research is neglecting social inequalities and power issues related to knowledge production (Mack, 2010).

The term intersectionality is associated with Kimberlé Crenshaw's *Mapping the Margins: Intersectionality, Identity Politics, and Violence against Women of Color* (1991) and Black feminism, especially Combahee River Collective's 'A Black Feminist Statement (1979). They argued that African American women's lives, cannot be understood only by looking at the oppression based on race or only based on gender. They argue that race, class, gender, and sexuality all shape the living experiences and realities of Black women.

Intersectionality refers to the "critical insight that race, class, gender, sexuality, ethnicity, nation, ability, and age operate not as unitary, mutually exclusive entities, but rather as reciprocally constructing phenomena" (Collins, 2015, p. 1). Intersectionality theory offers an understanding of the multiplicity of identities for both oppressed and privileged identities (Cole, 2009), which exist within a context of connected systems and structures of power, such as laws, policies, state governments, political and economic unions, religious institutions, and media (Hankivsky, 2014). People can experience privilege and oppression simultaneously, depending on their different identities, social positionality and the specific context they are in (Hankivsky, 2014). Intersectionality theory acknowledges how multiple social locations interact, defining the position of a person in the society, their location on the privilege-discrimination spectrum and access to social services and opportunities.

As of Jemiah, the participant in my research, quoted above, said about the syndicalist movement Jemiah's grandmother was a part of in Colombia, the class struggle was the primary one for the movement, while sexism and patriarchy within the movement were left unacknowledged. bell hooks was one of the first feminist theorists who wrote about intersecting dimensions of sexism and racism (hooks, 1981). At the time when critical pedagogy was predominantly focused on class issues, she cast a light on the intersections of class, of race and gender.

Therefore, intersectionality as a perspective has developed to acknowledge that oppressions based on gender, race, and class, and later sexual orientation and gender identity, and other locations cannot be undrestood as separated, and are interrelated. These oppressions are experienced simultaneously by those who live on the margins (Combahee River Collective, 1979; Crenshaw, 1991).

### 1.2 *Adult Education for Social Change*

As already noted, in this book I use the terms social justice educator and adult educator for social change interchangeably, and as synonyms, because both refer to the progressive social change work in the field of education that activists who are participants of my reseach are engaged in. However, I would like to position my book and the research I conducted on the topic of activist identity development of TGNC social justice educators and activists, in the field of adult education for social change.

In the adult education literature, adult education for social change is most often understood as "critical, emancipatory, transformative, strategic, socially critical, liberal, radical or revolutionary" (Foley, 2007) and described with values of "social justice, greater social and economic equality, the promotion of a critical democracy [and] a vision of a better, fairer world" (Johnston, 2006, p. 409). However, that does not mean that adult education for social change is conceptualized as a monolithic and universal notion of social justice (Hoff & Hickling-Hudson, 2011). It is instead the ideological position of the actors aiming to achieve social change what determines the content of adult education for social change (ibid.). That can vary, from progressive efforts such as challenging economic injustices and exploitation; combating homophobia, transphobia, racism, environmental destruction, HIV related stigma, etc., to the neoliberal developmental model and conservative efforts, such as the introduction of religious values into all forms of governance (ibid.).

I would agree with Hoff and Hickling-Hudson (2011), who proposed, on the basis of postcolonial theory, a complex of five interrelating elements, when talking about the role of international Non-Governmental Organizations in promoting adult education for social change. These five elements are:

1. *Representation* – in theory and practice. The Eurocentric famework of the established research, which marginalizes the voices of the oppressed, is apparent at the theoretical level (epistemic violence) and reflected in practice.
2. *Transformational potential* – Through social change education, such as learner-centered and critical pedagogy popularized by Paulo Freire (2000), marginalized people can reflect on and examine how to take their power back.

3. *Multiple perspectives* – Depiction of the histories of oppression in binary terms, such as oppressed vs. oppressor, North vs. South, dominant vs. subaltern is too simplistic (Venn, 2006). Postcolonial theory [along with the intersectionality theory and queer theory when it comes to gender issues[8]], supports the understanding of the subjects and identities in their complexity and multiplicity.
4. *Multi-causality* – Because the existing economic, political, and social conditions shape the content and the aims of adult education for social change curricula, progressive social change which aims at their transformation through adult education, is context-specific.
5. *Historicism* – Adult education for social change calls for historical contextualization and analysis of the dominant ideologies that shape the construction of the normative discourses and understandings of "reality".

In this book, when talking about adult education for social change, I refer to this type of provision that has these five elements as cornerstones of socially transformative work.

As already highlighted, when talking about my research participants, I use the terms "adult educator and activist for social change", and "social justice educator and activist" simultaneously and interchangeably. That is also because some of my research participants who identify as social activists, would not identify as adult educators for social change, even though their work is undoubtedly of an adult educator for social change. From my activist experience, the terms (social) activist and social justice educator, are widespread among people who identify as activists, while the term "adult educator for social change" is more frequent in the professional (including academic) circles of people whose educational background is in adult education. Moreover, not every adult educator is an activist or adult educator for social change (or social justice educator). What distinguishes social justice oriented adult educators and activists for social change from adult educators in general, can be understood through the already described concept of critical consciousness. Some authors argue that the acquisition of critical consciousness is a crucial aspect of political development, which involves learning and gaining of knowledge to (1) critically analyze the status quo and its socially unjust nature, and (2) understand and imagine society from radically alternative viewpoints directed toward social liberation (e.g., Freire, 1970; Reicher, 2004).

## 1.3  Epistemic Injustice

The value of critical and intersectionality theory in grounding this book can be better understood through the concept of epistemic injustice (Fricker, 2007) since this book and the research presented aim to raise the visibility of trans epistemologies, and are a platform for trans activists so their voices can be heard. According to the ground-breaking work of Miranda Fricker on epistemic injustice (ibid.), social understanding and individual's understanding of their own social experiences, belong to a sphere of epistemic activity, where relations of identity and power can create a specific kind of epistemic injustice. That implies that marginalized social groups often have difficulties challenging distorted social understandings of their identities, lived realities and social experiences.

Fricker distinguishes between two types of epistemic injustice: *testimonial injustice* and *hermeneutical injustice*. Both imply "a wrong done to someone specifically in their capacity as a knower" (ibid., p. 1). She centers the analysis of both types of injustice on the concept of social power, which she understands as "a socially situated capacity to control others' action" (ibid.), and which includes incredulity, misinterpretation, and silencing. Flicker particularly reflects upon "identity power" (ibid., p. 4) and its harmful effects when it involves identity prejudices which deny credibility to/from speakers who are members of a minority social groups. She argues that hermeneutical injustice implies having some significant area of one's social experience hidden from collective understanding due to a structural prejudice, when "a gap in collective interpretive resources puts someone at an unfair disadvantage when it comes to making sense of their social experiences" (ibid., p. 1).

The biggest harm of hermeneutical injustice lies in the fact that the individual or the group holding a minority identity are unfairly disadvantaged by a lack of collective understanding of their lived realities. That is directly related to the construction of a social identity, for example, an identity of TGNC social activist, which will be elaborated in chapters below. Hermeneutical injustice can mean, in certain social contexts, that someone is socially constituted as something they are not, and is prevented from becoming who they really are as is often the case with TGNC people. The lack of visibility and representation in the positions of power, agency, and influence that TGNC people experience, seems to be related to the concept of epistemic injustice and its specific form of hermeneutical injustice. Especially, having in mind that TGNC people's gender identity is very often socially invalidated, pathologized, disqualified and not legally recognized in many countries in Europe.

Furthermore, another type of epistemic injustice, testimonial injustice, occurs when "prejudice causes a hearer to give a deflated level of credibility to a speaker's word" (ibid., p. 1).

That means that members of minority social groups are often not acknowledged as subjects of knowledge, and therefore are harmed in their self-development (ibid., p. 5). Fricker suggests that in that sense, people are prevented from becoming who they are (ibid.). The lack of presence and visibility of trans-related topics in education, including adult education for social change and social justice education literature, research and practice, is an overt example of testimonial injustice and erasure of trans epistemologies. Together with hermeneutical injustice and the lack of visibility, factual and actual understanding of trans and GNC people's lives, needs and struggles, epistemic injustice becomes a concept central to this book, and to the research presented in Chapter 2.

1.3.1     Queer Epistemology and Epistemic Injustice

From the perspective of queer epistemology, testimonial injustice refers not only to silencing those who do not conform to the "norm", of what is considered to be "normal", "usual" in one country or a context, but also to perpetuating epistemic injustice by pressuring the Othered to occupy a certain identity category, and define themselves in relation to what is considered to be the norm, as in the case when people are not heterosexual or cisgender (Hall, 2017). The Queer theory radically questions fixed, binary categories of gender and sexuality (Sullivan, 2006). According to Hall (2017), queer theory destabilizes two predominant assumptions about sexuality in Western contexts: (1) that sexuality is fixed part of the innate human nature and (2) that person's sexuality exists in an independent way and is established before a person's need to understand it and name it. Queer theory is interested in understanding how power relations influence a person's understanding of their sexuality and gender. People who are not heterosexual and cisgender are pressured to come out and reveal to the world their sexual orientation and/or gender identity. They are often asked how they know they are who they say they are, and are asked to define themselves in "acceptable" binary terms of sexuality (homosexual or heterosexual) and gender (often referred as (biological) sex, seen as a binary category: male or female). Queer theory challenges binary notions of gender and sexuality and understands both as a spectrum. The term queer refers both to sexualities and gender identities outside of the binaries. It is often used by people who don't identify with binary gender roles, such as trans and gender non-conforming people and/or with the binary concepts of sexuality (pansexuality, for example, is a capacity to feel attraction towards people of various gender identities). Furthermore, when referring to a community, queer is used as an umbrella term referring to the whole LGBTQI community, as opposed to saying "gay community", because not everyone in the community is, what is considered to be the norm, a cisgender, gay man.

*Willful Hermeneutic Injustice* is a concept coined by Gaile Pohlhaus, Jr. (2012) to address the reconception of the hermeneutic injustice from the queer perspective.

According to Pohlhaus Jr. (ibid.) the problem is not only the absence of resources among marginally situated knowers to conceptualize their realities. The problem also lies in the refusal of knowers who are dominantly socially situated, to allow their understanding of the world to be impacted by the knowledge of those who are marginally situated, and which is coming from their lived realities, experiences, and understandings of the world.

Queer epistemologies do not understand knowledge to be the opposite of ignorance. Queer epistemologies don't essentialize and generalize sexualities and gender identities, assuming all people of the same sexuality and gender identity have the same experiences, and/or are a homogenous group, sharing a "common knowledge". Queer epistemologies value epistemic humility of not-knowing, or better said, of what remains unknown, which can be critically reflected upon, or possibly even unknowable (Hall, 2017). As Hall (2017) highlighted, although queer epistemologies might be understood as a "failure to know", or "failure of knowledge", they actually value the possibilities of existing and knowing differently, outside of the norm (ibid.). Queer epistemologies understand knowledge as a work in progress, through the process of deconstruction, revision, and re-construction. They aim at understanding how truth, desire, sexualities, and identities are shaped by the power relations in society, and the implications of that dynamic on the process of knowing and understanding oneself and others (Hall, 2017). Queer epistemologies value revision of what is known and critical reflection upon the current knowledge. According to Hall (2017), they value epistemically resistant rather than an epistemically assimilationist strategy of conforming to the norm of that is considered to be "normal" and the "natural" (ibid.). As such, queer theory and epistemologies belong to the body of critical theory and are complementary with intersectionality theory. For example, transgender gay migrant, who is a sex worker and a person of color, might suffer multiple discrimination, based on their gender identity, sexuality, migration status, ethnicity and/or race and sex work related stigma. Additionally, they can experience harassment from the police, and other state institutions, if they are not protected by the law. Therefore, assuming that they, as a trans person, have universally shared experiences with all trans people, implies erasure of the fact that transphobia they experience is shaped by racism, xenophobia, sex work stigma, anti-refugee discourses, and vice versa. If they decide to become a social justice activist, we cannot understand their activist identity development just by taking into account their gender identity or their occupation, and by understanding their gender identity in an essentialist way. Therefore, my understanding of gender identity and more specifically, trans identities and trans issues, in this book, comes from critical, queer and intersectionality theory, as it will be explained below in Section 2 (Key Concepts and Terms).

When it comes to the lack of presence of queer, and specifically trans epistemologies in academia and education, including in, paradoxically, adult education for social change and social justice education, I believe the critical question that needs to be asked is: "Who participates in the creation of hegemonic epistemologies, and in creation of what is considered a "common knowledge" in academia and education?

I would agree with Collins (2017) that hegemonic epistemologies are not created regardless of political and social factors, but are rather shaped by them, and further construct the social and the political domains. I would agree with Collins (ibid.) that the epistemological gate-keeping in academia is a result of the epistemic injustice perpetuated by the social inequity and epistemic oppression. Epistemic oppression negates or devalues the agency and validity of epistemologies of the marginally situated social groups, while promoting and privileging epistemic agency and legitimacy of the privileged, dominantly socially situated knowers in society, and consequently in academia, as well.

I would also agree with Collings (ibid.) that dominant epistemologies in academia have historically valued decontextualized, abstract, rational, "objective", and generalizable knowledge. In academic circles, that type of knowledge has gained legitimacy over time, over subjective knowledge, phenomenological and critical understandings of the knowledge production, multiple levels of subjectivity, coming from lived experiences, and face-to-to face interactions. It excludes emotionality, corporality, and not just rational ways of knowing. It is not surprising that to this day women and people of feminine gender identities and expressions are often overrepresented in disciplines that are concerned with the "emotional", the "subjective", and with care, such as psychology, psychotherapy, nursing, teaching, etc. It is a result of the patriarchal *socialization for gender rolers and the* binary division on feminine and masculine "opposites". Epistemologies traditionally associated with masculinity (valuing the objective, rational, generalizable, quantitatively measured knowledge) are considered to be more valid and trustworthy. Social justice education and adult education for social change which are concerned with the lived personal and social experiences, should be inclusive of the knowledge that comes from lived experiences of marginally situated individuals and groups.

Collins (2017) highlights that within the academy which values objectivity seen as the antidote to bias associated with the subjectivity, knowledge production that comes from politics and ethics of actions of social justice is often delegitimized (unless it serves the interests of those in power).

I would agree with Collins (ibid.) in recognition that intersectionality is "socially constructed by the interpretive communities organized by the testimonial practices of their members" (p. 121), which often happens face-to-face, in case in trans activism and community organizing (even when means of online communications are used, interactions are personal and welcome the subjective experience). Meanwhile, in academia, according to Collins (ibid.) testimonial practices are organized in mediated ways, such as academic conferences, patterns of citation, articles selected to be published in academic journals. According to Collins (ibid.), in academia white men are more authoritative than persons of other gender identities, while theoretical knowledge is more valued over the practical experience.

Therefore, established testimonial interactions within the academy can reproduce epistemic inequality, injustice, and oppression, which explains the lack of trans epistemologies not just in academia, but in formal education as well, at all levels. In Chapter 5 I provide my personal reflection on the lack of trans epistemologies in academia and education for social change, due to privileging the epistemology of the well-established social actors.

## 2   Key Concepts and Terms

### 2.1   *Transgender, Trans and Gender Non-Conforming*

Consistent with past transgender research (Beemyn & Rankin, 2011) in this I book use transgender or trans as an all-encompassing term used to refer to people whose gender identity does not align with the sex assigned to them at birth. This umbrella term includes different subgroups often referred to in the literature as MTF (male to female) and FTM (female to male) transsexual (individuals seeking gender-affirming surgeries and/or hormone replacement therapy (HRT) to align their body with their internal sense of gender identity); gender non-conforming (individuals who do not conform to societal gender roles), and gender non-binary (a person who doesn't identify either as a man or a woman. They can identify as both, for example, a bigender person; or they can be a genderqueer person who does not identify with gender labels; or agender person who does not identify with any gender, etc.).

As already described in the Section 1.3.1 in the Introduction, I adopt the position which comes from the queer theory and which sees gender as a spectrum rather than two opposed binary categories. Therefore, I use in this book terms transgender and gender non-conforming (TGNC) simultaneously, to refer to people who do not conform to societal norms they are expected to perform when it comes to their gender identity, acknowledging the diversity of transgender identities and gender diversity in general.

Furthermore, I use the term cisgender to refer to individuals who are not transgender, which is a common practice within queer activist communities. It is important to acknowledge that trans individuals may choose to use pronouns to refer to themselves that do not match the pronouns one might assume they use. When referring to my concrete participants, I use the pronouns of their choice. In addition, a singular pronoun *they* is used instead of he and she, referring to a single person, as an example of inclusive language and the use of pronouns that do not endorse gender binary, acknowledging non-binary identities, as recommended by the Maltese education policy *Trans, Gender variant and Intersex students in schools* (Ministry for Education and Employment of Malta, 2015, p. 4). For example, instead of saying: "As he stated, his family attitudes have changed ...", I would say: "As they stated, their family attitudes have changed ..." referring to a single individual, using *They* as a singular pronoun.

### 2.2   *Social Justice Activism*

Social justice activism refers to "disrupting and subverting arrangements that promote marginalization and exclusionary processes" (Theoharis, 2007, p. 223). According to Goldfarb and Grinberg, this can involve "actively engaging in reclaiming, appropriating, sustaining, and advancing inherent human rights of equity, equality, and fairness in social, economic, education, and personal dimensions" (quoted in Theoharis, 2007, p. 223).

Social justice activism aims to "directly, or indirectly improve individual lives through strategic initiatives that impact the domains of power" (Pratt-Clarke, 2010, p. 41).

Pratt-Clarke (2010) presented the Transdisciplinary Applied Social Justice Model (TASJ model), in the book *Critical race, feminism, and education* (pp. 40–41). The model is both the theoretical and the methodological tool for engaging in social justice research and practice. In this book, social justice activism is understood through the lens of TASJ model.

TASJ model includes the four domains of power: hegemonic, structural, disciplinary, and interpersonal. The hegemonic domain includes systems of ideology, thoughts, perspectives, values, beliefs, and stereotypes, that are often shaped by history. More specifically, this domain includes racism, sexism, classism, and other systems of oppression rooted in ideologies about individuals (homophobia, transphobia, etc.), as well as alternative ideologies that challenge these dominant standpoints. The disciplinary domain includes invisible and visible laws, policies, practices, procedures, regulations, which are in alignment with ideologies from the hegemonic domain. This domain legitimizes the hegemonic domain by turning ideologies into concrete policies and practices. This disciplinary domain is applied directly within the structural domain, which includes institutions, systems, and structures ("state", and systems within the state, such as the education system, the legal system, the healthcare system, etc.). The interpersonal domain involves individuals and their daily interactions, including the individuals who are in the role of leaders and gatekeepers (who are empowered and legitimized to implement policies and procedures in the disciplinary domain). All these domains are shaped by individuals and groups with mutually interwoven identities, which dynamically influence each other through different levels of agency (race, gender identity, class, ethnicity, nationality, sexuality, disability, social location, etc.). These identities carry various levels of entitlement, privilege, socially affirmed dominance, and unearned advantage comparing to others (ibid.). These identities shape life experiences of individuals, which is reflected in their life stories, narratives, and discourses, that are formed within specific contexts. The legitimacy of these narratives is often questioned, ignored, silenced, or they are re-shaped, and told by the voices of those who hold bigger social and epistemic agency in the given context. According to Pratt-Clarke (2010), these narratives are of the vital importance for understanding social justice activism, and they must inform the social justice activism.

I agree with the understanding of activism offered by Pratt-Clarke (2010, p. 4), according to which social justice activism aims to "directly or indirectly improve individual lives through strategic initiatives that impact the domains of power". Throughout the book, I tackle all four domains of power presented in the TASJ model: hegemonic, structural, disciplinary, and interpersonal. I elaborate on how each domain of power influences trans and gender non-conforming people's life experiences, so that the narratives of participants of my research could be understood in their complexity and depth. Throughout the chapters of this book, I elaborate on all domains of power that influence trans people's social situatedness, and agency in society: from dominant ideologies reflected in the laws, policies, procedures implemented by the states and state's institutions; to state's gatekeepers who determine knowledge production and epistemic legitimacy of the knowledge of those who are marginally situated.

It is important to take into consideration when discussing social justice activism, that trans people who are marginally situated in society based on different minority identities, can often be considered minorities within the LGBTQI communities (Hagen, Hoover & Morrow, 2018). The issues faced by White, cisgender, able-bodied, gay men tend to have more visibility, while trans people of multiple minority diverse identities based on ethnicity, race, sex characteristics, ability, religion, etc., tend to be less visible and represented within the queer movement (ibid.). Moreover, transgender women have historically been excluded from women-only activist spaces (Gamson, 1997) because of cisgender and separatist women's biases (Stone, 2009).

## 2.3   *Activist Identity Development*

Being an activist, an adult educator for social change and a leader means taking on an active role in enacting social change to the benefit of humankind (Komives, Lucas, & McMahon, 2007).

While there is numerous research done on the leadership identity development, especially focusing on stage models of identity development (Komives et al., 2005, 2006, 2007), one of the most influential theories in social identity development is Cross's Nigrescence Theory (Cross, 1971, 1991, 1995; Cross & Vandiver, 2001), related to the development of a Black social identity (as opposed to personal identity; in reference to other group members). It has been used throughout the years by different scholars researching different social identities, such as feminist identity, LGBT identity, Latino identity, and of importance to this book, transgender identity development (Gagné, Tewksbury, & McGaughey, 1997).

Cross and Vandiver (2001) understood identity development as a result of socialization that occurs in a lifespan, from infancy to adulthood, but also as a result of experiences or encounters that catalyze change. In this book, I adopt this understanding of social identity development, which will be elaborated in more detail in Chapter 2. While there is a body of research on the relationship between LGBT identity and activist and leadership identity, the research and the literature on the social justice activist identity development among transgender and gender non-conforming people specifically is still scarce (Hagen, Hoover & Morrow, 2018).

Activist identity development, especially in relation to development of the identities of LGBTQI people is a topic that has been gaining momentum in the last decade, specifically in relation to LGBTQI college students' identities and experiences (Renn, 2007) and LGBTQI students' leadership (Renn & Bilodeau, 2005a, 2005b; Renn & Ozaki, 2005). Most of the studies conducted use qualitative methodology to explore the issue of LGBTQI identity development and leadership development of LGBTQI people, focusing on university and college students. However, research on LGBTQI identity development and leadership development often focuses exclusively on the experiences of cisgender LGB people, while excluding TGNC people (Renn, 2007).[9] Moreover, most research involving the LGBT community tends to concentrate primarily on gay men, which is then generalized to the entire LGBTQI community (Chang & Chung, 2015). According to Nadal et al. (2012), one of the major problems with these studies lies in the fact that they tend to focus primarily on cis lesbian and gay participants, failing to recognize the unique experiences of transgender people. Very often in the studies conducted, if they include transgender people, they do not acknowledge the diversity of transgender identities and heterogeneity of trans communities. Instead, often they focus only on people who have undergone medical transition,[10] and/or who identify as transgender man or woman excluding genderqueer, gender non-binary people (ibid.).

## 3    Conclusion

It becomes clear that learning about the development of the identity of social justice adult educator and activist for social change among transgender and GNC people, is important for the reparation of epistemic injustice that TGNC people face in academia and specifically in the field of education. The research presented in Chapter 2 brings novelty to the field of education, especially adult education for social change and social justice education theory, research and practice in several ways, by:

1. Filling the gap in education literature and research in relation to gender identities beyond gender binaries such as trans and GNC identities and in relation to the development of the identity of adult educator and activist for social change of TGNC people.
2. Raising awareness among educators and academics on how to develop trans-affirming education provision and curricula, taking into account recommendations provided in Chapter 6.
3. Critically working towards more inclusive adult and social justice education theory, provision and research which values critical and intersectional approach, taking into account power structures, power relations in the given society that influence knowledge production and produce epistemic injustice towards those who are marginally situated. That includes carrying out research "with" rather than "on" marginally situated people in order to empower research participants to use their agential power to change oppressive conditions (Hoff & Hickling-Hudson, 2011).

### Notes

1   Trans is an umbrella term referring to transgender and gender non-conforming people, whose sense of gender identity differs from the sex assigned to them at birth.
2   Lesbian, Gay, Bisexual, Transgender, Queer and Intersex. Queer refers to gender identities outside of the gender binary (people who don't identify with binary gender roles), but is also used to refer to sexuality which is not binary, such as pansexuality for example (a capacity to feel attraction towards people of various gender identities). Furthermore, when used to refer to a community, queer is used as an

INTRODUCTION

umbrella term for the whole LGBTQI community. As opposed to saying "gay community", because not everyone in the community are gay men, in this book I use the term queer as an umbrella tern. Intersex refers to variations in sex characteristics, and bodily diversity, and is an affirming term used instead of an outdated, stigmatizing term hermaphrodite.

3  Except for the Open University of Cyprus which delivered courses online.
4  Member organizations (their representatives) are gathered once per year in different European countries at the Annual Members Conference (AMC), which was formerly called General Assembly. They represent the highest decision making body of the organization. Every year they elect members of the Executive Board of the Network, consisting of 6–8 people from member organizations from different European countries, aged at the time of the election between 18 and 30 years, out of which two serve the role of the Co-Chairs. Members of the Executive Board are elected for a 2-year mandate. The Executive Board employs the Secretariat of the Organization, to implement the work of the network.
5  Reparative justice refers to political practices of reparation towards individuals and groups who have been misstreated and oppressed in various ways, whether by moral/etical wrongding done to them, or wrongdoing of authorities who failed to provide justice towards them, or through political and/or social oppression. The concept of reparative justice includes the reparative possibilities and responsibilities that institutions such as universities, churches, governments, corporations can do to make amends for the wrong doing both in symbolic and material ways (Walker, 2010).
6  Not transgender.
7  Queer theory radically questions fixed, binary categories of gender and sexuality (Sullivan, 2006).
8  While acknowledging the need to challange reproduction of patriarchal gender related stereotypes and oppression in society and in adult education, it is important to remember that the picture is not as simple and binary as: 'white men who opress white women', although that is also important to address. Gender, seen as a spectrum, can intersect with different indentities and material realities. If we want to challange oppression that for example, a trans woman who is a sex worker, and is also a person of color might face in their life, not only from white men but also from the middle class, cisgender, white women, and general society which reproduces structural and systemic inequality and oppression.
9  Often that is done by reinforcing the gender binary assumption that acknowledges the legitimacy of only 2 genders, assuming that all people must identify with the gender assigned to them at birth or if not, they have to identify as either man or woman.
10 Refers to gender affirming surgeries and/or hormone replacement therapy (HRT) to allign a person's body with their own sense of their gender identity.

CHAPTER 2

# The Research

This chapter presents a brief overview of the influential research on the topic of activist identity development among LGBT, and specifically trans people; transgender identity development and the intersections between them.[1] The existing research informs my research and is presented at the beginning of this chapter. This chapter further elaborates on my Master thesis research conducted in 2018 titled *Queering the Environment: The Development of the Identity of Adult Educator and Activist for Social Change among Transgender and Gender Non-Conforming People*. Finally, this chapter presents the main findings of my research: common themes and issues in activist identity development identified from the analysis of the interviews conducted between February and June 2018, with eight transgender and gender non-conforming (TGNC) people. All participants were from different countries,[2] and were at the time in leadership positions in organizations working on the advancement of LGBTQI human rights throughout Europe.

## 1 Review of the Existing Research

When reviewing the literature around the topic of my research, I was looking for research on topics such as activist identity development of LGBTQI people, activist development of TGNC people and transgender identity development. Therefore, I will present a brief overview of the studies related to each of the topics.

### 1.1 Transgender Identity Development

The studies reviewed below provide a brief overview of the research done on transgender identity development. Some of the presented models of transgender identity development have similarities with the stages of Expanded Theory of Nigrescence (Cross & Vandiver, 2001), which is one of the most influential theories of social identity development, and is developed from Cross's Nigrescence Theory (Cross, 1971, 1991, 1995; Cross & Vandiver, 2001). Cross and Vandiver (2001) formulated the Expanded Nigrescence Theory to explain the development of a Black social identity (in relation to other group members). They understood social identity development through socialization during a lifespan, from infancy to adulthood. Moreover, they acknowledged that social identity development can be influenced by experiences or encounters that enact change. Expanded theory of Nigrescence is particularly useful for understanding how activists with marginalized social identities might shift from organizing their identity around assimilation, miseducation, or self-hatred, to a sense of pride in who they are, resulting in deep engagement in social struggles their group faces.

The first stage of developing a Black identity, according to the Expanded Nigrescence Theory (Cross & Vandiver, 2001), is a Pre-Encounter, where an individual is disconnected from the Black culture through either assimilation (identifying only as American), self-hatred (hating Black people and culture), or miseducation (accepting attitudes held by dominant culture about Black people and their culture). The next stage, Encounter, happens when an individual becomes aware of the racialized world around them. The following stage is Immersion-Emersion. This stage is characterized by polarities, individuals present themselves as anti-White or are exclusively focused on Black culture. The third stage, when individuals accept and feel proud of their Black identity, is the Internalization stage. Individuals who have internalized their Black identity can focus on their Black culture and empowerment. Those who reach the Internalization stage can work with people of diverse identities, while simultaneously feeling proud of their Black heritage and culture.

This model of social identity development is used in the research of different minority groups and might serve as an interesting framework for thinking about transgender identity development, as well.

Gagné, Tewksbury, and McGaughey (1997) conducted research with 65 FTM (male-to-female) trans individuals and developed a four-step transgender identity development process. In the beginning, participants thought of their gender identities in terms of difference. They were pressured conform to gender roles related to sex assigned to them at birth, and conceal their true gender identity. Further, a Self-identification phase included finding others who had similar experiences of their gender identity, or learning the terminology related to their feelings about who they are. Social stigma about gender non-conformity would often lead participants to come out first to themselves. After that, they could come out to others, and express their true gender identity publically. This stage was characterized by the fear of how others would react to and cope with them coming out as trans. Researchers noted that trans participants in medical transition had less control over their coming out as they had to disclose their gender identity to therapists and physicians in order to obtain clearance and access to gender affirming surgeries (medical transition).

Finally, the last phase of transgender identity development included living as their true selves.

Bockting and Coleman (2007) created a five stage transgender identity development model, based on Coleman's (1982) gay identity development model. Similarly, the five stages are pre-coming out, coming out, exploration, intimacy, and identity integration. The researchers noted that with a newly established gender role, a person might be required to come out twice: first as transgender, and then in relation to their sexuality. Bockting and Coleman (2007) highlighted that not all trans people will go through the same stages outlined in transgender identity development models, linearly. The developmental process depends on a person's personality, level of resilience, support system, local community, etc.

Bilodeau and Renn (2005) warned that stage models should not be seen as hierarchical: the final stage doesn't represent the highest point that has to be achieved or which is achievable by everyone.

Morgan and Stevens (2012) interviewed six transgender adults and analyzed data from a lifespan perspective, identifying three prominent themes: an early sense of body-mind dissonance, managing and negotiating identities, and the process of transition. However, the concept of transition is complex in a sense that many transgender individuals use non-binary identities, such as genderqueer and gender non-binary and choose not to take hormone replacement therapy or undergo gender affirming surgeries (Kuper, Nussbaum, & Mustanski, 2012).

Katz-Wise et al. (2018) conducted a study to identify pathways of transgender identity development using narratives from both transgender and gender non-conforming (GNC) youth and their cisgender caregivers. The sample included 16 families, 16 trans and GNC youth, from 7 to 18 years old, and 29 cisgender caregivers. Trans and GNC youth represented diverse gender identities, including trans boy, trans girl, gender-fluid boy, and girlish boy. Caregivers included mothers, fathers, and one grandmother. The conceptual framework included seven main themes:

1. Trans identity development (a complex interplay of phenomena that constitute processes of being oneself, both internal and external; realization of transgender identity, both gradual and immediate, and transition processes),
2. Sociocultural influences/societal discourse (sociocultural norms and discourse about gender and transgender identity influenced youths' gender identity development and the ways in which caregivers responded and adjusted),

3. Biological influences (puberty as a developmental stage that both catalyzed transgender identity realization and complicated youths' sense of self, as their bodies changed in ways that were in dissonance with their affirmed gender identities),
4. Family adjustment/impact (the ways in which a family adjusts to and is impacted by a youth's transgender identity may affect the youth's identity development and access to support/resources related to their gender identity),
5. Stigma/cisnormativity (experiences of discrimination and hostility impacted the ways in which transgender youth coped with gender identity and expression across different contexts),
6. Support/resources (receiving social support: professional support, support groups, and interactions with other transgender youth and their families, and broader community support and being able to access resources shaped the ways in which youth came to understand their gender identity), and
7. Sender affirmation/actualization (ways in which caregivers supported their child in facilitating processes of gender actualization, by which TGN youth were fully affirmed in their gender identities, such as by seeking counseling and medical advice, influenced youth's identity development).

To conclude, research on transgender identity development mostly used stage models to conceptualize that development. A common limitation of predominant research proposing developmental models of transgender identity lies in the fact that it is often based on other minority identities development models (Cross & Vandiver, 2001; Coleman's, 1982) which were developed without including trans experiences (Renn, 2007). Luckily, more recent research (Katz-Wise et al., 2018) acknowledges the heterogeneity of the trans community, by including participants of various trans identities.

Furthermore, existing transgender identity developmental models often exclude gender-non-conforming individuals, and those with non-binary gender identities (Rahilly, 2015). Another limitation is that the existing body of research often doesn't take into account the heterogeneity of trans community and focuses primarily on the experiences of transgender individuals who are not people of color or of diverse ethnic background (Moradi et al., 2016). More research on transgender identity development among individuals of different racial and ethnic backgrounds, and other minority identitites and material realities is needed, because transgender identity development occurs not only in relation person's sense of their true Self, but also in relation to their social sphere (Levitt & Ippolito, 2014).

### 1.2 Intersections between Activist and TGNC Identity Development

The most apparent gap in the literature is reflected in the lack of research that examines the relationship between transgender and GNC identity on the one side, and activist and adult educator for social change identity development, on the other side.

There is a body of research on LGBT student activist identity development, and while some samples contain participants who identify as transgender, often the heterogeneity of the transgender community is not taken into account. Furthermore, trans participants are usually present in small samples.

Renn and Bilodeau (2005a) conducted a research that explored the relationship between LGBT identity and involvement in campus activism and leadership among 15 LGBT-identified leaders from three universities in the United States. Open-ended interviews were conducted and analyzed using grounded theory methodology against the Leadership Identity Development (LID) model developed by Komives et al. (2006). The research showed that the development of both activist/leadership and LGBT identities of the participants was a result of involvement in identity-based organizations on the campuses. In the first stage, Awareness, the participants recognized that coming out as LGB or T was sometimes connected with the existence of leadership and activism (Renn & Bilodeau, 2005a). In the next Exploration/Engagement stage, as they experimented with leadership, participants learned new skills and gained a sense of confidence.

Stages three and four, Leadership-Identified and Leadership-Differentiated, showed how participants in this study moved from seeing leadership as positional (stage three) to recognizing that leadership can come from anywhere in the group (stage four). As participants gradually started to perceive their engagement with the group as important and meaningful, througout the continuous involvement, their commitment to activism grew. In stage five, Generativity, commitment to the group turned to passion: participants were very active during this stage in sustaining their group and helping others to develop relevant skills and competencies. Understanding the wider purpose of their activist work and making a lifelong commitment to it, was a mark of the sixth stage named Internalization/Synthesis.

In another study, Renn and Bilodeau (2005b), explored participants' LGBT or queer identity development, looking at the intersections between engagement in leadership activities and LGBT/queer identity among seven undergraduates at the Michigan State University involved in planning an LGBT conference. They analyzed the data using D'Augelli's (1994) identity development model. Results showed that conference planning led to the development of positive and supportive social connections, which helped participants further establish their LGBT identities. The findings of this research showed that the identity-development processes interact with each other, rather than appearing separately in stages. For example, the participants developed both personal and social identities as LGBT people, along with developing an identity of an activist committed to a larger community of marginalized people.

Furthermore, Renn (2007) explored the interactions between gender identities and sexual orientations and leadership identity, using a grounded theory methodology. Interviews with 15 students were conducted at three institutions of higher education in the USA. Renn (2007) developed an involvement-identity cycle, as it became evident from the research that students' involvement in LGBT student organizations lead them to serving activist roles. Increased involvement in leadership and activism led to more visibility of their LGBT identities, which, in turn, established their leadership identities. An apparent link between participants' leader/activist and LGBT/queer identities was identified. Renn (2007) categorized merged identities into four types that differ along two dimensions – approach to sexual orientation/gender identity and style of leadership. Participants exhibited either LGB identity or queer identity (the latter is marked by the desire to challenge societal norms and dismantle categories of gender and sexuality). Along the other dimension, participants were either positional leaders or activists who lead aiming at social transformation.

The four identity types are: LGB(T) Leader, LGB(T) Activist, Queer Leader, and Queer Activist (Renn, 2007). LGB(T) Leader, consisted of lesbian or gay students who have a traditional view of leadership and work within the established norms of the system. This identity type did not include bisexual or transgender students from the sample. LGB(T) Activists understood sexual orientation similarly, but approached leadership with the desire to disrupt systems that marginalize people, not just those who are LGBT. These activists were often more experienced than LGB(T) leaders, and usually worked collaboratively to enact social change. The third identity type, Queer Leader, did not appear in this study's sample. Finally, Queer Activists, the fourth identity type, had merged their LGBT and leadership identities. Interestingly enough, transgender participants belonged to this identity type. They worked to transform oppressive systems completely therefore aiming at social transformation and not simple social change, and challenged the normative understanding of sexuality and gender. Queer activists had a "sense of urgency" (Renn, 2007, p. 324) to their work. They wanted to create change through engagement in politics, committee work, and organizing protests, and to work in solidarity with other marginalized communities. During the course of the study, six participants moved from one identity dimension to another, for example from being LGB to queer, from leader to activist, or both (LGB Leader to Queer Activist). As Renn (2007) highlighted, the queer identity should not be understood as more developed than LGB identity. The difference lies in the leadership style: activist/transformational leadership style is more advanced than the positional one.

The presented research focused on exploring the relationship between queer and activist/leadership identity development, but none of this research was focused specifically on trans and GNC people and their activist identity development, although they were included in the research samples (often in small number).

Moreover, a common limitation of the presented research lies in the fact that it often uses gay identity development models (Coleman, 1982; D'Augelli, 1994) which are then generalized to the LGBTQI community, while these models were developed without including trans experiences, or with a narrow understanding of trans identities (Renn, 2007). Finally, none of the research presented acknowledged the heterogeneity of trans communities, taking into account the social situatedness of trans activists and the impact of the multiplicity of their identities on their activist identity development.

The research conducted by Hagen et al. (2018) focused on the intersection between social activism, sexual orientation, and gender identity among twenty sexual minority women (SMW) and transgender persons (mostly focusing on sexual minority, White, well-educated women). The research sought to develop an empirical model to explain social justice activism and its diverse meanings among SMW and transgender individuals. It acknowledged the relationship between the meaning of social activism that persons have and their social situatedness, resulting in their life experiences, and experiences of oppression and privilege. The results showed that social justice activism was intensely relational, and had multiple benefits for the participants (such as: decreased internalized oppression, increased empowerment, resilience, and social support, leading to trauma healing, hope, pride, and joy while engaging in social justice activism). However, researchers highlighted that social justice activism involved marginalization within the social justice movement and the queer community. This is in relation to social situatedness of the activists based on their experiences of oppression from within and outside of activist communities (exclusion of transgender women from cisgender women-only activists spaces, and the lack of inclusion of people of color in LGBTQI activist spaces).

Therefore, the research presented in this book in the following sections, addresses this gap by only inviting participants who identify as trans and GNC, and by taking into account their multiple identities which determine their social situatedness. This is an important step toward reparative justice, especially in theory, research and provision of social justice education and adult education for social change.

## 2  The Research on TGNC Activist Identity Development

My qualitative narrative research, grounded in critical educational research paradigm and intersectionality theory sought to understand how the development of the identity of adult educator and activist for social change was experienced among TGNC participants. Specifically, I was interested in the exploration of how was that development mediated through gender identity of my participants, as well as through other intersecting identities, and the role these other identities together with significant life events (experiences of social injustices) played in activist identity development.

As the research showed, different factors may intersect with person's gender identity, shaping their social situatedness, their social agency and access to social services and opportunities, such as: sexual orientation, bodily diversity/ sex characteristics, age, disability, race, ethnicity, migration status, religious background, educational attainment level, socio-economic background, geographical location. Therefore, intersectionality theory informed my understanding and interpretation of the gathered empirical data. As explained in the first chapter, intersectionality theory offers an understanding of the multiplicity of identities for both oppressed and privileged identities (Cole, 2009), which exist within a context of connected systems and structures of power, such as laws, policies, state governments, political and economic unions, religious institutions, and media (Hankivsky, 2014).

The critical educational research paradigm informed my understanding and interpretation of power structures, relations, and inequalities in societies that, shape identity formation and development of a social justice activist. It also helped me to challenge them by raising critical questions, aiming towards fostering critical consciousness, by questioning dominant cultural, political, and social domains (Mack, 2010). This is in alignment with the chosen methodology of narrative inquiry, which focuses on the experiences of one or more individuals, and exploration of the experiences of these individuals, both personal and social, since the individual is interacting with others (Creswell, 2012).

Finally, since I was familiar with intersectionality theory prior to conducting the research was not atheoretical in nature. My knowledge of intersectionality comes from my professional/activist experience, and personal experience as a gender non-binary queer activist. The chosen theoretical framework had ontological and epistemological relevance, but it did not constrain the research findings. In other words, the theoretical background was to cast a light on the data analysis and help interpret data.

The main research question of my research was: How is the development of the identity of adult educator and activist for social change experienced among transgender and gender non-conforming people?

The specific research questions were[3]:

1. How do transgender and GNC adult educators and activists for social change experience the intersection between their gender and activist identities?
2. How do gender identities of transgender and GNC adult educators and activists for social change affect their identities as activists?
3. What roles do other identities (e.g., race, ethnicity, socio-economic status, migration status, sexual orientation, sex characteristics, etc.) play at the intersection of adult educators and activists' for social change gender identities and activist identities?
4. What are the main life events that motivated them to become activists and adult educators for social change?

## 2.1 *Researcher's Position*

This study was approached from the critical educational research paradigm (CERP), which comes from critical theory and the belief that research should be conducted for "the emancipation of individuals and groups in an egalitarian society" (Cohen et al., 2007, p. 26). As discussed in Chapter 1, critical theory is not a settled body of practices, but rather a framework, a way of thinking and a way of problematizing. It can be understood as an umbrella for a range of other theories: critical race theory, critical pedagogy, critical disability theory (Cohen et al., 2011) and of relevance to this study, intersectionality theory. This research paradigm originated from the criticism that educational research is neglecting social inequalities and power issues related to knowledge production (Mack, 2010). It acknowledges that knowledge which is considered worthwhile is "determined by the social and positional power of the advocates of that knowledge" (Cohen et al., 2007, p. 27), which is related to the concept of epistemic justice (see Chapter 1, Section 1.3). CERP recognizes that knowledge production is an "expression of power rather than truth" (Mack, 2010, p. 10). It aims to challenge reproductions of inequalities in knowledge production and the way they shape identity formation and development, and the presence of trans epistemologies in education. Critical researcher's aim is not only to understand and interpret these power relations and inequalities in societies that influence identity formation and development, but to challenge them by questioning dominant cultural, political, and social domains (ibid.). I position myself as a critical education researcher, not just because the ontological and epistemological underpinnings of my research are reflected in the chosen theoretical background (intersectionality theory), but also because my research focuses exclusively on the minority social group that suffers epistemic injustice, aiming towards reparative justice. I see this book as a step toward the acknowledgement of trans epistemologies in education theory, reseach and practice, from which they have been systematically and systemically erased. My critical stance is reflected in all stages of this research: from the chosen theoretical framework, population, methodology (method and data collection tool) to interpretation of the collected data and approach to research ethics.

Throughout all the stages of the research, I have been aware and reflexive of my social situatedness and positionality in regards to the participants of my research. I am aware that I am privileged in many ways: I am White, endosex[4] able-bodied person, of higher education attainment level, and my body appearance is within the "norm" of the body size in society I live in. Therefore, I haven't experienced racism, interphobia,[5] disability-related discrimination, or fatphobia, as some participants of my research have. As a gender non-binary queer person who is not seeking gender-affirming surgeries or hormone-replacement therapy, I haven't experienced pathologization of my gender identity or oppression from the medical system. I was never in the position to turn to medical and mental health professionals for these reasons. Moreover, I am in enrolled in the five year long postgraduate training program to become a psychotherapist, I am certified psychodrama counselor, and I hold Bachelor's and Master's degree in Adult Education. Therefore, I am privileged because my word has credibility, because of my higher education attainment level, and I am considered to be a trustworthy source of information in the social contexts I live within. Moreover, I am of good mental health and I am trained (through my training in psychotherapy) to be resilient, which is a luxury that many of participants of this research did not have. I do have access to education and employment opportunities in my home country, although due to the type of social justice work I am involved in, which goes "against the grain", I have experienced unemployment and felt unemployable in the the context of neo-liberal labor market of the economy in my country, which is led by the right-wing totalitarian government. Furthermore, as I don't struggle with legal recognition of my gender identity the way that trans people who are in the medical transition do, who often have to wait for prolonged periods of time to have their gender identity legally recognized in official documents, as Chapter 4 shows, I don't experience barriers to employment in that sense. On the other side, I am aware of the points of my marginalization, and my social situatedness in relation to participants of my research. I come from Eastern Europe, from Serbia, a country which is not in the European Union (EU), and therefore my employment opportunities outside of my country are hindered (employers within the EU can employ a person from non-EU countries only if there are no qualified candidates for a certain job position from the EU countries). Therefore, I do feel my access to work-related opportunities outside of my home country is hindered due to my citizenship. Because of my citizenship (not having an EU citizenship), my travel mobility within the EU is limited (the number of days I can stay within the EU as a tourist is limited to 90 days within 6 months). Most of the participants of my research don't experience these barriers (except for one). Furthermore, my gender identity/gender non-conformity is questioned, and in the context of my home country, it is not even considered real and valid by the general public and by the law. Trans and non-binary gender identities are not recognized by the law in Serbia. As a non-binary person of, what is read as feminine gender expression, I am perceived and treated as a cisgender woman, because sex assigned to me at birth was female (and my gender expression is read as feminine). Because of that, I am exposed to a complete erasure of my gender identity, and am exposed to the intense sexism and covert and overt forms of violence, physical, psychological and sexual harassment. My home country is a highly patriarchal society and violence towards those who are perceived as feminine (including gay men, trans and cisgender women), and towards gender non-conforming people is normalized. Violence is especially normalized towards persons whose sexuality is queer (I identify as pansexual), as Serbia is a highly homophobic and transphobic society.

Hence, taking into account my position on the discrimination-privilege spectrum, and the impact of my social positionality and resulting life experiences on the way I perceive, interpret and understand the world, I decided to share the analytical power I have as a researcher (which is enhanced by my epistemic agency coming from my social situatedness and resulting privileges), with the participants. That way this research becomes a platform so they can tell their life stories. To do justice to my research participants, I chose to provide extensive quotations from their accounts, so that their stories are represented in an authentic way, the way they shared them with me. Finally, I chose to share my analytical power (that I have in the role of the researcher) with my participants through data collection, data interpretation, and the presentation of the results of my research, as it will be described in paragraphs below.

## 2.2 Research Design

Since the research has suggested that qualitative inquiry is appropriate when phenomena have not been previously studied (Morrow & Smith, 2000) and because narrative research is particularly indicated for research about identity development (Riessman, 1993), I chose a narrative approach to explore the development of the identity of adult educator and activist for social change among transgender and GNC people. This qualitative method is particularly appropriate taking into consideration the complex nature of gender identities, as well as the complex nature of sexual orientations and other identities[6] gender intersects with, because in narrative research, the focus is on the experiences of one or more individuals, and exploration of the experiences of these individuals, which are both personal and social, since the individual is interacting with others (Creswell, 2012).

Furthermore, a narrative inquiry is in alignment with intersectionality theory, because it acknowledges the interconnectedness of individual and cultural narratives (Rossiter, 1999). As Rossiter (1999) pointed out, individual life narratives are situated within a myriad of overlapping familial, religious, socio-economic and cultural contexts. Therefore, individual narratives are dependednt on the context, since they are an expression of, an embodiment of systems of meaning within which the person lives (ibid.), as both narrative inquiry and intersectionality theory postulate. Additionally, because narratives allow participants voices to be heard and their lived experiences to be analyzed (Zamani-Gallaher & Choudhuri, 2016, p. 49), this chosen method is in alignment with the "bottom up" approach valued by intersectionality theory, which proposes starting research by asking people how they experience their lives and their identities (Hankivsky, 2014).

There are two approaches to the narrative inquiry: analyzing participants' stories by looking for themes across their narratives, or forming a narrative from participants' descriptions or stories of their experiences (Connelly & Clandinin, 1990). I chose the first approach. I was not looking to formulate a linear or a phase model of activist identity development, but rather to identify common emerging themes, as well as differences among the narratives.

As the review of the relevant research on social identity development showed, stage and phase models of development have been dominating understanding of identity development and identity change in adulthood. But, their generalizability to populations different from those on which they were originally based, is questioned (Rossiter, 1999). Developmental variations might be connected to gender, class, and cultural differences (ibid.), which is not necessarily taken into account when developing these models. Rossiter (ibid.) highlighted that universality in prevalent adult development theory, which is based on stage and phase models, reflects dominant cultural values and leads to a devaluation of alternative developmental paths.

Since this research was conducted with a population who suffers, as already presented, human rights, social and epistemic injustice, and taking into account that my sample was small and participants were from diverse socio-cultural backgrounds, socio-economic statuses, geographical locations, and of different gender identities on the transgender spectrum, I was not interested in creating a developmental phase-model of activist identity development, since its generalizability and validity would be questionable. My direction was quite the opposite: I wanted to look at the development of an identity of adult educator and activist for social change *in retrospective*, from the position of reflecting back on the developmental process and path of identity formation. The narrative of the life course is central to the construction of the meaning, because a narrative interview reconstructs a person's life story, in a way that provides unity, purpose, and meaning (McAdams & McLean, 2013).

## 2.3  *Data Collection*

A type of narrative interview, the Life Story Interview (Foley Center, 2009), was used and adapted to the research topic. The reason why this specific data collection tool was chosen is because it enables the interviewee to take ownership of the interview process, while analytical power is distributed, it is not only in the hands of the researcher (Adriansen, 2010). That is possible because unlike the "conventional interview", in which the interviewer asks very specific questions, guiding the direction of the conversation, in the Life Story Interview, the way I applied it, using a timeline tool for the first chapter, it is very important that the interviewer has active listening skills and can tolerate *being* silent, not taking over the interview process by asking too many questions (ibid.). Although the researcher eventually offers their interpretation in the form of published research, still the interviewee is invited to participate in "constructing the story" (ibid.). Because thematic questions asked were quite broad, as it will be explained further on, the interviewee could decide what they want to share, hence, they could direct the conversation. Therefore, the choice of a data collection tool reflects the critical research paradigm being applied to methodology: by giving the power to participants to share their stories, take as much time as they need to share their understanding of their activist identity development.

### 2.3.1 The Structure of the Life Story Interview

The life story Interview I conducted is divided into several chapters. In the first chapter, named Life chapters, the interviewee is asked to think about the development of the identity of activist and educator for social change, as if it was a book, and to divide it into several chapters with its main events. They were encouraged to do that in ways that suit them: by drawing, or drawing a timeline in the middle of the paper, horizontally, or just by writing on a piece of paper. The chronological ordering of events is the guiding principle of this chapter. The reason why I chose to apply a timeline tool to this chapter is because it is the tool for "untangling the story and for engaging the interviewee in constructing this story" (Adriansen, 2010, p. 3).

The next chapter of the interview was about the Key Scenes in Life Story (high point, low point, a turning point; positive and negative childhood memory; vivid adult memory, wisdom event; religious, mystical and spiritual experience). Questions were broad,[7] allowing the interviewee to decide what they want to share.

Furthermore, in the Future Script chapter, the interviewee was asked: how they envision the next chapter of their life; about dreams, hopes and plans for the future; and to describe a life project they are working on. I added two questions to this chapter, in accordance with the topic of my research, asking the interviewee:

1. *What support do you need so that you can carry out your activism and education work for social change?*
2. *How do you envision the societal impact of your work?*

The next chapter focuses on the challenges (the greatest life challenge, health-related challenge, major loss, and failure and regret).

I added one additional question in this chapter, in accordance with the research topic. The interviewee was asked:

3. *What are the main challenges that you as transgender or gender non-conforming person and activist face?*

The next chapter of the Life Story Interview focuses on Personal Ideology[8] (religious/ethical values; political and social values; change and development of religious and political views over time, and a single most important life value). Then, the interviewees were asked to identify a central life theme and to name it.

Finally, the Reflection chapter included questions related to feelings of interviewees during the interview, and how they think the interview affected them. In addition, they were given an opportunity to add something they haven't been asked or they want to share.

## 2.4 Data Analysis

Each interview was audio recorded with the consent of the participant and transcribed for further analysis. I noted not just the words, but the emotions as well: laughter, uncertainty, sadness, anger and anxiety.

Collected data was analyzed using the combination of three approaches: (1) individual thematic data analysis, (2) cross-individual thematic data analysis and (3) visual approach and analysis of metaphors. The Thematic Data Analysis (TDA) method involves categorizing the data on the basis of the themes related to the research questions and theoretical framework (Smith, Breakwell, & Wright, 2012). Visual approach refers to tools such as drawings and metaphors to illustrate data, connect and integrate meanings and add emotional, personal relevance (Miles & Huberman 1994).

TDA allows categories to emerge from the data and is qualitative, unlike the content analysis, which starts with predefined categories and is quasi-statistical, seeking to identify the frequency of certain words, inter-correlation between categories, and to express them quantitatively (Saldana, 2009; Creswell, 2012). Since my focus, was to identify the main common emerging themes between the participants' narratives and not to seek for pre-defined categories in my data, I chose thematic over content data analysis. There are two primary ways of identifying themes in thematic data analysis: inductive and deductive (Braun & Clarke, 2006). I chose the inductive approach to identify and describe the categories that emerge from the data. Types of thematic analysis conducted in this research are individual and cross-individual analysis (Smith, Breakwell, & Wright, 2012). Coding of data was based on the analysis proposed by Saldana (2009):

1. Open, In Vivo coding: words or phrases from the actual language in the data.
2. Second cycle coding: pattern coding to identify emerging themes.

Writing analytic memos as a reflection tool on my coding process, code choices, emerging patterns, categories, sub-categories, and themes followed this process from the beginning (ibid.).

Overall, my data analysis included the following steps:

1. Carrying out TDA to identify codes, categories and emerging themes in each transcript (Open, In Vivo coding).
2. Writing analytical memos throughout the entire process.
3. Subjecting individual transcripts to second coding: pattern coding to identify themes.
4. Looking at the emerging data in relation to the research questions.
5. Creating maps of activist identity development for each transcript to visually represent the process.

6. Cross-individual thematic analysis: comparing identified themes, subthemes and categories between the narratives.
7. Re-organizing themes: merging categories, separating categories and sub themes.
8. Again, looking at the emerging data in relation to the research questions.
9. Creating final common themes and one summative map of activist identity development, to include and represent emerging pathways and themes.

2.4.1 Participants

This research focused on transgender and GNC adult educators and activists for social change from different countries. In order to participate in the research, the participant needed to be:

1. Older than 18 years.
2. Self-identify as trans and/or gender non-conforming.
3. Self-identify as an activist and/or adult educator for social change.
4. Be in the leadership position in the organization working on the advancement of LGBTQI human rights (currently or in the recent past).
5. Be each from a different country.
6. Give written consent confirming that they understand that this research involves sharing sensitive personal issues.
7. Give written consent confirming that they have access to psychological support in case of the distress after the interview.

Because traveling to different countries to interview participants required significant time, and financial resources, and having in mind the given time frame for conducting this research (one semester), eight participants were interviewed, from the following countries: Slovenia, Romania, Serbia, Sweden, the USA, Ireland, Iceland, and Greece. The gender identitites of my participants are: trans man (two participants), gender non-binary and trans (four participants),[9] queer and trans (one participant), and trans and intersex (one participant). One participant identified as a person of color. Five participants were from the European continent, one emigrated from South America, and one was from the United States of America, living in Europe at the time the research was conducted. In terms of sexual orientation, three participants identified as pansexual, two participants identified as queer, one as queer or bisexual, one identified as heterosexual and one as non-monogamous/queer. When it comes to educational attainment level, seven out of eight participants had advanced degrees. These are educational backgrounds of the participants of my research: B.A and M.A in Film and TV Editing; B.A. in Sociology; Upper secondary high school, B.A, in Community and International Development and M.A. in Education; B.A. in Social Work and M.A. in Gender Studies; B.A. Archeology & M.A. International Relations; B.A. Sociology and Gender Studies and M.A. in Gender Studies; and B.A. in Psychology. When it comes to religious affiliation, five participants identified as non-religious, one as agnostic, one as atheist and one as Christian-Protestant. Other relevant identities, material realities and experiences participants felt are important for them to share, which impacted their activist identity development are: two participants were of lower socio-economic status, and stressed out poverty as a hindering factor in their life; two participants shared they have a passing privilege (would not be perceived as trans); one participant was an asylum seeker; two participants shared experiences of fatshaming throughout their lives. Participants were of the following age: 45, 28, 24, 33, 33, 30, 27 and 24 years old.

2.4.2   Context

I met, throughout my engagement with IGLYO (International LGBTQI Youth and Student Organization), serving the role of a member of the Executive Board from 2015–2016 and of a Co-Chair of the organization from 2016–2017, transgender and gender non-conforming activists and educators for social change, from the pan-European region. Those who were in leadership positions serving either as presidents, in case the organization was a trans-specific community-based organization, or program coordinators of trans-specific programs within community-based LGBTQI organizations, were invited to participate in the research. Therefore, since I had a chance to meet potential participants of the research at the international LGBTQI conferences, seminars, and study sessions, and in certain cases I cooperated with them in the past, without any conflicts of interest, I decided to apply the purposive sampling technique and reach out to them directly via email, informing them about my research. However, as I explained in the introduction of this book, the research I conducted was limited by time and financial factors. As I didn't have a research travel grant, I had to rely only on my monthly scholarship when traveling to interview participants (which impacted the choice of my participants), during the time frame for conducting this research (one semester). Another limiting factor was time availability of my potential interviewees, as all my participants were very busy and were engaged in social justice work not only in the countries they live and work in, but also on the international level. Had I had more time and resources, I would invite more trans activists to participate in my research and of more diverse identities (especially in terms of race, ability, religious affiliation and variations in sex characteristics).

### 2.4.3 Sample

Non-probability sampling technique, purposive sampling was applied. While applying a purposive sample, a researcher uses a particular knowledge or expertise about some group to select subjects who represent the population (Berg, 2001).

First, I specifically sought participants who I knew have different gender identities on the trans spectrum, to include both those who seek gender-affirming surgeries, and/or hormone replacement therapy, and those who don't want any medical interventions, but do identify as trans and/or GNC. I sought to identify participants of different ability, health, mental health, migrant statuses; different socio-economic statuses, religion, race and ethnicities, each from a different country. The reason for choosing each participant from a different country comes from my activist work experience: I realized that trans and GNC people report facing very similar forms of societal oppression, regardless of their geographic location and how progressive or regressive their country is considered to be when it comes to protection of queer people's human rights. Therefore I wanted to explore if similar topics would emerge from the narratives when it comes to experiences of their activist identity development. A diverse sample was important because of the intersectional frame of this research, and I tried to gather as diverse sample as I could.

### 2.5    *Steps in Recruitment and Data Collection*

First, I sent an email to potential participants informing them about my research. Consent Form and Plain Language Statement were shared with them via an online survey tool, SurveyMonkey. When potential participants responded, I introduced them to the ethical considerations of the study, including the anonymity and confidentiality of this research. They were informed they would be referred to in my research using the pseudonym of their choice. Two participants wanted their names to be used instead of a pseudonym and their identities to be revealed, and their written consent was obtained about that. Furthermore, participation in this research required obtaining written consent from the participants, confirming: (a) they understand this research is of a high risk for experiencing distress, due to sharing sensitive personal material; and (b) they have access to and are willing to seek support of a mental health professional, in case they become distressed after the interview. Participants were told they are free to ask questions about the research before, during and after the interview and it was made clear that they can withdraw at any time. They were informed that the interview will be audio-recorded for the purposes of transcription and further analysis, and written consent about it was obtained. At this stage, participants were also informed that research will be used further for education and advocacy purposes (to advocate for human rights of transgender and GNC people by presenting this research at international conferences, possibly witting academic papers and book), and written consent was obtained accordingly through the Consent form.

Second, with participants who accepted to take part in the research, a discussion around scheduling an interview in person in the city of their residence followed via email. I decided to conduct each interview face-to-face, due to the sensitivity of the topic.

Participants were not provided with financial compensation. The possible educational and social value of this research constituted a psychological incentive for the participants. Several activists outside of the pool of contacted potential participants, who heard about my research reached out to me expressing their interested to participate in the research. In my opinion, that shows the "urgency" to increase the visibility of trans issues and trans epistemologies. Unfortunately, as already elaborated, due to limited financial resources and given a timeframe for thesis submission, I couldn't include more than 8 participants.

Third, participants were interviewed in the cities of their residence and at the location of their choice that we agreed upon beforehand. We met in the facility that could provide confidential and uninterrupted interviewing and which was safe both for the participant and for me. For example, the workplace of the participant, or a study room at the local University library. Icelandic participant was interviewed via Skype, due to my inability to travel to meet them, for financial reasons. I conducted all interviews during the spring/summer semester of 2018.

Finally, meeting in person with participants was organized within three consecutive days. On the first day, we discussed one more time the purpose of the research, the structure, and the length of the interview, along with all ethical issues. It was a pre-interview, "warm-up" meeting. On the second day, one-on-one interview was conducted and recorded, lasting usually between an hour and a half and three hours. The possibility to meet me on the third day was offered to the participants, in case they felt triggered by the interview or had the need to talk about it for closure. During the interview, my role was of a listener who would ask broad, thematic questions. I kept the conversation going by asking for examples, clarifications, or asking other probing questions. The critical educational research paradigm was applied to the way the interview was conducted. It was a space for participants to tell their stories. I would let participants speak without the interruptions characteristic of "conventional" interviews with a standardized set of questions (Riessman, 1993).

Participants chose what they wanted to share, and interviews had an organic flow, becoming a joint construction (Connelly & Clandinin, 1990). I noticed a pattern during the data collection process. Several participants asked me if I think the interview was successful and if it was useful for me. They had the feeling they might not give me "what I wanted and what I was looking for", since the interview was centered on them, and not so much on my standardized set of questions. Some participants even expressed concern that I might not find "anything valuable" in their accounts in relation to my research topic, because they had the freedom to choose what they want to share. Again, the participants were activists in leadership positions in organizations they work with. I understood their concerns as a consequence of their experiences of being deined an epistemic and testimonial agency, throughout their personal life and social justice activism. As accounts of my participants, quoted below in Section 3 of on research findings, will show, many of my participants are used to being in the position in which they have to say what the other wants to hear (to the psychiatrist, the doctor), so they can be granted access to trans-affirming healthcare they might need, or believed when it comes to their gender identity.

During and after the interview I checked in with participants to see how they are feeling, giving them the opportunity to ask me any questions (Josselson, 2007). After the interview, I notified participants that the results of this research and their transcripts will be available to them in written form.

## 2.6  Ethical Considerations

This research was approved by the University of Glasgow School of Education Ethics Committee.

It was my ethical duty to: ensure appropriate relationships with my participants, ask for their consent, ensure confidentiality, and think about their wellbeing (Josselson, 2007).

To ensure confidentiality, I de-identified[10] the collected data, and replaced identifiers with a code, to which I retained the key, in a secure location, on my personal computer (Josselson, 2007). Electronic access to participant's files was available by password only, and only I had access to them. To ensure anonymity, each participant was referred to this research by a pseudonym of their choice, apart from two participants who wanted their name and identities to be revealed, as they consider visibility to be an important aspect of their activism. Written consent about it was obtained, and nevertheless, I was mindful of the data I would share from the narratives of the participants who are not anonymous. Due to my ethical concerns, I included in the Research findings chapter only narratives by one of them. Other ethical issues which required written consent are presented in the parahraph above on Steps in Recruitment and Data Collection. My positionality as a researcher and reflections on the impact of my social situatedness and resulting epistemic agency on different phases of this research was discussed above in this chapter in the paragraph on Researcher's position. Therefore, I will focus on the following issues: my reflexivity as a researcher, my relationship with participants, and mine and their well-being.

The literature says that in narrative inquiry the relationship between the researcher and participants should be rooted in trust and equality (Connelly & Clandinin, 1990). For the reasons provided in the paragraph on the Researcher's position, I would argue that equality is hardly achievable if we think in terms of social situatednes and positionality, especially when participants have multiple minority identitites. Since I already knew participants of the research from my activist work, and since I as well belong to the queer community, I would describe my relationship with participants as one of trust and respect. I was perceived as an insider, not an outsider, which impacted their belief in my "right" intentions and ethical reasons for conducting this research. The fact they knew me allowed them to share their stories deeply and intimately, which they highlighted as well. On the other side, precisely that made some of them feel, as Alex said: "weird, because I already know you and you know so much about me". Knowing my participants was at the same time a valuable and sometimes a hindering factor. However, my worry was not if I would be biased as a result of knowing them, in the interpretation of the results of my research, as I wasn't aiming at scientific objectivity, decontextualized, generalizable knowledge, but I was rather aiming at raising the visibility of testimonial practices of TGNC activists and sharing with them my epistemic agency. I was more concerned and reflective about my social positionality and resulting epistemic agency, and the ways it can be used for reparative justice, through giving participants the space to tell their stories the way it feels right for them, during the interviews; sharing participants' authentic accounts in the results of the research, and offering them a possibility for a meeting on the third day of the interview process, for the purposes of closure after the interview, in case they felt distressed.

One of my main ethical questions was: "was our interaction one of fairness?" After all, participants were sharing sensitive personal information with me while being emotionally exposed, and I was listening, not sharing anything personal. It is important to acknowledge that ultimately, as a researcher, I have the final power of interpretation. That analytical power was present from the beginning, as I had to decide who is a relevant interviewee, whose stories will be included in the findings of my research and how will they be interpreted (ibid.). I tried to mitigate that analytical power, by choosing a data collection tool which allowed "giving the power back" or at least sharing that power with the participants, as described earlier in this chapter.

When doing research with multiple marginalized identities, even if the researcher belongs to the same minority group, still because the researcher role is a power position, there is a danger for a researcher of falling into a role of savior to participants (Glesne & Peshkin, 1992). On the one side, narrative inquiry often requires a close connection between the researcher and the participant, especially when they have experiences in common (Connelly & Clandinin, 2006). Therefore, I would argue that it is important for the researcher to cultivate critical consciousness, critical reflexivity, and awareness of their social situatedness, epistemic agency, motives, privileges and power dynamics present in the relationship with participants. It was important to me to acknowledge the power dynamics inherited in different positions on the spectrum of privilege-discrimination between the participants and myself. To increase the authenticity of their voices and share analytical power with them, I decided to use more extensive quotations from their narratives, descriptive of their experiences.

That led me to the next ethical question: "could the interview become harmful to any of my participants?" The answer is: "Yes". At least they could have felt embarrassed, exposed, vulnerable (and sometimes they had), triggered, or traumatized at worst (which didn't happen). My background in psychotherapy education[11] gave me the confidence to conduct this research, since I am trained to actively listen and remain focused for longer periods of time, holding a space for people to share their stories, and containing challenging emotions. Therefore, measures I have taken against the potential harm of the interview process on the participants are: occasionally, but not too often, asking them how they feel during the interview; affirming courage and honesty; undoing shame by conveying empathy and non-judgment; offering them to omit data and not answer my question; reviewing given consent by reminding them of the right to withdraw at any time and highlighting that withdrawal would not hinder our relationship in any way (Glesne & Peshkin, 1992).

That led me to the next ethical question: "was this research professionally or personally risky for me as a researcher?" The answer is: "Yes". Working on the research with a minority social group which faces extreme minority stress, social oppression and pathologization of mental health and gender diversity, and being a member of that community myself while conducting this research alone, was emotionally challenging, on occasions. Holding space for participants' sharing of sensitive, sometimes emotionally challenging material, included sometimes feeling their, and my own, embodied and emotional pain. As a psychotherapy student, I am trained to contain challenging emotions around the universality of human suffering, but this research included not listening about universality of suffering as such, but listening all over again about accounts of suffering because of systemic oppression that doesn't have to be, but it persists across the countries, when it comes to TGNC people. As I was actively involved in my psychotherapy training while conducting this research, I used that space to work on my emotions and affective aspect of conducting this research, so that I can preserve my capacity to be present and emotionally and cognitively available to my participants.

## 2.7 *The Validity of the Research*

I relied on methods for validation of narrative research (Riessman, 1993): correspondence, coherence, persuasiveness, and pragmatic use, to increase the trustworthiness of my research. I offered participants to review the transcriptions to make sure they correspond with what they meant. Unfortunately, due to the length of an interview itself, most of the participants said they will rely on my judgment and trust that I transcribed what they said. As for coherence, I aimed to have participants' goals, and what they shared verbally in alignment with the themes identified. In order for a narrative study to be persuasive, I aimed to write an interpretation that is based on the evidence, providing quotations from participant's narration. The pragmatic use of this research is described throughout Section 2 of this chapter.

## 3 Research Findings

This research presented in this section aimed to understand how the development of the identity of adult educator and activist for social change was experienced among trans and gender non-conforming participants of my research. Furthermore, the study explored how that development was mediated through one's intersecting identities, significant life events, and the role they played on the activist identity development of the research participants.

As a result of cross-individual thematic data analysis, the following major themes have emerged across the narratives:
1. *Main life events* that impacted the formation and development of activist identity.
2. *Main challenges* that impacted the formation and development of activist identity.
3. *Support factors* needed for the sustainability of activism and adult education for social change.
4. Applying the *critical framework* to social justice work.

Each of these themes will be explained in more detail below.

### 3.1 *Main Life Events That Impacted the Formation and Development of Activist Identity*

Within this theme, two subthemes were identified: gender identity related and non-gender identity related life events.

Among *Gender-identity-related* life events, realizing gender non-conformity; medical and social transition into one's true gender identity; dealing with "coming-out", took a significant portion of the activist identity development journey. For example, Ugla a trans and gender non-binary activist from Iceland, currently living in the UK (who wanted their identity to remain disclosed), explained how they became an "accidental activist" and advocate for trans people:

> I don't think I saw myself as an activist or an advocate, or as a spokesperson until I was seventeen, when I came out. That was when I went to visit a doctor for the first time. I told them I was trans, and I want to pursue a medical transition. The doctor didn't know what trans was, and they sent me to a psychologist who also didn't know, and sent me to someone else. And they didn't know. I kept going to different people and no one actually knew what to do. That's when I realized that I have to do something. I needed to start educating people, starting with this doctor. I started a support group for trans people in the town I was living in. The ball started to roll and the media started to get interested. Reykjavik Pride did an interview with me for their magazine. And within a single night, everyone in the entire country knew who I was. And that's why I called it "an accidental advocate".

Experiencing bullying because of one's gender identity and/or expression was another gender-identity-related life event that emerged across the narratives. Aiden, a trans man, shared how he experienced bullying in school because of his gender expression, and for another reason: fat-shaming.

> When I was eight years old, I was allowed to choose a hairstyle. I chose to cut my long hair completely and chose the "bowl" haircut. At the same time, I had giant glasses with plastic frames. And I loved them! In this period things changed for me in school, drastically. Kids started to treat me differently. That was the first time I started getting the question from my peers: "Are you a boy or a girl?" This period is characterized by those memories: being happy about being able to express myself and having parents who were supportive of that, but not having peers who are supportive of that. After I turned eleven, bullying in school got a lot more intense, and biology and hormonal changes made it tougher for me. The

kids at school were really mean to me. When I played soccer, I played with a mixed-gender team. I had the option to play for all girls team, and I choose the mix-gender team, it was more appealing to me. I was a large kid. I was always "the fat kid". I didn't conform to body-size norms, along with gender expression norms and I guess kids really didn't like that. The girls were awful towards me. They shaved their legs and arms and I didn't. So they would tease me about that. When we had a gym class, we had to change from the clothes we would normally wear, to our gym clothes. And I would wear my gym clothes to school that day, when we had a gym class, so that I don't have to change my clothes in locker rooms. Because that was really traumatizing for me, being in locker rooms with girls. Gender identity issues were not things I knew about at this time. I knew about lesbian and gay people, but I didn't know about trans issues. When I was 16, life got harder. My body went through changes, estrogen hormones, and I had really intense gender dysphoria.[12] I was binding my breasts from the first moment. Fortunately, I had my best friend who was going through the same experience. That was really important to have a peer who got it, who knew how it feels. I went through a period of self-harm and depression, which was super intense, but I had him and the other three friends who were supportive. They got me through that period of time when I was experiencing bullying. At the age of sixteen, I had gotten a driving licence. Soon I drove my best friend and myself to the weekly support youth group at the LGBT center in our town. And mentors were incredibly supportive. The message: "Who you are is OK" is what came through from these meaningful adults in my life. That was an empowering experience for me which lead me to activism. My best friend and I became Co-presidents of our schools' Gay-Straight Alliance (GSA). We were the Co-presidents for two years. At the time we left, we had the largest group they have ever had in GSA! Between 20–30 participants, and we started with 8. We did trainings for the staff, trainings in the community, a lot of stuff around International Day of Silence and Trans Day of Remembrance, we were at the Pride and so on. That was the rainbow period of my life.

Both examples of Aiden and Ugla show how coming into terms with one's gender identity led to involvement in activism. For some other participants, *non-gender-identity-related life events*, such as witnessing and experiencing injustices in life, dealing with an interpersonal loss, or relocation, led them to activism, and exploration of their gender identity. Fiachra described how experiencing poverty and domestic violence shaped their activist development.

I grew up in a house that was emotionally violent and in some cases physically violent, with constant screaming and shouting at me and my mother. My father's alcoholism was a big part of that. I didn't know how to deal with my anger. I turned that inwards and tried to have a sense of control, so I developed an eating disorder. But for me, this was actually one of the biggest formative times of my life, because I became incredibly introspective. It really led me to developing a deep sense of empathy and understanding of the sensitivity of others. At the same time, I was starting to realize I was generally different. I was queer: assigned female at birth, attracted primarily to women. I would later come out as trans, but at this stage, I was very tomboyish, a queer goth from the working class, in a small school, in a small town. I would get angry at my father because he was violent and unjust. In school, I would be very quiet, unless someone said something really racist or homophobic. It wasn't until my college when I figured out what I wanted to do in life, because I felt that my world is falling apart. My father developed alcohol-related dementia. I had a few heartbreaking breakups. At the same time, fortunately, I have been involved with a youth group for LGBT people and that improved my confidence in some ways. There I met my first queer friends and that was most probably the only thing before college that gave me some sense of belonging. A sense of solidarity. Throughout college, I was working so much that the amount of volunteering I could do was minimal. I took a year off after it, did three jobs, some volunteering for some charities. I started volunteering with international youth and student organization. I was trying to build up the experience. Then I went to the West Bank for 3 months to work as a volunteer human rights manager and ecumenical accompanier, working on the issues where people are experiencing human rights abuses every day. We were staying at the Palestinian town, trying to make it safer, just by being there. Protective presence it's called. Behind the town, there was an Israeli settlement. They are illegal under international law, as they were built under an occupied territory. You can't transfer your population outside of your territory and this is what these settlements are. And Palestinians are not allowed in by walk or cars. It's an Israeli-only road. That was my first time in the field, which I loved. It really mattered to me: really feeling connected to people and feeling that impact. I think after this role I went back home. I was an intern with Amnesty International for 5–6 months, and had a great time there: did a lot of campaigning, lots of petitioning against torture. Then worked with another organization against unfair treatment of asylum seekers and refugees. After that, I had an internship with another organization, where I

> was working on providing guidelines on shelters for humanitarian emergencies for the people working in Sierra Leone and Liberia. And this was a research role. Pacifism is my ultimate ideal. As I grew up being queer in a poor family in a small town, understanding the struggles of marginalized people, who have experienced force used against them, and personally growing up in a household where violence was used against me, these experiences had influenced my strong pacifist orientation and my activist development.

Another participant, Sebastian said it was only when he suffered a big loss: his father's abandonment and mother's death due to her terminal illness, that he gave himself the permission to think about himself, including thinking about his gender identity.

> My activist call appeared in my fight for my mother's life. My dad left us when I was 13 years old, and until I was 19 my mission was to help my mother stay in life, however I can. I even got enrolled in medical secondary school, wanting to help her somehow. She had cancer. It was only me and her. I had to deal with her illness and health care system which has always been … failing people, especially in the 90s. This is when my activist call appeared. My mother died when I was 19 years old and somehow that gave me permission to think about myself. It was only me who was left of that family. I started with the medical transition. I was alone in that process, only had the support of my friend from high school. That's how my wish to support others who are going through similar experiences, emerged. So, through a friend I got in touch with an activist from the local LGBT organization and started working on trans issues 12 years ago, when it was a quite neglected topic in activism here. I had experiences of dealing with doctors, medical professionals, so I became the contact person for them, while simultaneously having contact with trans people, their families, and partners. I started facilitating support groups and counseling for trans people, started cooperating with organizations from the neighboring countries. The first support group I formed was in my home country. Afterward, I formed support groups in 2 neighboring countries and helped the creation of a support group in another country. Today, 12 years later, more than 150 trans and gender non-conforming people went through the support group here, and we started it only with 4 trans men.

For some other participants, like River and Alex, other *non-gender-identity-related life events*, such as relocation to another city or country, played an important role in their activist identity development and exploration of their gender identity, specifically because it led to meeting like-minded people. For Alex it was a formative experience:

> I moved to the capital city from the rural area, when I got enrolled in University. When I got to the capital, I started getting involved in environmental and animal rights activism. That's when I met this friend of mine. She was vegan, older than me, around 30 years old. I was 20. I admired her so much. She introduced me to the world of animal rights activism. She was a feminist, involved in a grassroots group, a collective of people who organized projections, discussions. We became really good friends, and we decided to move in together. Other people from the collective wanted to live with us as well, so we ended up renting 2 houses, which were next to each other. We all moved in together. On the ground floor of one of the houses, we created an alternative library. It was one of the most formative periods of my life. I became more political. I started thinking about systemic oppression and my part in it: learning about feminism, human rights, anti-racism. It was one of the most important periods of my life because I started exploring my queerness. I met a lot of interesting people through that collective, who were coming from other countries. Anarchists, activists, feminists. No one really cared I was queer. I never really needed to come out to this group. You just date whomever you want and that's it. So that was really great.

For River, relocating to the capital city, which was followed by several relocations to different countries and meeting like-minded people, lead to involvement in activism and exploring their gender identity.

> It was interesting how, as soon as I stopped living with my mother when I was 19, I started exploring my identity. First I thought I was a lesbian. Someone said to me: "Oh you should come to one youth camp", which was organized by the main LGBT organization here. And that was the first time I met so many LGBT people, mostly LG though, but still, I really liked it. I started volunteering with that organization. They organized a youth exchange. That was my first youth exchange. It was a couple of other countries and us and the topic was LGBT topics in the school curriculum and school environment. I was just like: "Wooow, there are all these LGBT people from all these places! I had no idea they existed!" I still remember it so much! So impactful. Then I started doing some volunteer work with Pride, an organization that was formed, and I was with the team from the

start. We would meet once or twice per week for 6 months. But looking back at it, I was mostly quiet. I went to all the meetings, I just didn't have a voice, because I didn't feel I have enough knowledge to form opinions. I was very young. I just had this massive thirst for knowledge. So I started applying to everything I could. I discovered the SALTO database. Part of it was not even LGBT, just youth work. But I grew so much. I traveled, met such different people, cultures. I also experienced a lot of homophobia. I went to Egypt, Turkey … many places where I was the only person who applied through an LGBT organization. But it shaped me a lot. I gained many skills. It was an important period. I also did my EVS,[13] moved around a lot. I lived in Germany for 8 months, in England for 6 months, and it had a big impact on me. I did my Master's in Gender Studies in another country, and that part was really important for me. Because through all these trainings and traveling I started meeting trans and non-binary people and started thinking about my own gender identity. I first came out as genderqueer and later on non-binary, which is the term I identify with today. Before I just didn't have the language to express my gender. I started using gender-neutral pronouns, because I was exposed to a language [English] where I was able to do this. It was easier than in my home country. We had to write a lot of papers for my Master's and I chose to do every assignment on LGBT topics, mostly trans. Now when I reflect on that, that was super important. It gave me tools and theoretical knowledge, which I think I am using in my activism very well. The form of activism I am doing is intersectional and norm-critical, and for that, you need a massive understanding. Then I went to a conference on Intersectionality, and I remember putting in an action plan during the conference "start trans support group". When I got back to my home country, I started co-facilitating a trans support group with the local LGBT organization I volunteered with. I remember crying after it a lot because people in it were so gender binary and I was very strongly in my academic bubble and needed to step out of it and see this is real activism now. It was just awful. I felt completely invalidated as a non-binary person. It took a long to feel comfortable as a non-binary activist, because there are not many of us here, especially those who are not medically transitioning. I felt I had so many ideas and opinions and I knew they have to start coming out. So I created a Facebook page by myself and just started writing. I would find a trans article, post it and write my opinion in my native language. And I went to every feminist, LGBT, human rights event possible. Eventually, I founded a first trans-specific organization in my country [and became its president].

These are some of the main life events that have impacted the formation and development of activist identity, and exploration of one's gender identity among participants of this research. As it can be seen from the presented themes, it was possible to discern between: a) Activist development with the queer community and b) Activist development working with non-queer related identities.

The following paragraphs will present the next common topics in activist identity development.

## 3.2 Main Challenges That Impacted the Formation and Development of Activist Identity

One of the central challenges that participants experienced is systemic oppression, related to navigating the healthcare system and dealing with the pathologization of gender non-conformity.

Ugla reports navigating health care as one of the biggest challenges.

> At the time when I needed it, if you wanted health care as a trans person in Iceland, you needed to play a certain role, a role of a "perfect woman" or a "perfect man". It meant proving to a bunch of people, who are stuck in outdated gender roles, that you are of the gender you identify with. They want to hear that you knew you were trans since you were a child, that you played with girls, in case you are a trans woman, and you didn't like playing with boys, and doing "boys activities". If you are a trans woman, and you needed an estrogen, you needed to prove to medical health professionals that you are a perfect woman in every sense of the word. When I started my medical transition, I visited a psychiatrist for the first time. There is a trans team at the hospital that gives you access to hormone blockers, name change and so on. And in the first session I had with him, he asked me a series of questions, one of them being what sort of underwear I was wearing at that point. And then he continued asking me if I had sex, with whom and what have I done. I was 18 years old and had to describe to a complete stranger these questions, in detail. This is just an example of how the system is failing trans people and how outdated it is when it comes to trans issues. I remember sitting in the psychiatrist's office and thinking: "Why is this relevant?" and feeling so afraid, if I didn't respond I wouldn't get access to what I needed: access to estrogen, name change, many sets of surgeries that I might want. So I felt forced to answer this strange questions. If you want to get access to trans-related healthcare you have to play that role. And I think, for a

while, I did. I took that identity as well. And the challenge was breaking away from that identity, that role. Once I've gone through that healthcare system and navigated it, I could finally be myself. I could actually say: "This is all fake, now I can be myself". So for me, the biggest challenge was going from pretending to be a boy,[14] to pretending to be this stereotypical woman, to actually being myself.

Aiden shares a similar experience.

> In San Francisco, I started going to the community health center. They had Thursday nights drop-in for gender non-conforming kids who had medical questions. I went to check it out and the nurse was amazing! She was in a relationship with a trans guy, amazing! I went there for the entire time I have been living in San Francisco, which was 6–7 years, and in all that time I saw the doctor once. San Francisco is quite progressive. This woman genuinely cared about and listened to people who came there. So I started asking questions about what I need to do to start taking hormones. I have decided to see a therapist, to be able to have access to hormones, because this clinic, although very progressive, still used Harry Benjamin protocols for standards of care.[15] But I didn't really connect to the therapist. Maybe because I knew I was required to talk to him before taking hormones, so I was more concerned with convincing him that I was mentally sound so that he would approve my hormones. I was more concerned with that than with getting my stuff figured out through therapy. And I think a lot about this. Even to this day. Why am I saying what am I saying? To prove someone that I am … who I know that I am, who I am saying I am? Whenever you talk about gender identity, the discourse is framed in that way that you have to "prove it". I am solid with my identity as a trans man, and I think my identity would always be trans-masculine, if we look at the gender identity spectrum. But then you have a spectrum within trans-masculine. It took me a while to give myself permission to be the way I want to, to say to myself: "you don't have to be more trans-masculine just to prove to the outside world that you are a trans man". I always felt that I have to "convince" doctors and therapists how much trans I was. I learned that you have to tell the therapist what they want to hear. In 2011, I had an opportunity to have a top surgery and I needed to have a letter from a psychiatrist. This guy was great. He was through the University. I went to him and I said: "Look, I am trans and I have been on hormones for 7 years [at that point]. I know who I am, I

am solid in my identity, I have an opportunity to have a top surgery and I need a letter from a therapist". And he said: "Done". That was it. On the one hand, he was amazing. But once again I needed to use his signature, to get what I need. I went with my dad and my best friend to do my top surgery. At the time it was not covered by the health insurance, my dad paid for it. My granddad had died, so he got some money from there. At the time, no health insurance that I knew of, would cover the top surgery. Nowadays, there are insurance policies that cover top surgery, bottom surgery is rarer to be covered, but it's changing.

During the time I was serving at the Peace Corps in Southeast Asia, I had some medical issues with my uterus. And I was in the waiting room with only pregnant women. But the doctors did the best they could. The doctors from the Peace Corps went to the hospital beforehand and talked with the doctors there. It was all very secretive: "We have a transgender patient coming here. We need to make sure that everything is OK". But in their attempt to be respectful, or to maintain the secrecy that I didn't really want, they asked me to sit outside instead of the main waiting room. And when it was my turn to come in, they opened a back door and sneaked me in the clinic. I was like: should I be offended or honored? And to this day I don't know, I haven't decided. Because I get what they were trying to do: they were doing what THEY thought was the best and respectful for me. But it felt weird, and a bit … dehumanizing. I was hidden behind this curtain … and I had to have this super painful ultrasound. I have been medically evacuated to the States because they thought it wouldn't be safe for me to have surgery in that country. So whenever you are medically evacuated from the Peace Corps, you have 45 days to prove that you are medically fit to return. So I had to recover from it enough to pass the doctor's evaluation within 45 days. Once again, another doctor whom I had to prove that I was fit. By the way, when I was applying for the Peace Corps, I had to go back to the therapist that I've seen at the University, who gave me the letter of approval for my top surgery. I asked him to give me a psychiatric evaluation for the Peace Corps. And this is interesting: According to the Harry Benjamin standards of care, before I got hormones, I should have been diagnosed with what was then called gender identity disorder and was considered back then a mental health disorder. But because the clinic I went to in San Francisco was so progressive, they were not really into diagnosing me. So now, in order for me to be able to serve in the Peace Corps, I had to be diagnosed with a mental health disorder.

Sebastian, who underwent medical transition in his youth, faced challenging health care system one more time in 2015, when he had to do a series of medical analyses because of a health issue: thrombus on the eye. After a series of analysis, he discovered that he is in fact intersex.[16] This is what he shared about issues that intersex people face with medicalization.

> Intersex children are discriminated against from a very young age from medical professionals, through forced surgical interventions and medicalization. For example, babies with penises smaller than 2 cm, which is considered "too small" are assigned the female gender by the doctors and genitals are reconstructed to look female, while clitorises larger than 0.9 cm are considered "too big" and are reduced in size. So doctors assign the male gender to the baby in that case. That is against the Convention on the Rights of the Child, and the right to bodily integrity and autonomy. No surgeries can be done on those who cannot give consent, and babies and young children are one of these people. Doctors often justify to the parents that surgeries are necessary, saying the child's health is in the stake. And parents give their consent.[17] But what is forgotten is that while they, doctors, decide with the consent of the parents who don't have enough knowledge on the issue, what the gender of the child will be, they cannot really know how will the child identify in terms of their gender when they grow up. And the harm is already done. And the trauma stays. After realizing I am intersex, I founded an organization, the first one in my country working on intersex issues specifically. Intersex people I work with have experiences of being physically abused because of the medical interventions performed on them. That trauma can happen from the preverbal period, when the child is still young and can't remember it, as in the case of one-month-old babies. And that trauma is not recognized by the society and healthcare system. Therefore, there is a veil of silence around intersex issues. That's the most painful aspect of it for me. And it starts with those who hold the biggest power: doctors. There is a culture of silence on intersex issues and what has been done to intersex children, even among medical professionals. Parents keep that secret from the children, and from other parents. Children keep that secret from other children, because of the stigma. This society recognizes the word hermaphrodite and not intersex. Intersex is the right term, which has been used in academic circles recently, but still, it is seen as a condition, and not as human beings who have variations in sex characteristics.

THE RESEARCH	57

Apart from systemic oppression faced in dealing with the healthcare system, several participants described systemic oppression faced in activist work related to legislative, policy and bureaucratic challenges. Ugla shared their experience.

> In 2015–2016, another activist and I received an email from one of the political parties in Iceland. They said they have been working on the consultation on "third gender" and wanted to create legislation to propose it to the Parliament. We read it and it was completely out of touch with the reality of what trans people in Iceland needed. It mentioned two-spirit people [which is related to indigenous North American context], the third gender in Africa, India and all these contexts that are not representative of what being trans in Iceland is like. So my friend and I realized that we have to form our own group of people, to work on legislation that we are going to present to political parties. We established a meeting with all political parties in Iceland, because Iceland is such a small country, so it was easy to set that meeting. We started working with one of the political parties on comprehensive legislation about trans and intersex rights. It has been in work for two and a half years now [since 2015, and is still in the progress due to various levels of resistance], and it will be presented to the Parliament this year [2018], in the next couple of months. If it passes, it will be the most comprehensive legislation on trans and intersex rights in the world.[18] So we realized we can not count on anyone else except for ourselves to know best what kind of change we need. We needed to tell them how to do things, so we took the power, realized we are the experts on this topic, and the political parties have to work with us if they want to create a meaningful change on trans rights in this country. That was quite empowering to say that to the political parties: "we are going to do this, and you are here to help us however you can". They are not the experts on trans people's rights and needs, we are.

Fiachra shared their experience of working with one of the United Nations agencies, in one country in Asia.

> That country, while it doesn't criminalize LGBTQI people, is still very conservative, it doesn't accept LGBTQI people socially, politically and morally. Part of that is based on religious grounds. We were supporting research in that country, and other countries, on what the legal reality was for legal gender recognition of trans people and employment discrimination of

trans people. Just the facts on the ground. And there was a right-wing, religious movement there that was gaining momentum, scapegoating and focusing more and more on LGBTQI people, saying that we were promoting homosexuality, while we were actually doing research. In the end, it came down that the government said to the UN: If you don't stop this program working here, we are going to kick out the rest of your programs. These are programs that work on everything from environmental impact to poverty alleviation, other human rights violations, just … huge problems. Because this is a developing country. So we had to pull out. And for me, that was disheartening, not just on the personal level, but also on the professional level. Because we have been working with the local activists, whom we called our partners on the ground, who have been involved in the research. They felt abandoned, betrayed and lost faith in the work we have been doing. And my team was mostly queer team, nearly all of us were LGBT and a couple of allies in the team. We had to leave and we didn't have a choice in that matter. Because when you work on LGBTQI rights, or the rights that people often find unacceptable, you know it's easy for people to drift away. It is symptomatic of how working with minorities is often approached. It's like: "it's great as long as it's sexy". You don't hear international corporations supporting LGBTQI rights in countries that are not LGBTQI supportive, or that have policies that are prohibiting. And I understand why they made that decision, because you have to have a permission of the country to operate there. But often politics can get in the way of helping people especially something which is as sensitive as LGBTQI rights when bureaucracy is getting in the way, which happens with multi-national, international organizations, where there is a lot of funding from the outside sources. Often you can't release reports because of politics or the lack of will from somebody who isn't an LGBTQI ally. I found that very difficult. But that's a part of the work.

These were some of the participant's experiences related to systemic oppression. Another sub-theme of experienced challenges is related to the lack of supportive environments, such as community, family, friends, and partners. Jemiah shared their experience with their stepfather.

When I was 18 years old, I moved out of the family home. I had a conservative fundamentalist stepfather, who had mental health issues that no one ever spoke about or told me about. I knew about it because he would be in mental health institutions. My mom would always try not to hit me or use corporal punishment, but it did happen on occasions, by my stepfather who always hated me. He always wanted to punish me physically. I think he hated me because I am queer. I would be upset because of the way he sees the world: a patriarchal guy who because of the mental health issues would never be a family provider, that would always be my mom. But he would always act like: "women are not allowed this, and men are allowed to do that". I would challenge him on this stuff, even about the Bible, because he is a Christian fundamentalist, always referring to the Bible to justify himself. He would refer to the Old Testament saying that being queer is not OK. So I would always challenge him on gender issues, patriarchy in the society we live in. And he would be upset with me. If I leave the plates on the table, he would make a fuzz out of it and my mom would be in front of the two of us trying to protect me. But sometimes, when my mom was not there, he would hit me. And everyone in my family was protective of him, because of his mental health issues. He also hated Muslims, and I am a really strong anti-racist and I would always argue with him, calling him out for Islamophobia. If it would happen during the family dinner, everyone would try to stop that, not to have him angry. Because he is a man, and no one wanted to see him angry.

My mom was basically fed up with me and wanted me to leave. So I left. I remember that day and how I felt. I packed one bag and left, super dramatic. I didn't tell my mother where I'm going to be. And on the commuter train, I called my friend and asked if I can live with her. That was the low part of leaving my family. The good part was that I found a home and stability where fighting was not a norm, where I didn't feel hated and where I could be myself 24/7. It showed me beautiful parts of coming out and allowing yourself to love yourself, basically. But it also showed me what is like to choose between your self-worth, your life, and your family. It is very very difficult for me to choose between. For me is almost the same. My worth is in having a family. After I left, my mom would see me in the media, in the articles about the Pride for example. She would be super upset and write me evil stuff, so I haven't talked to her for two years.

Aiden shared that when he decided to come out as trans to his family, his sister threatened him, saying that if he decides to transition, she will never talk to him again, or allow him to see his nephew who he loves. Alex shared a similar experience:

> Once I was on the national television, talking about my experience of being queer, so my father and extended family found about it through the media. My mother was traveling back home from Italy. The family called her and informed her about it. I remember she told me: "I would rather have my plane crushed than having to face this".

River reported having a very unsupportive first romantic partner, who was queer herself, but not in favor of River's life as an outed[19] queer and activist in becoming. River also shared that their friends reacted negatively when River decided to come out as genderqueer: they laughed.

Furthermore, one of the common challenges that participants reported facing, which emerged as another sub-theme is: dealing with internalized transphobia, impostor syndrome, and feeling of "not being enough". Ugla shared how coming into terms with their gender identity and letting go of shame and feeling "less than" has been their greatest challenge.

> Learning to celebrate myself and learning to love things I am shamed for, is my biggest challenge. Trans people are usually seen as objects of disgust, or undesirable or seen to have weird bodies. When I was in secondary school there were three brothers who were raised in the same area as me. They made a song for a song contest in the school. The song was about a guy who was involved with a girl and later realized she has a penis, that she is a trans woman. It was a big joke and everybody laughed, considering that disgusting. At that moment I didn't realize why that was wrong. I had such internalized shame that I was like: "Yeah, of course, that's weird". I wasn't able to challenge transphobia back then, because I had such internalized shame, that I didn't realize back then It was wrong. So the biggest challenge was to be able to celebrate myself, celebrate my body, celebrate being trans and being proud of that. Not wanting to hide that, not thinking I'm undesirable and that it's OK for people to treat me wrongly because I am trans.

Aiden described how he struggled with the feeling of "not being enough".

> There is always that feeling of a fraud: either I am not trans enough, as in this case when I served in the Peace Corps, I was thinking if I am acting cis enough, am I "passing"[20] as cis man enough. I got accepted to work in the "Children, Youth and Family" sector of the Peace Corps. I got assigned to work in a very small community. My job was to work with people who are on their social welfare system. I went there as a trans man and was

told by the doctors that it is best for me to keep my gender identity for myself, for the risk of violence. It is a very religious country. The community I was living in was very religious, Catholic. Because I was going there not for myself but for the community, I decided to keep my gender identity a secret. If I had decided to be open about it, it would erode a lot of trust and relationships I was trying to build.

On the other side, within the queer community, I feel I have to prove that I am queer enough. I feel like when I was perceived as a butch lesbian, before the transition, I was accepted in the queer community. But once I started passing as a man, when I was not visibly queer … it was harder to find and sustain that community. Every time I go to a queer space I have to out myself: to justify why I am in the queer space. I have to prove that I am queer enough for that space. If I don't immediately say: "Hey, I am a trans guy", then I am not welcome in that community. And that sucks.

Jemiah, a queer person of color, described how they had to make a conscious effort to see themselves as deserving of opportunities, status, success, and overcome what they described as the impostor syndrome.

I try to achieve stuff by launching myself into it. And in the past 3 years, I've been trying to achieve stuff by going for them. I applied to this Secretary General position in an organization. It is well paid and cool position, I would never dream of three years ago, because of an impostor syndrome, I think. And now I see opportunities that I haven't been able to see before, because of racial and other social structures. I manage to allow myself to grow. Because of my impostor syndrome and being afraid of succeeding or being powerful and having power, now I want to allow myself to experience all these opportunities. It's not that I don't have the capacity, knowledge or skills, because I do have them. It's because the society is sending you a message: "you are not good enough for this". It's about the race as well. This is a super racist and racialized country, although people wouldn't say that, but it's highly racist. From street harassment to employment possibilities. It's structural, it is everywhere in the society. Sometimes when I do a training facilitation job and I get paid for it, I look at my bank account and feel like: "There is something wrong with my bank account. Someone is putting money there that doesn't belong to me. I don't deserve this money, I've always been so poor". And then I say to myself: "I earned this money because of my merit and my work". I definitely think if society tells us we are not worthy of love, acceptance, job opportunities, success, it's more difficult for us to internalize the "go and get it" attitude.

Another common subtheme within the experienced challenges is the lack of visibility and validation of GNC identities.

Alex shared how they felt not visible and validated as a gender non-binary person.

> It's challenging for me because most languages are gendered and binary. These young people I work with barely speak English, so gender-neutral pronouns are not close to their reality. When I ask colleagues to use gender-neutral pronouns, they might use it when I ask them to, but forget about it afterward. But every time somebody genders me, especially when they use female pronouns, when they misgender me, I feel it very deeply. It leads to a feeling that my identity is not valid – as I always have to explain it. Sometimes I feel excluded from the trans community because I don't want gender-affirming surgeries or hormonal therapy. Being seen as not really trans, or not trans enough, feels like I don't belong there, but I don't belong to the cisgender community either. Many cis friends rather don't tackle this subject with me. Actually many people trans or cis, colleagues or friends, don't really ask how it is for me to be gender non-binary in order to understand me better. We ignore this topic or talk about it superficially. The only people who ask me are those who see me as a "living book", an object of interest.

It was already described in the paragraph on how relocation as a life event can influence activist identity development, how River felt invalidated as a gender non-binary person, when they started facilitating a trans support group. That was one of the motivating factors for founding the first trans-specific organization in their country, working on the advancement of trans and GNC people's rights.

Ugla reported how invalidated they felt during an interview for the UK TV program, Good Morning Britain.

> Together with my partner, who is also an activist and a non-binary trans person, I went for an interview with Piers Morgan and Susana Reid about what is it like to be non-binary, on Good Morning Britain. This interview was a complete disaster because he wasn't acknowledging non-binary people at all. Honestly, we weren't brought there to talk about non-binary

issues. We were brought there to be ridiculed and humiliated by him on TV because he thought we were just a bunch of weirdoes who identify as "neither men or women". That was actually the longest interview in the UK media on non-binary issues. It demonstrated how non-binary people aren't taken seriously by the media and how we are ridiculed and humiliated, compared to animals, you know? Piers said at some point that being non-binary is contagious! I told him the exact argument has been used about homosexuality in the past, and he said it's not the same. He said if people can identify however they want in terms of their gender, that means he could identify as an elephant and go to a London Zoo, or he could identify as a black woman! I think he did it for the media attention. Because we weren't arguing with him, he needed and wanted to make it crazy.

The last common sub-theme within the experienced challenges that shaped participants' activist identity development is the *Effects of experienced discrimination and oppression on mental health*.

As presented above, Aiden shared how he struggled with depression and self-harm, while experiencing bullying in school because of gender non-conformity and not fitting into body-size norms. River said: "the older I get, the more I am in activism, the harder work-related situations I face, the more I am living vividly most of my identities, the more affected my mental health is. I have anxiety and depression". Fiachra shared how they started facing mental health challenges after their father was diagnosed with Alzheimer's and how they struggled with it because they didn't want to be "double stigmatized".

> My father going into permanent care is what triggered my obsessive-compulsive disorder. I had a complicated relationship with my father. His condition makes grieving hard, because it feels like a slow death. My anxiety level went through the roof. I was diagnosed with Obsessive-Compulsive Disorder (OCD). The positive part is that I can be compassionate toward other people who are struggling with mental health issues, because I know it's hard. But, you know, people like to pathologize trans people. And people like to say I'm mentally ill because I am trans. And I'm about to say that I have a mental health issue, but it's not about me being trans. I have OCD. I would rather focus on understanding that, than having pathologized healthy aspects of me.

Alex shared they used to experience panic attacks and anxiety because with more activist related work they'd became more anxious. They said they can't differentiate anymore if its anxiety or "modus operandi" related to the challenges of activist work.

Jemiah shared how after leaving parental home because of being queer and after breaking up with their partner, they started facing mental health problems, as a result of the stress related to homelessness.

> I started drinking a lot. Which is what a lot of us queers do when it comes to coping. I went really bad down road spiral of drinking, depression, homelessness. I would go from one apartment to another, stay with some friends. I was feeling really bad. I was like … this is what it means to be queer. Because we, queer people, always face these issues. We always say how trans women are overrepresented in homelessness or social exclusion. And I always thought that can't happen to me because I know the white gay movement, that has more money, resources and stability than trans people, at least from my experience. I realized that being broke, having problems with alcohol and not having a stable home, family or a support system, you can really just go down, really quick.

Ugla shared how impacted they were by a recent loss of a friend, a fellow trans activist, who died of suicide.

> One of the close friends of mine committed suicide recently. She was also an activist and did so many great things. She was one of the people who run a web page called *A Trans Teen Survival Guide* which is a blog on Tumblr. And that was a place where trans teens could send in questions, thoughts, express if they need support. She helped so many people come into terms with who they are. And she has always been very good at that. She supported so many people and yet, she was not able to support herself. And that was the saddest moment. She had a lot going on: being trans, media in the UK being hostile. But she was keeping it all in. And that's one of the reasons why my partner and I made a book that we are going to publish. It's called Trans Teen Survival Guide,[21] which is going to be dedicated to her.

Another issue that all participants reported facing in relation to their mental health, is activist burn-out. All participants highlighted that being in the role of constantly educating people is emotionally draining. Jemiah said that because they are a person of color, they are always expected to educate people on race and colonialism: "Just knowing that EVERY time you go to some space [educational or representational event], you have to teach someone what is it to be trans or why is important to be racially sensitive. It's tiring". Aiden shared they got tired of proving they are "enough" [queer enough, trans enough, passing enough]:

> The problem which involves being out about my gender identity in non-queer spaces is: I automatically become somehow less of a person and more of an object of inquisition. The first thing everyone wants to know about me when they hear that I am trans is about my anatomy! As an activist, I am happy to share my experiences and knowledge with others, but there is a difference between someone asking me questions respectfully and someone objectifying me, by what they think my gender identity means. Also, it can be discouraging to have to re-face battles [with the system], all over again. It drains your soul to have to fight, for example, for the right to use a public toilet. One should never have to fight for that, it should be a given. Having a gender-neutral toilet is not that difficult.

Alex said that because of the activist burn-out they suffered, they changed a job. Now they are more focused on education and training facilitation than leadership positions in queer activism.

These presented challenges lead to another common theme which emerged from the data: *Support factors that participants need so they can carry out their social change work.*

### 3.3 Support Factors Needed for the Continuation of Activism and Adult Education for Social Change

One of the most frequent support factors that participants of this study highlighted is the need for a network of like-minded and supportive people. That topic was evident throughout previously shared statements about formative life events and challenges that influenced activist identity development. Aiden shared how having supportive friends helped him deal with school bullying and how meeting like-minded queer people through volunteering, was influential for coming into terms with his gender identity. The later was also highlighted by all the participants. Sebastian and Ugla shared that having a supportive partner with whom they can share their activist achievements is important to them. Sebastian said he needs support from new activists who will continue the work. River shared the same-the importance of not being alone and having a team of people who can eventually continue their work. Interestingly enough, both of them are leaders of the organizations they founded. Having a supportive social network of activists from different countries is something that River, Sebastian, Ugla, Fiachra shared they need. Fiachra and Jemiah highlighted the importance of having a supportive family environment. Jemiah said:

> The family is the safety net we so desperately need when we face institutionalized discrimination – when the court and legal systems can't protect us. On the other hand, the family can also be the offender or the source of violence. Many young trans or GNC people are lost without the sense of a family. Some of us choose to have our own, self-defined family, and some of us are forced into being all by ourselves.

The next sub-theme within support factors is about having access to safe and gender-affirming spaces. As it can be seen from participants' statements in the previous paragraphs, having a safe school environment free of transphobic bullying is of paramount importance for them. They also highlighted some more specific factors, such as having trans and GNC-affirming facilities (for example, gender-neutral toilets), so that they don't have to fear for their safety and be exposed to harassment.

Access to social services and opportunities is another common sub-theme within needed support factors, specifically related to employment without discrimination; simplified gender recognition procedures,[22] access to trans-affirming healthcare based on informed consent. Jemiah said that it is: "difficult enough to find a good job where you feel welcome, you're accepted and not afraid of unequal or uncool workplace culture".

Ugla highlighted that representation and validation of trans and GNC people is important both in terms of employment opportunities and creating accessible trans-affirming health care. They said:

> Trans people are not being taken seriously or seen as the experts on their lives, capable of knowing themselves and what they need. Often other people, from politicians to doctors and the general public, are telling us who they think we are, what they think we need, and how they think we need access to certain social services. But in reality we know exactly what we need, we live it every single day. The biggest challenge is to make people recognize it and listen. If we are going to create laws, trans-affirming policies, better healthcare, and improve society, we have to be able to voice out what needs to change and to be taken seriously. We need to have agency in that social change. And it goes beyond just advocacy, it goes into representation in entertainment, theatre, books, arts, careers, education. Everything. Trans people need to be leading conversations

about trans people and trans people's needs. That needs to be seen as a plus, as a good thing: the fact that we are the experts on our lives who should be seen as such, as opposed to being seen as trouble. If you don't have trans people involved in a trans-related project or initiative, you are not going to make things good. Nothing for us without us.

All participants highlighted access to trans-affirming healthcare, based on informed consent, as an important support factor. Several participants highlighted the need to have access to trans-affirming mental health – psychotherapy and counseling, as a safe space to address the challenges that come with activist work, such as burn-out and working under systemic oppression. Sebastian said that having a good therapist is one of his priorities when it comes to supporting factors needed for his work. Another important support factor is access to simplified legal gender recognition procedures based on self-determination instead of medicalization and pathologization.

Participants of lower socio-economic status, with experience of poverty, shared the importance of having paid job, because volunteer work they can engage in depends on that.

Another common topic within support factors is continuous work on self-development, personal growth, and learning. Jemiah said they want to set higher standards for the queer movement, in terms of learning about other marginalized people's struggles:

> We need to align with other movements. For example, I can be an ally for the disability rights movement. I can ask: "what can I do and how I can help?". And if I do something which is insensitive due to my lack of knowledge, I'm not gonna start crying, or asking them to educate me or comfort me, because I know that power structures related to ablism exist within our movement as well. So if I can manage to face my privilege, standing in solidarity with people who face different struggles, I can learn more and do better. That's what I would ask our community: to educate ourselves and to hold ourselves accountable. We are killing our own activists by excluding them. By not being a good ally. We have to educate ourselves. "When we know better, we do better", Maya Angelou said.

Ugla highlighted the importance of learning how to love oneself:

> Everything I have done is based on "personal is political", and based on emotional intelligence, compassion and learning to love myself. Being radical in what you do, while being vulnerable at the same time, is

important because vulnerability straightens that, it is an important part of activist learning. Often in our societies, we don't see vulnerability as a strength, but I see it as a huge strength, it's incredibly empowering.

River shared something similar, which they named as: un-learn, learn and re-learn:

> Learning how to be myself. How to unlearn, re-learn and learn ... freedom, I guess. Act in radical vulnerability. For me, that means the capacity or a decision to learn to express yourself for yourself, but also for others to feel that they are not alone. It's about how to be a member of the queer community, while at the same time building, forming that community. You can't form a community if you are not vulnerable with them, because they are not going to attach themselves to someone whom they are not feeling as a person.

For Alex, continually investing in personal development and self-awareness is equally important as having a supportive social network.

### 3.4   *Applying the Critical Framework to Social Justice Work*

All participants reported applying an intersectional and critical framework to their activist and social justice education work and shared similar ethical values (compassion, justice, radical vulnerability, and kindness), political orientations (leftist, socialist) and social values, such as justice, freedom, and equity, valuing intersectional feminism, anti-capitalist, anti-racist, anti-oppressive, norm-critical, human rights-based approach to adult education for social change and social transformation. The development of this critical consciousness is described through participants' witnessing and experiencing injustices in life, both personal and those faced by other people who belong to minority social groups. Furthermore, working with non-queer communities and meeting people of different minority identities through activist work, is described as a learning experience that shaped the development of their critical consciousness. A sense of solidarity with the struggles of other minorities and alliance with them is seen by the participants as an important aspect of applying the critical framework to their work, together with envisioning a radically transformed society.

When talking about the most influential contexts for their activist identity development, participants stressed the importance of: volunteering (focusing on, for example, homeless people, animal rights activism, environmental activism); doing internships in various fields aiming at social transformation (for example, LGBTQI rights, refugees and displaced people); formal education (Bachelor's and Master's degrees which contribute to better understanding of social issues and inequity, such as gender studies, international relations, community development) and non-formal education (summer camps and summer schools, conferences, seminars, both related to queer and non-queer issues), which allowed them to explore their gender identity and learn about other people's struggles.

However, not all participants envisioned their future activist work focusing only on gender issues and trans and GNC people's rights. Some of them want to focus primarily on the affirmation of trans and GNC people's rights, and dismantling binary gender norms, while working intersectionally to address the multiplicity of societal oppressions. Other participants want to primarily focus on the rights of other minority social groups: refugee rights, poverty reduction, and community organizing of minority social groups. Nevertheless, all of them acknowledge the interrelatedness of different systems of oppression leading to social exclusion and aim to give their contribution to creating progressive social change for all.

## 4  Discussion and Conclusions

The purpose of this research was to explore the development of the identity of adult educator and activist for social change, among transgender and GNC participants from different countries, who were at the time the research was done, or in the recent past prior to the interviews, in the leadership positions in the organizations working on the advancement of LGBTQI human rights throughout Europe.

This research was conducted to address the gap in adult education theory, research, and provision in relation to gender identities beyond gender binaries and in relation to the development of the identity of adult educator and activist for social change among TGNC people. More specifically, I saw this research as a step towards the reparation of epistemic injustice done to trans and GNC people, which facilitates and is facilitated by systemic and systematic oppression. That epistemic injustice is reflected in the lack of trans epistemologies in education, both formal and non-formal social justice education. The research was approached from the critical educational research paradigm, seeking to understand how is activist identity development mediated through one's intersecting identities, and experiences of social injustices and the role they played in that intersection. The findings of this research and the recommendations provided in Chapter 6 can be used to create adult education, social justice education, and general formal education practice that is affirming of transgender and GNC people.

Some of the participants came to activism and adult education for social change because of the challenges they faced due to being trans and GNC, which is a finding supported by the reviewed literature (Bockting & Coleman, 2007); others because of witnessing and experiencing non-trans related injustices in life. Some participants gave themselves permission to explore their gender identity with the support of the activist spaces they belonged to. That is in alignment with the previous research done, which highlights that through meeting other like-minded people participants explore their gender identity and eventually come out as trans (Gagné et al., 1997). Furthermore, participants shared how exploring their identity and coming out as trans led them to involvement in activism and increased commitment to social change, which previous research also confirmed (Renn & Bilodeau, 2005a, 2005b; Renn, 2007), and vice versa: increased involvement in activism led to more visibility of their queer identities, which, in turn, firmly established them in activism (ibid.).

To summarize, gender identity exploration/development and activist identity development were influenced by each other as previous research confirms, as the one conducted by Renn and Bilodeau (2005a) who found that involvement in identity-based organizations on campuses led to the development of both activist/leadership and LGBT identities of the participants; and that the identity-development processes interact with each other, rather than appearing sequentially in stages (Renn & Bilodeau, 2005b).

Presented narratives show how activist identity development is shaped by different life events, such as experiencing injustices in life or having or lacking supportive environments. Challenges that participants reported facing, correspond to those found in the literature: transgender and GNC people experience discrimination, harassment, and hostile climates in education, employment, healthcare (Bilodeau, 2009; Beemyn et al., 2005; Beemyn & Rankin, 2011; Rankin, 2003; FRA, 2014; Wilchins et al., 1997; McKinney, 2005, UN, 2018). Issues that trans people face in their daily life are elaborated in Chapter 3 while issues that trans activists face in their work are elaborated in more detail in Chapter 5.

These experiences negatively affected participants' mental health, as the research also confirms. It is widely acknowledged by the research that trans and gender-variant people experience higher suicide rates, suicide ideation, depression, and anxiety than the general population (Bilodeau, 2009; Meyer, 2003; Haas et al., 2014; Bockting et al., 2013; Cochran, 2001; Effrig et al., 2011; Clements-Nolle et al., 2006; Marshall et al., 2015; Haas et al., 2014) and worse overall mental health (Bockting et al., 2013). The research on that topic will be presented in more detail in Chapter 3.

Among the specific challenges, participants of my research reported facing is the lack of support in the family environment, which affected their mental health and well-being. That finding is in accordance with the previous research done which shows that trans participants who experienced high levels of family rejection are more than three times as likely to have attempted suicide, and two and a half times more likely to have engaged in substance misuse (Klein & Colub, 2016). Research also highlights that greater levels of support from family members are related to higher life satisfaction of trans and GNC people (Erich et al., 2008). Aiden and Sebastian reported that only after their parent died, they give themselves permission to explore their gender identity and eventually, transition. That is in accordance with the research which shows that many trans participants reported delaying their gender transition to minimize family conflict (Von Doussa, Power, & Riggs, 2017).

In accordance with the previous research (Riggs et al., 2018), the participants of this research reported witnessing domestic violence, and experiences of such violence were related to reported depressive symptomology, and lower experienced levels of social support. Therefore, the importance of family acceptance of trans and GNC people is obvious.

Another common topic that participants of this research shared are microaggressions related to the use of gender-based pronouns. Incorrect pronouns use differs toward those gender binary participants who underwent medical transition and experience misgendering based on the use of incorrect gender pronoun before, during and/or after their social and/or medical transition; and toward those participants who identify as gender non-binary, using a pronoun "they" as a singular gender pronoun. Alex and River shared how being called a "woman" doesn't match their view of themselves and makes them feel invisible and invalidated. Literature review on trans and GNC specific microaggressions provided by Chang and Chung (2015) highlighted this problem.

In relation to feeling invisible and having the legitimacy of their gender identity questioned, another common theme emerged among the participants: a feeling of not being enough, as highlighted by Aiden, Alex, Ugla, and Jemiah. Participants shared how in order to be validated as a trans person, they were expected by the medical professionals[23] and the general population, to feel, think and act in ways that are the "exact opposite" from those socially expected for the gender they were assigned at birth, which is also confirmed by the research (Bilodeau, 2009). That is in alignment with the previous research that shows how trans people are expected to be or to act in gender-conforming ways (in alignment with the sex assigned at birth) and were denied their transgender identities (Nadal et al., 2012, p. 67).

Several participants of my research who did go through medical and hormonal transition[24] would still identify as gender non-binary or gender non-conforming, because they do not or conform to binary gender roles and stereotypical behaviors associated with them.

Aiden shared how because of his passing privilege, of being perceived as a cisgender man after the transition, he was never assumed to be trans both within the queer community and among cis people, which led to having to prove constantly, especially to the queer community, that he belongs there. Other participants who didn't feel the need to go through gender-affirming surgeries and/or hormonal therapy, but wanted to only, for example, to use the pronoun "they" and/or change their name, shared the feeling of "not being enough", because they were not perceived as trans enough by the trans community and didn't feel they belong to the cis community, either, like Alex for example. Research has also identified this problem (Pearce, 2012). River reported being laughed at when coming out as gender non-binary to their queer friends. That topic is present in the literature review on trans-specific microaggressions by Chang and Chung (2015) which highlights that gender non-conforming individuals may be ridiculed for not conforming to societal expectations of gender roles. Beemyn and Rankin (2011) highlighted how students who identified outside of the gender binary, found it particularly challenging to conform to the many gender-segregated policies and practices on university campuses. Aiden shared how he struggled in school when placed in locker-rooms for girls, or how having to fight for the right to go to the toilet in accordance with his gender, can be an exhausting and invalidating experience.

Other common topics that all the participants of my research shared were: applying the critical framework to their social justice activist work; valuing intersectional feminism, anti-capitalist, anti-racist, anti-oppressive, norm-critical, human rights-based approach to social justice activism. That corresponds with the research findings (Renn, 2007), which show that trans participants who merged their LGBT and leadership identities, fell into a category which was named "queer activist" and was marked by the desire to challenge societal norms and dismantle categories of gender and sexuality. They were dedicated to challenging normative approaches to sexuality and gender while working to transform oppressive systems completely, the same as participants of my research, who saw connections with other marginalized communities being an important aspect of their work.

## 4.1　*Intersectional Complexity*

Participants of my research reported that other intersecting identities and material realities influenced their activist and adult educator for social change identity development. These are: skin color/race, ethnicity, lower socio-economic status/poverty, religious affiliation, bodily diversity/sex characteristics (intersex status), mental health status, educational attainment level, and body size norms, to name a few. The complexity of the intersections between these identities is visible when looking at how their importance shifts in a different context. Important differences between participants' activist identity developmental paths seem to be related to the ways in which these other identities and material realities intersect with their gender identity, defining their position in the society and access to social opportunities and services. Jemiah highlighted several times how navigating racism and homelessness while being queer, was challenging. Fiachra said their activist identity development was shaped by the fact they were raised in poverty and had to work while studying, so the number of volunteer activities they could take on was limited, in addition to suffering from/witnessing domestic violence. Aiden and River highlighted that they experienced not just transphobia, but also fat-shaming as they didn't conform to the body size norms as well, so they were "double stigmatized". Sebastian shared how being trans and intersex shaped their activist identity development. A passing privilege that Aiden spoke about helped him to avoid the potential harassment because he is perceived as a cisgender man. The multiplicity of people's identities is what theoretical framework of this research, intersectionality theory, acknowledges, suggesting that these identities determine person's social situatedness, resulting in experiences of privilege and marginalization, which happen simultaneously, shaping peoples' lives (Combahee River Collective, 1979; Crenshaw, 1991; Collins, 2015), as this research showed.

To summarize, gender identity intersects with other relevant identities and material realities, and together with meaningful life events, and experiences of injustices and societal oppression, as well as privileges, influence social justice activist and educator identity development. Finally, in order to understand the whole person and their life, in the richness of the totality of who they are, without reducing them to a single identity such as their gender identity, we need to critically reflect on person's social situatedness, in relation to their social justice educator and activist identity development. We need to acknowledge and take into account power structures, power relations in the given society to understand how 'various social injustices, oppressions, and privileges interact and are enacted by the function of multiple identities' (Nishida, 2016).

Because this qualitative research was conducted with a small sample, with participants who are of diverse socio-cultural backgrounds, socio-economic statuses, geographical locations, and of different gender identities on the transgender spectrum, I cannot claim the generalizability of my research findings. Nevertheless, common identified themes are in accordance with the previous research done on the relationship between activist identity development and queer identities. The value of this research is in its specific focus: a minority social group that suffers epistemic and human rights injustices. Therefore, the contribution of this research to education theory, practice and research can be seen in the light of repairing that epistemic injustice. The narrative approach allowed me to explore the research topic taking into account the richness of participant's lived experiences, while theoretical framework-intersectionality theory, allowed me to interpret them taking into account the totality of who my participants are as human beings, without reducing them to their gender identity, and therefore, objectifying them. The critical educational research paradigm was applied throughout the whole research, from the choice of the research topic, through choosing the research population, to choosing a methodological approach, approach to data analysis and finally, interpretation of the collected data. This paradigm allowed me not only to understand and interpret power relations and inequalities in societies that influence activist identity formation and development, but to challenge them by questioning dominant power structures. Finally, conducting this research was a life-enriching experience because of the readiness of my participants to be exposed, vulnerable, brave, honest, and open with me while sharing some of their most challenging life experiences. If there is any value of this research, it is in participants' unique existences, and the fact that they keep on working to improve the lives of many people, and the society in general. For the better.

### Notes

1 The literature review was concluded in May 2019, as this book was submitted to the publisher in its final form on June 1, 2019.
2 Slovenia, Romania, Serbia, Sweden, USA, Ireland, Iceland and Greece.
3 Specific research questions (the first 3) were developed on the basis of the research questions set by Johnson (2014) who conducted a doctoral research on the intersections between college students' transgender and activist identities in the urban university context in the USA.

THE RESEARCH                                                                                                                    75

4   Not intersex. Other word used to refer to non-intersex people is dyadic.
5   Irrational fear, and emotionally charged negative attitude towards intersex people, mostly experienced by endosex/dyadic people (those who are not intersex).
6   Such as age, ability status, mental health status, race, ethnicity, migration status, religious background, educational attainment level, socio-economic background, geography, etc.
7   For example: Please describe a scene, an episode, or a moment in your life that stands out as an especially positive experience. This might be the high point scene of your entire life, or else an especially happy, joyous, exciting, or wonderful moment in the story. Please describe this high point scene in detail. What happened, when and where, who was involved, and what were you thinking and feeling? Also, please say a word or two about why you think this particular moment was so good and what the scene may say about who you are as a person.
8   For example: "How do you approach political or social issues? Do you have a particular political point of view? Are there particular social issues or causes you feel strongly about? Please explain".
9   It is important to highlight that I chose not to disclose which participants underwent medical transition, because I didn't want to reinforce the idea that the transition itself, makes a person "more trans". However, out of four participants who identified both as trans and non-binary, two of them underwent gender affirming surgeries and/or hormone replacement therapy, to align their body with their internal sense of gender identity, in addition to two pearticipants who identified as trans man, and one who identified both as trans and intersex.
10  I created a codebook for names, locations, organizations, etc. so that all identifying information could be excluded from the final narratives, but could be reconstructed in the future by me, in case I need it (Josselson, 2007).
11  I am certified psychodrama counselor by the Regional Association for Psychodrama and Integrative Psychotherapy (RAIP), which is a psychotherapy training institute in Serbia, where I am currently enrolled in the advanced level of a 5 years long postgraduate training program in group psychotherapy.
12  A term referring to gender incongruence. After June 18, 2018 the World Health Organization removed gender identity issues from the list of mental health disorders, naming them "gender incongruence" and assigning them to the chapter on Conditions related to sexual health (TGEU, 2018a). But American Psychological Association (APA, 2013) still counts gender incongruence as mental health disorder, although the most recent additions of the DSM have changed the term to "gender dysphoria".
13  European Voluntary Service.
14  They were assigned male at birth.

15 Protocols regarding the treatment for individuals who wish to undergo hormonal and/or medical transition, based on which medical doctors make decisions regarding access to health care for trans and GNC people. First clinical guidelines were created by the former Harry Benjamin International Gender Dysphoria Association, which is today called World Professional Association for Transgender Health and works on setting protocols within the medical model of approaching trans issues.
16 It is important to make a distinction between intersex and trans people. Intersex individuals are persons who cannot be classified according to the medical norms of so-called male and female bodies with regard to their chromosomal, gonadal or anatomical sex. The latter becomes evident, for example, in secondary sex characteristics such as muscle mass, hair distribution and stature, or primary sex characteristics such as the inner and outer genitalia and/or the chromosomal and hormonal structure (Ghattas, 2013, p. 10). Trans individuals are those whose sex assigned at birth is not in alignment with gender they identify with.
17 IGLYO launched in 2018 the "Supporting your intersex child" toolkit for parents, carers, relatives and siblings of intersex children, written in collaboration with OII Europe and the European Parents' Association (EPA), which can be accessed at https://www.iglyo.com/iglyo-oii-europe-and-epa-launch-intersex-toolkit-for-parents/ (IGLYO, OII Europe, & EPA, 2018).
18 The Gender Identity Law, or Gender Authonomy Act was adopted by the Icelandic Parliament in June 2019 (Iceland Review, 2019). While it affirms the rights of trans people, including people who identify as gender non-binary, it is not without the shortcomings, according to the Icelandic activists (ibid.). The biggest critique of the law is that it left the rights of intersex people behind. As I have understood from a follow-up conversation with Ugla on this matter after the law was adopted by the Parliament, the proposed law sought to ensure protections both for trans and intersex people, specifically for intersex children; by aiming to forbid the practice of performing unnecessary surgeries on intersex children. These demands of the Icelandic activists working on the legislation did not make it into the final legislation, after the revisions made to the original proposed bill. Instead, the law prescribes the creation of a special committee to research a new law specifically for intersex adults and children, within a year's time.
19 Person living openly as who they are.
20 Passing privilege refers to be perceived by others as cisgender, not being "visibly trans" and therefore being at lesser risk of transphobia.
21 It was published a couple of months after the interview we had (Fisher & Fisher, 2018).

22 An opportunity to legally change name and gender marker in documents, without the compulsory psychiatric evaluation, sterilization, as some trans and GNC people might want to undergo these medical procedures, but others might not want to.
23 Medical professionals refers to professionals working in medical health care, such as doctors, nurses, administration personnel, etc.
24 Often refered to in the literature as transexual, which is a medical term.

CHAPTER 3

# Experiences of Transgender and Gender Non-Conforming People

In order to understand experiences of trans and gender non-conforming (GNC) adult educators and activists for social change, it is first necessary to understand how overt (discrimination in education, employment, lack of access to health care, and social services, therefore systemic oppression) and covert forms of bias and discrimination (microaggressions) affect transgender people's lives.

The purpose of this chapter is to provide a context for the research I have conducted, and to provide an overview of the issues that trans and gender non-conforming people face in their daily life, such as experienced discrimination in education contexts, the effects of the experienced discrimination and minority stress on mental health and well-being and experiences with mental health professionals; spectrum of privilege within trans and GNC communities, and visibility of trans and GNC identities. Readers who wish to learn more about trans peoples access to employment and education related to the legal gender recognition laws, policies, and procedures, and existing international legal and policy framework on trans issues which impacts access to education provision, are referred to Chapter 4. Those interested to learn more about the experiences of trans and gender non-conforming activists related to their social justice activist work, are referred to Chapter 5.

The chapter will focus on the experiences of trans people: experiences of trans and GNC students on campuses; issues of visibility of trans and GNC people; psychological effects of the oppression they experience and experiences with mental health professionals; the spectrum of privilege experienced within trans and GNC community and microaggressions experienced in everyday life. Readers interested in transgender and GNC identity development and activist identity development of trans people, are referred to Chapter 1.

## 1   Experiences of Trans and GNC Students

Until recently, there was not much available data on trans and GNC students' experiences in education, such as bullying, harassment, and exclusion in schools. During my work with International LGBTQI Youth and Student Organization (IGLYO), while I was serving the role of the member of the Executive Board of the Network, IGLYO launched a campaign called No More Hiding, during UNESCO's international ministerial conference Out in the Open (IGLYO, 2016). A photo exhibition and a film about LGBTQI young people's experiences of homophobia and transphobia in education (ibid.) were launched during the event, and IGLYO had two representatives of queer youth to share their experience of homophobic bullying in formal education, and to call ministers of the countries present to take LGBTQI related harassment in education seriously. UNESCO published *Out in the Open: Education Sector Responses to Violence Based on Sexual Orientation and Gender Identity/Expression* (UNESCO, 2016b) and outlined several recommendations, related to the response of the educational sector on the topic. UNESCO stated that a comprehensive education approach is needed to prevent and address homophobic, biphobic, transphobic and interphobic bullying (UNESCO, 2016a). This includes the implementation of (1) LGBTQI affirming national policies and/or action plans, (2) LGBTQI inclusive curricula and learning materials, (3) training for educational staff on LGBTQI issues, (4) support for queer students and families, (5) partnerships with civil society organizations, and (6) monitoring of discrimination based on SOGIESC[1] and evaluating the executed measures.

Furthermore, research worldwide showed that experienced discrimination based on SOGIESC in education increases the risk of drop out from school (UNESCO, 2016; Jones et al., 2016; GLSEN, 2016; WHO, 2015a). A study in New Zealand showed that trans secondary school students were almost five times more likely to be bullied on a weekly basis than their cisgender peers (Clark et al., 2014). The survey carried out by the European Union Agency for Fundamental Rights (FRA, 2014) found that a quarter of trans respondents who attended school/university themselves or had a child/children in school/at university, felt personally discriminated against by school or university personnel in the 12 months preceding the survey, but when looking at trans students only, the number rises to 29% (FRA, 2014, p. 21).

Research done on the experiences of transgender students in education, showed that transgender students experience a sense of not belonging, feelings of isolation, or having to hide a crucial aspect of their identity because of the fear for personal safety (Rankin, 2003; Meyer, 2004; Beemyn & Rankin, 2011). Psychological effects of experienced discrimination in education based on SOGIESC include thoughts of dropping out, psychological distress, self-harm, and even suicide attempts and suicide ideation (Bilodeau, 2009; Effrig, Bieschke, & Locke, 2011). Transgender students attending colleges in the United States report facing harassment, discrimination, hostile climates on college campuses and exclusion (McKinney, 2005; Beemyn, Curtis, Davis, & Tubbs, 2005; Rankin, 2003, 2005; Bilodeau, 2009).

Bilodeau (2009) developed a theory of *genderism* – institutional discrimination, coming from privileging a gender binary system in higher education. Based on 10 semi-structured interviews conducted with transgender students at two universities in the United States of America, Bilodeau identified four themes to describe how genderism in the higher education context shapes the experiences of transgender students. First, because of social labeling, students were considered either male or female. Therefore, one of two binary gender categories were assigned to them without their consent. For trans students because of being trans, their membership within the assigned category would always be questioned. The next theme was identified as social accountability and it showed that those conforming to the binary system of gender were rewarded, while those not conforming to the binary gender norms were punished, in the areas of gender-segregated facilities, academics, and employment. The third theme showed that because of favoring the gender binary system in education, students who don't conform to the binary gender norms faced marginalization. Students' lives within the formal education setting and outside of the campuses were affected by relationships with their peers and faculty. Their work in student organizations, and their plans for their future careers were also impacted by these relationships. The last theme that Bilodeau identified showed that social isolation had negative psychological effects on the participants of the research. Students who did not conform to the gender binary system felt invisible. For some, a coping mechanism was to conform to the gender binary, to avoid being constantly asked to explain and justify their existence. This research cast a light on some of the challenges that transgender students face because of systemic genderism in the university context. It showed the need for universities to support a spectrum of gender identities and expressions, not just those that fit into the gender binary of the so-called "two opposite genders". This research highlighted the need for policy changes within education. For example, to enable trans and gender non-conforming students to change their name and gender marker within institutional systems, and to add the "gender identity and gender expression" as protective grounds from discrimination in university nondiscrimination statements and policies. This research also called for: developing LGBTQI affirming education provision and practice, which includes trans-affirming facilities and locker-rooms, allowing trans students to use bathroom according to their lived gender and not sex assigned at birth; providing a training for the University staff on LGBTQI issues and trans identities (training on gender and sexual diversity), to name the few.

## 2  Visibility of Trans and GNC Students in Education

For the purposes of the research described in *Campus climate for gay, lesbian, bisexual, and transgender people: A national Perspective*, Sue Rankin (2003) invited thirty higher education institutions in the USA to participate in the research. Twenty agreed and fourteen completed the surveys. Rankin wanted to learn more about the experiences of LGBT people on campuses and campus climates, more specifically personal campus experiences for LGBT students, perception of the campus climate for LGBT members of the academic community, and their perceptions of institutional actions, including administrative policies and academic initiatives regarding LGBT issues and concerns on campus (p. 4). Results showed that more than one third (36%) of LGBT undergraduate students have experienced harassment. Those who experienced harassment reported that derogatory remarks were the most common forms of harassment (89%) and that fellow students were most often the perpetrators (79%). Fifty-one percent of respondents hid their gender identity or sexuality to avoid intimidation, and 20% feared for their safety because of their gender identity or sexual orientation. One of the limitations of this study was that it didn't provide options for participants who identify as gender non-conforming to state their gender identity. Participants could choose between identifying as male, female and transgender. It is important to have in mind that some transgender people, who identify within the gender binary (as a man or a woman), would not necessarily identify as "transgender" unless trans identity and visibility is important to them personally and politically. The results of Beemyn and Rankin's (2011) national, mixed-methods study showed that trans people who were "out"[2] experienced more harassment (40%) and feared more for their safety (58%) compared to those who were closeted (who didn't disclose their gender identity) or were out to only a few friends. Participants of this study stated they would hide their gender identity to avoid harassment. Those college students who identified outside the gender binary, such as genderqueer students, reported facing challenges to conform to the many gender-segregated practices and policies on campus (ibid.).

## 3  Psychological Consequences of the Experienced Discrimination

It is widely acknowledged by the research that trans and gender diverse people experience higher suicide rates, suicide ideation, depression, and anxiety than the general population (Bilodeau, 2009; Meyer, 2003; Haas et al., 2014; Bockting et al., 2013; Cochran, 2001; Effrig et al., 2011; Clements-Nolle et al., 2006; Marshall et al., 2015) and worse overall mental health (Bockting et al., 2013) especially those who wish to, but are unable to, access gender affirming surgeries and/or hormone replacement therapy to be able to live in their self-defined gender (Heylens, 2013; Colton Meier et al., 2011; Yadegarfard et al., 2014).

The higher risk for developing mental health issues among LGBTQI people is linked to stressful experiences of discrimination and stigma that accompany a minority social identity (Hatzenbuehler, 2009). The growing body of research has recognized that microaggressions against marginalized people are a form of trauma, and there is evidence of the connection between experienced societal oppression and the experience of trauma (Johnson, 2017a, p. 65).

Effrig, Bieschke, and Locke (2011) conducted an empirical study in the United States with two research samples nationwide, with the aim to examine harassment and discrimination that transgender college students face on campuses, and the impact it has on their psychological health. Research samples included students from the general population and students seeking counseling services. Transgender college students, both those seeking mental health treatment (clinical group) and those not in the treatment (non-clinical group), were compared with their cisgender (not transgender) peers. The clinical sample consisted of 27,616 participants, 40 of whom identified as transgender, and the nonclinical sample consisted of 21,686 participants, while 68 of them identified as transgender. The first part of the research the studied the difference of experienced distress (suicidal thoughts, suicide attempts, and self-harm) and victimization (experienced harassing, controlling, or abusive behavior and unwanted sexual contact) between both samples (clinical and nonclinical) of transgender students, as well as between transgender and cisgender students. The results showed that treatment-seeking transgender students had significantly higher rates of suicidal ideation. Rates of self-harm, suicide attempts, or victimization between the clinical and nonclinical samples of transgender students were not significantly different. Additionally, the data revealed that trans participants, both from the clinical and nonclinical sample, had experienced significantly higher rates of distress and victimization in all areas than cisgender participants. The second part of the study explored the differences between transgender and cisgender participants within the clinical and nonclinical samples on the CCAPS subscales, which includes items such as anxiety, depression, substance use, eating concerns, the hostility, and distress. Two important differences were identified, regardless of the fact that the difference in sample sizes between transgender and cisgender participants made analyzing the data more challenging. The mean scores of transgender participants from the clinical sample were significantly higher than of cisgender participants from the same sample, on the Family Distress CCAPS subscale. Moreover, transgender participants from the nonclinical sample showed higher mean scores on the Family Distress and Generalized Anxiety scale than cisgender participants from the nonclinical sample. While acknowledging that this study's limitation lies in the small sample sizes of trans people, the results clearly showed higher rates of experienced psychological distress and victimization among the students who identify as transgender. Another limitation of this study is the lack of diverse gender options in the application forms that students filled in when registering to higher education institutions or registering for counseling services. For the first sample gender options available were: man, woman, transgender and "other", while for the second sample gender options available were: male, female, transgender, and an option not to disclose. Therefore, the variety of transgender and gender non-conforming identities remained invisible, as there was not an option to state one's gender identity outside of the gender binary. Nevertheless, this study is significant not just because it showed the effects of the experienced discrimination on mental health and well-being, and the differences between experienced distress among transgender and cisgender students, but it created a space for the future research in relation to exploring the relationship between experienced victimization and psychological distress. It would be interesting to examine why transgender students from the non-clinical sample, did not seek clininal counseling treatment, when the study showed they experienced high rates of psychological distress and victimization. The fact that trans people around the world have been subjected to the pathologization of their mental health for being trans,[3] together with the stigma around mental health issues, and social stigma because of gender non-conformity, might be the possible explanations which give an indication for further research.

The relationship between family rejection and psychological distress among trans people is a topic that has been gaining more research interest in the last decade. Factor and Rothblum (2008) reported that trans men and women experienced statistically lower levels of support from family members than their cisgender siblings. Erich et al. (2008) found that greater levels of support from family members were related to higher life satisfaction. Klein and Colub (2016) reported that trans participants who experienced high levels of family rejection were more than three times as likely to have attempted suicide, and two and a half times more likely to have engaged in substance misuse. Clements-Nolle et al. (2006) examined the impact of gender-based discrimination and victimization on the rate of attempted suicides among transgender persons. The sample consisted of 515 persons and approximately one half of them had attempted suicide. Risk factors for transgender and GNC persons such as lack of family and social support are especially salient taking into account the history of stigma and pathologization related to their gender identity. Clements-Nolle et al. (2006) hypothesized that the discrimination experienced by transgender persons is higher than of cisgender LGB individuals because, in the case of trans people, both their sexuality and gender identity might challenge binary societal norms around gender and sexuality. Von Doussa, Power, and Riggs (2017) reported that many of trans participants of their research reported delaying their gender transition to minimize family conflict. Finally, research by Riggs et al. (2018) found that within a sample of 504 people of diverse genders and/or sexualities, transgender and non-binary participants were statistically more likely to have experienced family violence, and experiences of such violence were related to higher levels of depressive symptomology, and lower perceived levels of social support.

The importance of family acceptance for trans and GNC people becomes obvious.

## 4  Experiences with Mental Health Professionals

TGNC persons encounter significant barriers when seeking mental health counseling services (Benson, 2013; Bowers et al., 2005), including the stigma and fear associated with receiving mental health services (Shipherd et al., 2010) and lack of knowledge and sensitivity to TGNC clients by mental health practitioners (MHPs) (Elder, 2016; Hunt, 2014). The stigma toward TGNC people may increase the prospects that they will seek mental health services at a rate similar to sexual minority populations (Bieschke, McClanahan, Tozer, Grzegorek, & Park, 2000). Research shows that MHPs are often not adequately prepared to work with TGNC clients (Israel, Gorcheva, Burnes, & Walther, 2008; Shipherd, Green, & Abramovitz, 2010; Sperber et al., 2005). Bias perpetrated towards TGNC individuals by MHPs during counseling can be covert and subtle or overt and blatant (Bowers, Plummer, & Minichiello, 2005). Transphobia, also known as transprejudice, an irrational fear, disgust or emotional repulsion towards TGNC people (Hill & Willoughby, 2005) fuels the discrimination towards TGNC persons. MHPs cannot escape the impact of the systemic oppression of TGNC people, and they may sometimes unwillingly send derogatory or negative messages to their TGNC clients, without knowing and recognizing they are doing harm and perpetuating the systemic oppression (McCullough et al., 2017). These are transgender microaggressions[4] and can be especially harmful when coming from people who are expected to provide support and a safe space, as counselors and psychotherapists are. They can have good intentions towards the client, but at the same time, they can perpetuate pathologization and othering of trans persons through counseling, due to their own biases (Nadal, Rivera, & Corpus, 2010; Sue, 2010). Sperber et al. (2005) found that TGNC persons experienced overt discrimination from MHPs, such as MHPs' avoidance of any discussions on gender identity and/or refusal to acknowledge their client's correct pronoun. TGNC participants stated that therapists uninformed about gender issues contributed to their negative experiences of mental health services (Elder, 2016; Hunt, 2014). Benson (2013) found that TGNC participants felt they had to educate their MHPs about TGNC issues, or that MHPs did not understand the difference between sexual orientation and gender identity. Other negative experiences include MHPs overfocusing on gender issues, assuming gender issues were the reason TGNC clients sought mental health services and not focusing on presented issues that client reports suffering from (Elder, 2016; Hunt, 2014).

When clients of mental health services feel undervalued or misunderstood they self-disclose less and therefore, positive therapeutic outcomes are less likely (Shelton & Delgado-Romero, 2011; Sue et al., 2007). Some studies showed that TGNC individuals preferred MHPs who were already familiar with, knowledgeable of, and had the experience of working with TGNC clients (Benson, 2013; Rachlin, 2002). According to Bess and Stabb (2009), TGNC persons preferred MHPs who did not use diagnostic labels such as gender identity disorder. Rachlin (2002) identified four helpful ways in which psychotherapists affirmed these clients: acceptance, respect for chosen gender identity, treatment flexibility, and practitioner's connection to the TGNC community. Still, additional trans-affirming counseling and psychotherapy practices must be developed to better support TGNC clients (McCullough et al., 2017). The trans-affirmative approach means "accepting, advocating or educating people about concerns of transgender and gender non-conforming (TGNC) people" (ACA, 2010; APA, 2017). The trans-affirmative approach to counselling and psychotherapy means not just the lack of discrimination and bias towards the client, but applying counselling interventions that are validating and affirming of trans person's identity and lived experiences of discrimination and oppression, resulting from their social positionality, social stigma, and systemic oppression. TGNC people of color experience increased discrimination due to multiple minority identities (Grant et al., 2011). Therefore, it is vital that MHPs are knowledgeable and responsive to the needs of clients with multiple minority backgrounds (McCullough et al., 2017). MHPs must better understand the living realities of their TGNC clients, who live under systemic oppression, so they can better connect with them and distinguish between affirmative and oppressive practices (McCullough et al., 2017).

Mixed-method research (Dispenza et al., 2013) on the preparedness of counselors in training to work with transgender clients looked for the strengths and gaps in counselor preparedness regarding working with transgender individuals. The study gathered 87 counselors in training from an urban university in the southeastern United States who completed a questionnaire on transgender counseling competence. Additionally, through focus groups, the study explored education experiences of diverse counselors in training. The results of the research identified five main themes that emerged from the focus group interviews: (1) terminology regarding trans identities, (2) sources of information and knowledge on trans issues, (3) approaches to working with transgender people, (4) counselor in training characteristics, and (5) recommendations for the development of trans-affirming practice. Research showed that counsellors highlighted they are confused in regards to terminology around trans identities, which is in part, as they stated, a result of a lack of exposure and conversations on gender diversity in formal counseling courses and programs. Participants identified two particular sources of information regarding trans issues available to them: informal and formal. As said, formal education lacks trans-affirming curricula. Informal sources referred to personally knowing someone who is trans. Counsellors participating in the study stated that they learn about trans issues through the media representations of transgender issues (news, TV shows including drag shows), and through sharing information through social relationships. All participants of focus groups shared they felt incompetent to work with trans persons because of a exposure and knowledge on trans issues. When talking about their personal characteristics that lead them to work on counseling transgender persons, participants highlighted self-awareness that gender is not a binary category and awareness that socialization influences understandings of gender identities and sexuality. Counsellors' recommendations were towards attending focus groups to develop competence and awareness on trans issues, participating in small group discussions, and the need for their educators to promote transgender topics in the classroom. The research outlined recommendations for counselor educators and supervisors, the first one being the importance of providing educational opportunities on trans issues for the counselors they train and supervise, so that counsellors in training can explore their attitudes and biases toward trans people and issues. Recommendations highlighted that exploring bias in education, research, practice, media, and society, could help practicing counselors and counselor trainees to develop their awareness on issues of privilege and marginalization in society in relation to gender identity. Finally, the researchers (ibid.) acknowledged that facilitating a dialogue on trans issues in counsellor programs can also provide opportunities for students to explore their own gender identity and understand how sociopolitical factors impact a person's understanding of gender and gender diversity. Without this critical examination, the counsellor can perpetuate epistemic injustice (Fricker, 2007) that TGNC people already face. That is supported by the research as well (Bryan, 2018), which shows there are several types of microaggressions that LGBTQI people face in counselor education programs and that counselor educators may show LGBTQI related bias in their work, specifically prejudice and behavioral bias (Miller et al., 2007).

5     The Spectrum of Privilege within Trans and GNC Community

Just as people in one society are socially positioned in different ways, based on their identities and material realities (socio-economic status, race, gender, sexual orientation, ethnicity, educational attainment level, etc.), people within LGBTQI communities, and specifically trans communities, can be marginally situated and hold different levels of privilege. The effects of different interlocking systems of oppression, such as transphobia, homophobia, sexism, racism, classism, xenophobia, anti-sex worker sentiment, ableism, are present not just outside of trans and GNC communities, but also within them. These systems of oppression are especially affecting the experiences of trans and GNC individuals with multiple, marginalized identities. For example, very often individuals with non-binary genders (e.g., genderqueer, agender, gender fluid, etc.) are considered "not real", and not valid (Pearce, 2012), which places them lower on the spectrum of privilege within trans community. Trans women are overly sexualized, seen as in need of psychiatric help, and negatively portrayed in the media (Serano, 2007).

A 2015 survey conducted in the US showed that the unemployment rate among trans people was three times higher than the unemployment rate in the US population at the time; for transgender people of color, it was four times higher (Rankin et al., 2016). Surveys of approximately 6,500 transgender people in the United States showed that transgender people of color experience higher rates of police harassment, homelessness, violence, unemployment, and denial of healthcare (Grant et al., 2011). Meyer (2010) conducted semi-structured interviews with 44 participants in New York City for a study on two groups of victims of LGBT hate crimes – (a) white, middle-class and (b) poor, working-class people of color. Results of the study showed that the group of poor/working-class LGBT people of color experienced more violence than the White, middle-class group. Moreover, poor/working class people of color would rarely seek professional support after the traumatizing events, and would describe hate crimes as a widespread issue in their community, because they knew others who had experienced them.

Research indicates that discrimination, violence, and harassment against transgender women, LGBT people of color and sex workers are perpetuated at disproportionally higher rates. For example, the National Coalition of Anti-Violence Programs (NCAVP, 2016) published a Hate Violence Report which showed that, similar to the reports from the years prior to 2016, the majority of reported and recorded homicides of LGBTQ people in the USA were of people of color. In 2016, 77 total homicides of LGBTQ people were recorded, including the 49 lives lost at Pulse Night Club in Orlando, Florida on June 12th, 2016, where the majority of the victims were LGBTQ and Latinx[5] (ibid., p. 28). Out of the rest of the recorded homicides of LGBTQ people, 79% were people of color: 64% were Black and 15% were Latinx.

Transgender Europe published a report (TGEU, 2017a) which shows that trans and gender-diverse sex workers, make up 62% of the reported murders of trans and gender-diverse people whose profession is known (p. 18). According to the Trans Murder Monitoring Project (TMM) which systematically monitors, collects and analyzes reports of homicides of trans and gender-diverse people worldwide (TvT Research Project, 2018), more than 2,982 trans and gender-diverse people in 72 countries were killed between January 2008 and September 2018, while 271 were killed in 2018, which is an increase compared to previous years (ibid.). It is important to note that the data collected show only those cases which have been reported, and there is no data and no estimates available for unreported cases. Only those that can be found on the Internet, reported murders by the local activists and TMT partner organizations are counted. The majority of the murders occurred in Brazil, Mexico, the United States, Colombia (ibid.). According to the Transgender Europe publication *The vicious circle of violence: Trans and gender-diverse people, migration, and sex work*, in the United States, the victims are predominantly trans women of color and/or Native American trans women (TGEU, 2017a, p. 18). Research (Stotzer, 2008) showed that hate crimes toward transgender and gender non-conforming people are especially violent, and that transgender victims are targeted for violence for more complex reasons than their gender variance alone. In Europe, according to TMM data, Turkey has reported 51 trans women, the majority being sex workers, murdered in the last ten years (TvT Research Project, 2018, p. 2). In addition, the most (55%) of the murdered transgender migrants in Europe come from Brazil (TGEU, 2017a, p. 18). In Italy, 16 of the 22 murdered trans migrants were from Brazil, and of those Brazilian trans migrants, 12 were sex workers or 75% (ibid.). TMM project shows that transphobic hate crimes are especially violent, as the most prevalent causes of death in homicides of trans and gender-diverse people are: shot, stabbed, beaten, strangled/hanged, stoned, asphyxiated/smoke inhalation/suffocated, decapitated/dismembered, burned, throat cut, tortured, run-over by a car (TvT Research Project, 2018). The UN Special Rapporteur on Violence against Women highlighted that activists working in this field are targeted because they "do not conform to stereotypes of gender sexuality and/or identity, thus becoming victims of homophobic crimes" (UN Human Rights Council, 2012, p. 18).

## 6  Discrimination and Microaggressions

While much of the research is focused on major discriminatory events that LGBTQI and specifically trans people experience, such as discrimination in the job market (European Union Agency for Fundamental Rights (FRA), 2014; Rankin et al., 2016; Grant et al., 2011), experienced physical and psychological harassment because of one's sexual orientation and gender identity (Wilchins, Lombardi, Priesing, & Malouf, 1997), to name a few, more recent research began to examine microaggressions that occur in daily life. Microaggressions are "brief and commonplace daily verbal, behavioral, or environmental indignities, whether intentional or unintentional, that communicate hostile, derogatory, or negative slights and insults" toward members of oppressed groups (Sue et al., 2007, p. 271). Interpersonal exchanges involving microaggressions may not be perceived as discriminatory by perpetrators, who may believe their actions are harmless or innocent and may not understand the potential impact of these behaviors on recipients (Smith, Allen, & Danley, 2007; Sue et al., 2007). Nevertheless, such exchanges have negative consequences on the mental health of the person experiencing and suffering from them. As already highlighted, research has recognized that microaggressions against marginalized people are a form of trauma, and there is a body of evidence of the connection between experienced societal oppression and the experience of trauma (Johnson, 2017a, p. 65). Kira et al. (2013) understood oppression as a form of collective trauma perpetrated between social groups, which exists on a continuum from microaggressions to macroaggressions.

While there are empirical studies examining discrimination towards LGBTQI people, few of them have focused on discrimination through the microaggressions framework and specifically focusing on microaggressions that trans and GNC face (Nadal et al., 2012; Chang & Chung, 2015; Pulice-Farrow et al., 2017a,

2017b). Microaggression literature addresses not just interpersonal but also systemic microaggressions which describe various ways that systems, institutions, and environments can be microaggressive in nature (Nadal, 2012). For example, racist, sexist, transphobic and other discriminatory legislation (ibid.).

Nadal et al. (2012) conducted a qualitative, focus group study with nine participants[6] to identify types of microaggressions that transgender people experience in their everyday life.

Twelve categories of microaggressions were identified:
1. Use of transphobic and/or incorrect gendered terminology: Experiences involving the use of denigrating language, incorrect gender pronouns, or both.
2. The assumption of universal transgender experience: Interactions in which individuals assume that all transgender persons are the same (e.g., assuming that all transgender people undergo gender-affirming surgeries).
3. Exoticization: Encounters in which transgender persons are dehumanized or treated as objects (e.g., people treating a transgender person as a "token" because of their transgender identity).
4. Discomfort/disapproval of transgender experience: Occurrences in which transgender persons are treated with disrespect or condemnation.
5. Endorsement of gender normative and binary culture of behaviors: Statements and behaviors that communicate that a transgender person is expected to be or act in gender-conforming ways and is denied their transgender identity.
6. Denial of the existence of transphobia[7]: Instances when cisgender individuals invalidate a transgender person by denying that transphobic experiences exist.
7. The assumption of sexual pathology or abnormality: Incidents involving the treatment of transgender persons as psychologically abnormal or sexually deviant.
8. Physical threat or harassment: Experiences in which transgender persons are teased, intimidated, or bullied because of their gender identity.
9. Denial of individual transphobia: Instances in which a cisgender person denies that they have transphobic biases.
10. Denial of personal body privacy: Statements or behaviors in which cisgender people objectify a transgender person's body (e.g., a stranger asking intrusive questions about one's genitals).
11. Familial microaggressions: Subtle or unintentional forms of discrimination that occur within the family.

12. Systemic and environmental microaggressions: Covert forms of discrimination that occur on an institutional or community level.

Under the theme of systemic and environmental microaggressions, four subthemes were identified: (a) public restrooms (e.g., transgender persons must make a frequent decision when gender-neutral restrooms are not available), (b) the criminal legal system (e.g., transgender persons experience dehumanizing treatment from law enforcement), (c) health care (e.g., offensive comments or the use of an inappropriate gender pronoun by health practitioners), and (d) government-issued identification (e.g., difficulty with changing one's legal name and gender marker on legal documents[8] to access public assistance).

The study showed that transgender individuals experience several types of systemic injustice and discrimination from various sectors: the criminal justice system, healthcare, employment, education, family, and other public accommodations and service providers.

Nadal, Davidoff, Davis, and Wong (2014) conducted a study involving secondary analysis of a previous data, that examined transgender people's experiences with microaggressions (Nadal et al., 2012). The study used directed content analysis to examine transgender people's psychological processes and coping mechanisms when gender identity microaggressions occur in their lives. Participants' perspectives were categorized into 3 major domains: (a) emotional reactions: anger, betrayal, distress, hopelessness, and exhaustion, feeling invalidated and misunderstood; (b) cognitive reactions: rationalization, double-bind, vigilance and self-preservation, resiliency and empowerment; and (c) behavioral reactions: direct confrontation, indirect confrontation, passive coping.

Presented research clearly indicates the presence of minority stress resulting from systemic oppression, both covert and overt, and reflected in transphobia, transprejudice, hate crimes, discrimination in education and microaggressions in daily life.

Existing literature on transgender and GNC persons' experience with microaggressions is very limited. The main limitation of the current research is that it treats transgender and GNC persons as a homogenous group, while in reality there is a large degree of heterogeneity within the transgender communities and microaggression experiences may be unique to those with different transgender identities (Chang & Chung, 2015). Gender non-conforming individuals may be expected to conform to societal expectations of what it means to be either a "man" or a "woman" and expected to adhere to a socially accepted gender roles (ibid.).

Furthermore, GNC, genderqueer and gender non-binary persons might experience microaggressions related to the use of gender-based pronouns, which is different from binary trans persons' experience with microaggressions based on using incorrect gender reference before, during or after their social and/or medical transition. Gender non-conforming individuals do not identify with gender labels assigned to them, so being called a "man" or a "woman" (and "he" or "she") may not match their internal sense of gender identity (Chang & Chung, 2015). They might use the pronoun *They*, as a singular, gender-neutral pronoun. Chung (2015) highlighted when reviewing the literature on trans and GNC specific microaggressions, that exploring the diverse experiences of the various gender identities is necessary for developing a greater understanding of the heterogeneity of the transgender community.

### Notes

1 Sexual Orientation, Gender Identity, Gender Expression and variations in Sex Characteristics.
2 Coming out (of the closet) metaphor, or shorter "outing", being "out", refers to revealing one's own sexual orientation, gender identity or intersex trans to their environment.
3 Trans identities have been pathologized by the World Health Organization, medical and mental health professionals around the world, on the basis of 10th version of the International Classification of Diseases of the World Health Organization. In the newest online version of the International Classification of Diseases, ICD-11, that The World Health Organization has released on June 18, 2018, and which is adopted by the WHO General Assembly on May 2019, trans identities are removed from the mental health disorders chapter. A new chapter is added to ICD named "Conditions related to sexual health" and it includes a new diagnosis of Gender incongruence. This important change gives access to gender-affirming health care for people of trans identities, while ending a long history of medical and psychological pathologization of trans identities, through: so-called "conversion therapies", forced medicalization, forced hospitalization, and forced sterilization for trans and gender diverse people (TGEU, 2018a).
4 Microaggressions are "brief and commonplace daily verbal, behavioral, or environmental indignities, whether intentional or unintentional, that communicate hostile, derogatory, or negative slights and insults" toward members of oppressed groups (Sue et al., 2007, p. 71).
5 Gender neutral term refering to people from Latin-American background.

6 Three identified as transgender men, 6 identified as transgender woman. Five participants identified as Latinx, two as Multiracial, one as White, and one as Black/African American. Two participants identified as middle-class, whereas the remaining seven were working class or struggling with poverty.
7 Transphobia, also known as transprejudice, consists of emotional repulsion, hate, discrimination, and aggression towards individuals who are gender non-conforming and those whose gender identity does not align with the sex assigned to them at birth (Hill & Willoughby, 2005).
8 Legal gender recognition in many countries in Europe is not based on self-determination and requires that a trans person goes through compulsory sterilization, and/or hormonal treatment, and/or psychiatric evaluation, in order to have an access to name change and change of the gender marker in their documents (TGEU, 2016a). Gender recognition procedures are important non-discrimination measures. Malta, Ireland, Denmark and Norway set the path when they listened to trans people and established quick, transparent and accessible procedures based on self-determination (ibid, p. 6).

CHAPTER 4

# Legal and Policy Framework: Examples of Good Practice

## 1   Introduction to Legal and Policy Framework

Laws and policies in one country can be changed not only through advocacy efforts on a local and national level, but also through international mechanisms. Through my past role as a Co-Chair of the International LGBTQI Youth and Student Organization (IGLYO), I became familiar with the international mechanisms, especially through international networking and external representation of the organization. These external representations included, for example, participating in panel discussions and moderating panels at events, such as the conferences organized by the Council of Europe, World Health Organization, and World Pride, on topics such as gender and sexuality diversity in education; creating legal equality for LGBTQI people in Europe; prevention of homophobic and transphobic bullying in education and prevention of hate speech and hate crimes based on SOGIESC.[1] Through these events, I met with my colleagues working for international bodies, institutions, and organizations on the protection of human rights, and more specifically, LGBTQI people's rights. Therefore, I would like to dedicate this chapter to share what I have learned, to cast light on existing international legal frameworks, and provide examples of good practice of trans-affirming laws, policies, and practices that have direct or indirect, but relevant and significant, impact on trans peoples' access to education and the existence of LGBTQI affirming educational provisions. My hope is that this chapter will be of use to social justice activists and human rights defenders reading this book so that they can find ways to open a dialogue with, and assert pressure on, their governments where that is realistically possible. I also hope this chapter will be useful to social justice educators working toward progressive social change, to understand how (non-)existing national laws and policies related to trans people directly impact their educational work and their knowledge on LGBTQI (of specifically trans issues), affecting the support they can provide to trans students who need it. This chapter will help social justice activists, educators and general public reading this book, to better understand how legal and administrative challenges and/or non-visibility of trans issues in laws and policies, including educational ones, directly impact trans people's access to education and experiences throughout education, such as homophobic and transphobic bullying. Therefore, this chapter tackles all four domains of power discussed in Chapter 1, Section 2.2: hegemonic, structural, disciplinary, and interpersonal domain. The chapter will also provide examples of good practice across Europe and the world, so that educators reflect on the ways in which they can assert pressure on schools and local governments, to advocate for LGBTQI affirming school policies and education provision. These policies are needed for the development of LGBTQI affirming curricula and the development of support systems for trans students that can make schools safe environments, in which trans students can thrive and reach their full potential, instead of being spaces of their suffering. The examples of good practices in different countries, in the field of LGBTQI affirming education laws, policies, and provision, specifically Malta, Norway, and the Netherlands, are provided, for those educators working in school settings, to become aware of what can be done in relation to LGBTQI affirming education provision. However, for more details about the impact of experienced social exclusion and/or discrimination in education on trans students' mental health and well-being, refer to Chapter 3.

There are many thematic laws and policies relevant for the lives and daily existence of trans people (TGEU, 2018b), such as those related to asylum, prevention of transphobic hate speech and transphobic hate crimes (anti-discrimination laws, inclusive of gender identity, gender expression and sex characteristics as grounds for discrimination); laws that prevent discrimination of trans people in education and employment, as well as in health care, and specifically laws and policies that enable access to trans-affirming healthcare based on informed consent; laws that refer to family rights and parenthood recognition of trans people (often trans people around the world are required to divorce prior to obtaining legal gender recognition, especially in countries where marriage equality laws are not adopted[2]). However, this chapter will focus on the overview of the legal gender recognition laws and policies. It became evident and recognized both by the United Nations agencies and experts (United Nations, 2018) and the Council of Europe (2015) that when trans persons' gender identity and gender expression do not match their name and gender markers on their official documents, such as passports, identity documents (ID cards), or birth certificates, that makes everyday tasks more challenging. Opening a bank account, picking up a parcel at the post office, using a personalized public transport ticket becomes a source of struggle. It also hinders education and employment opportunities, because having educational or employment certificates that do not match one's name and gender, is a common cause of unemployment among transgender persons across Europe, and the world, together with the lack of legislation that explicitly prohibits discrimination based on

SOGIESC in regards to employment (Council of Europe, 2015, p. 5; UN, 2018, p. 8, 12; OHCHR, 2016a; International Labour Organization, 2016). To illustrate why focus on gender recognition laws in this chapter, I will provide an example from the real-life context. Many trans people I personally know from my country, my region (the Balkan peninsula) and overall European continent have shared with me, throughout the years, that they haven't gotten jobs they were qualified for, sometimes after actually being offered a job, when they disclosed to the employer that they are trans. Or that they were discredited during a job interview in a covert or an overt manner, when the employer would notice they are trans (those who do not have "passing privilege" and are visibly in the process of medical transition are automatically outed as trans). This type of employment-based discrimination happens due to societal stigma and pathologization of trans identities, when trans people are perceived and labeled not only as mentally ill, but also as a "public disgrace", an "offense to the public moral", "perverts", or interested only to spread so-called "gender ideology", a concept widely used in populist, right-wing discourses across the European continent (Beury & Yoursky, 2019, p. 153), as discussed in Chapter 5. In both of the mentioned scenarios, to avoid being accused of discrimination, employers can and did say, as my trans colleagues have shared with me, that they have many qualified candidates for the position, and they would get back to the trans candidate in a couple of days with their decision, which often, never happens (not all countries in Europe have adopted legislation that prohibit discrimination in the labor market on the grounds of gender identity and gender expression, and such discrimination is not easy to prove).

For example, during a public panel discussion on trans people's lived experiences in held in Belgrade in April 2019, a trans woman of Roma ethnicity, who was also a refugee from Kosovo, currently residing in Belgrade, Serbia (living in social welfare housing for youth without parental care, while finishing undergraduate studies at the University of Belgrade), shared she was offered a job as a Personal Care Assistant to a child with disabilities. After she successfully passed the interview with the child's parents, and got a job offer, she disclosed to the parents that she is a trans woman in medical transition. This was important to disclose as trans person's identity documents might not align with their lived gender identity and gender expression.[3] The parents' response to her was shocking: they told her they would get back to her, as they supposedly had other qualified candidates in mind, and needed time to decide. They never contacted her back.

Situations like this leave trans people vulnerable to homelessness, unemployment and under pressure to engage in sex work,[4] especially in contexts where gender-affirming surgeries (for those trans people who wish to undergo them) are not funded by the national, public health insurance, or are only covered partially. Furthermore, those trans people who engage in sex work in order to survive and/or cover the fees of their medical transition are additionally at risk, as sex work is criminalized throughout Europe (TGEU, 2016b). Transgender Europe (TGEU)'s Policy paper on Sex work (ibid., 2016) highlights that trans sex workers are burdened by transphobic and anti-sex worker laws making it difficult for them to escape persecution, in addition to being under extreme economic pressure. The organization, therefore, advocates for the decriminalization of sex work in the European context. It is important to make a distinction between legalization and decriminalization of sex work. The famous "Swedish Model" criminalizes sex workers' clients, and not sex workers themselves. Activists who advocate for it, see this model as a way to eradicate sex work, which they perceive as a form of male violence against women (TGEU, 2016b). According to this model, it is impossible to consent to "exploitation" (ibid.). However, this model and this perception of sex work are often heavily criticized by sex workers themselves, their collectives around Europe, and by the TGEU. The critiques argue that the Swedish model and perception of sex work as exploitation per se, denounce the agency and capacity to sex workers who are perceived as victims who need rescuing, regardless of their context, living conditions, and the fact that some people actually want to work as sex workers. I would agree with critics and argue that the denial of agency and capacity to sex workers to use their voices and tell us all what they want and need, represents a form of a savior complex, and testimonial quieting, often perpetuated, from my activist experience, by white, middle class, cisgender feminist women. Very often feminists are very vocal against sex work, believing they speak "in the name of all women" and perceive sex work as a form of exploitation, without necessarily reaching out to the collectives of sex workers asking them about their daily issues, struggles, needs, perceptions and understandings of their own work and life. Especially when it comes to the lived realities of transgender sex workers, of multiple minority identities, and those who also happen to be persons of color, speaking in "their name" without engaging with them in the decision-making processes around laws and policies on sex work, represents an overt epistemic injustice. Every policy and law has to be based on "Nothing for us without us" principle, and that sex workers need to take a lead in the social, political, legal and policy discussions concerning sex work. Trans people are enough deprived of agency over their body, privacy, sexuality, and gender by the state, therefore perceiving trans sex workers as victims who need rescuing further deprives trans sex workers of agency and contributes to their systemic erasure and epistemic injustice.

Even in countries where sex work is legalized, the state institutions and their representatives can harass sex workers, and use other means to fine them, such public moral laws and non-sex work related administrative offenses, such as violation of traffic regulations (TGEU, 2016b). In some countries, an estimated 43% of the transgender population had experiences of sex work (Hounsfield et al., 2007; Adebajo et al., 2013). That is not to say that all trans people engage in sex work but rather that they are in some contexts overrepresented in the population of sex workers or are more likely to engage in sex work due to systemic oppression, lack of employment opportunities and poverty. Furthermore, sex workers and trans people are globally disproportionately affected by HIV (19.1% of trans women worldwide are estimated to be living with HIV according to Baral et al., 2013). In contexts where sex work is criminalized and sex workers do not have access to health care and social security, it represents a serious problem. Trans Murder Monitoring Project shows that out of all murdered trans people globally, 65 percent of those whose profession was known were sex workers (TGEU, 2016b, p. 9).

While in the process of medical transition, trans people may not be able to hide they are trans, they are automatically outed and exposed to discriminative treatment which is confirmed by the report of the survey carried out by the European Union Agency for Fundamental Rights (FRA, 2014). The report shows that the level of discrimination EU trans respondents reported facing was alarming, especially in the area of employment and education. More than half of all trans respondents felt discriminated against or harassed in the labor market, because they were perceived as trans, in the year preceding the survey (ibid., p. 21). A quarter of trans respondents who attended school/university themselves or had a child/children in school/at university, reported they felt personally discriminated against by school or university personnel in the 12 months preceding the survey. When looking only at trans students, the number rises to 29% (ibid., p. 21). FRA called on EU Member States to ensure legal gender recognition of trans people, including the name change, social security number and gender marker change on personal identity documents, because not obtaining identity documents aligned with person's gender identity and expression hinders access to social services and opportunities for many trans respondents.

## 2  General Overview: International Mechanisms and Gender Recognition Laws

The United Nations (UN) human rights agencies and mechanisms can greatly influence international human rights standards and law, therefore influencing national laws and practice, and the advancement of human rights around the world. Trans people's human rights are relatively new to UN agencies and mechanisms, and have been treated as a part of the LGBTI umbrella until very recently (Chiam, 2017). However, the growing understanding of UN experts and agencies, together with the dedicated and passionate long-term engagement of trans human rights activists, has resulted in an increase of the attention of international bodies and institutions. Their resulting relevant recommendations and resources can be of use in national advocacy for trans people's rights done by the human rights defenders and educators.

Four UN human rights mechanisms have addressed legal gender recognition quite extensively: the Special Procedures, UN agencies, Treaty Bodies, and the Universal Periodic Review (Chiam, 2017).

### 2.1 *Special Procedures*

The Special Procedures are experts (individuals or groups), mandated by the UN Human Rights Council (UNHRC) to address country-specific situations or thematic issues (Chiam, 2017, p. 7). They are known as "Independent Experts" (such as the Independent Expert on the protection against violence and discrimination on the basis of sexual orientation or gender identity), "Special Rapporteur" or "Working Group" (such as the Working Group on discrimination against women).

The Special Procedures within their mandate, monitor, examine, advise and publicly inform on respect for human rights. This is based on the work they do conducting country visits and making recommendations to national authorities, preparing thematic reports, collating best practices, and responding to individual complaints. Their work is different from the work of Treaty Bodies (presented below), because their thematic mandates have a global scope, and can examine situations in any country (ibid.).

An example of the work of Special Procedures relevant to the topic of this chapter, is when the Special Rapporteur on Torture called upon UN Member States in 2013, to ban forced sterilization in all circumstances and particularly as a prerequisite for legal gender recognition of trans people (ibid.).

### 2.2 *United Nations Agencies*

Different UN agencies are responsible for different thematic issues, for example, the UN Refugee Agency (UNHCR) or the World Health Organization (WHO). They can have a significant influence on the governments, regardless of the fact that their recommendations are not legally binding on the Member States. When it comes to legal recognition of gender identity, the Office of the High Commissioner for Human Rights (OHCHR) is an important ally. It has offered best practices and guidance to the UN Member States on the basis of the analysis of legal gender recognition requirements across the world. The high Commissioner for Human Rights, who reports to the Human Rights Council, highlighted that Member States must respect the physical and psychological identity of trans persons by legally recognizing their gender identity without additional requirements that may violate human rights (Chiam, 2017, p. 9).

An example of good practice is when twelve UN agencies, including UNDP, UNESCO, UNAIDS, UNCHR, UN Women, UNICEF, and the WHO, called for legal gender recognition of trans people without imposing abusive requirements, in a joint statement on the rights of LGBTI people they released in 2015 (OHCHR, 2015).

### 2.3 *Treaty Bodies*

Treaty Bodies are appointed to review State compliance with binding international treaties (also known as "conventions"). When a State ratifies one of these instruments, they are legally binding and the State is obliged to implement the recommendations of the treaty under the international law, while the State's domestic legislation must not be in contradiction with the treaty. The States are periodically reviewed and are bound by the Treaty Body (Chiam, 2017, p. 9).

Treaty Bodies can make remarks on the unavailability of legal gender recognition procedures in the State which is under the review. In 2017, the Human Rights Committee expressed its concern that there is no legal gender recognition framework in Serbia and that trans persons cannot change their gender marker in personal documents without compulsory surgeries (Chiam, 2017, p. 10). Although my home country still to this day (May 2019) has not adopted a gender recognition law, it has made changes after these concerns were raised, thanks to the persistent efforts of the activists on the ground, and the support of international mechanisms. The changes were made to the law on Registry Books, which came into force in January 2019. According to the changes, a trans person on hormone replacement therapy, who has been visiting a psychiatrist for at least a year, can apply to change their gender marker and social security number in their documents, without surgeries as a requirement. While trans people's mental health is obviously still pathologized in my home country, and legal gender recognition is not very accessible (it requires a waiting period), the first step has been made: removing sterilization and surgeries as a requirement for changing the gender marker and social security number.

### 2.4 *Universal Periodic Review*

The Universal Periodic Review (UPR) is a UN Human Rights Council's mechanism, under which all UN Member States are peer-reviewed every 5 years on the entire spectrum of human rights issues. The Outcome Report based on UPR presents recommendations to the State to implement before their next UPR review. States can either accept or take note of recommendations. When recommendations are accepted, the UPR is a very useful tool for activists in their dialogue with their government, because activists and human rights defenders can hold their governments accountable for implementing recommendations (Chiam, 2017, p. 10).

For example, based on the recommendations of the Outcome Report in 2016, Belgium changed legislation to allow change of "civil identity" without medical requirements for legal gender recognition. In May 2017, the law that allowed legal gender recognition based on self-determination was adopted.

Now that we have an idea of how the UN human rights agencies and mechanisms can influence international and national human rights standards and laws, I will focus on a specific Special Procedure, which has contributed greatly to the visibility of importance of accessible legal gender recognition procedures to enjoyment of trans peoples' human rights, particularly those related to education and employment.

## 3  Examples of Relevant International Mechanisms

A Report of Victor Madrigal-Borloz, a UN Independent Expert, mandated by the United Nations Human Rights Council on protection against violence and discrimination based on sexual orientation and gender identity, was presented to the General Assembly of the United Nations on June 12, 2018 (UN, 2018). The report focused on two thematic areas. The first area was abandoning the classification of gender identity as a pathology (referred to by the Independent Expert and LGBTQI activists across the globe as "depathologization"). The second area referred on providing guidelines and recommendations to the Member States on how to ensure respect of gender identity of transgender and gender non-conforming/gender diverse people, and address violence and discrimination they suffer on the basis of their gender identity. This section draws on this report, along with other reports of relevant international bodies, organizations and institutions.[5] It points out severe human rights violations that trans and gender diverse people are exposed to, and highlights legal and policy issues that have a direct or indirect impact on: (a) TGNC peoples' access to education, (b) provision of education which is free from SOGIESC based discrimination, stereotypical and prejudicial portrayal, and homophobic and transphobic bullying, (c) developing educational practices which are affirming and inclusive of all students on the LGBTQI spectrum and (d) developing educational practice built on the curricula which is reflective of LGBTQI people's lived realities, portrayed with dignity and respect.

As acknowledged by Victor Madrigal-Borloz, a UN Independent Expert (UN, 2018), understanding of gender diversity differs across the world. Different cultures and traditions affirm gender diversity including Australia, Bangladesh, Canada, India, Nepal, New Zealand, and Pakistan. Together they represent a quarter of the world's population (ibid., p. 3). These countries recognize both in law and in cultural traditions genders other than male and female. Terms used when referring to trans identities are different across the countries (ibid.): hijra (Bangladesh, India, and Pakistan), travesti (Argentina and Brazil), waria (Indonesia), okule and agule (Democratic Republic of the Congo and Uganda) muxe (Mexico), fa'afafine (Samoa), kathoey (Thailand) and two-spirit (indigenous North Americans).

The right to legal recognition of a person's gender identity is linked to several international declarations, covenants and charters such as Universal Declaration of Human Rights, Article 6, the right to equal recognition before the law (UN, 2015, p. 14), and the International Covenant on Civil and Political Rights, Article 16 (UN, 1966, p. 177). It is present in international human rights law, other universal human rights treaties, and regional human rights instruments.[6] In reality, these are central tenets for the recognition of trans persons' rights and freedoms crucial for a dignified life, such as those related to health, education, housing, access to social security and employment (ibid.). For now, their actualization is dependent on the bureaucracy of a country in question and the identification of an individual (OHCHR, 2016a, p. 94). In reality of trans peoples' existence this means, as I have elaborated at the beginning of this chapter, when trans and gender-diverse people's gender identity is not adequately recognized by the State, by the law, they might suffer discrimination in everyday life. This discrimination includes exclusion and bullying in education contexts; discrimination in employment; denial or lack of access to the right to healthcare; housing and access to social security; violations of the rights of the child; and arbitrary restrictions on the rights to freedom of expression, peaceful assembly and association; the right to freedom of movement and residence, and the right to leave any country including one's own (UN, 2018, p. 8). It means that when trans person's name and gender marker in their official documents do not match their gender identity and expression, they are at risk of humiliation, harassment, violence, abuse, exclusion from school and labor market; restrictions of access to social services, health-care, housing, etc. Moreover, as recognized by United Nations human rights mechanisms, it means abuse or arrest upon attempting to seek police protection and report the attacks or discrimination (UN, 2018, p. 12).

Furthermore, the Parliamentary Assembly of the Council of Europe adopted a Resolution 2048 in 2015, titled *Discrimination against transgender people in Europe* (Council of Europe, 2015), which states that:

> The Assembly is concerned about the violations of fundamental rights, notably the right to private life and to physical integrity, faced by transgender people when applying for legal gender recognition; relevant procedures often require sterilization, divorce, a diagnosis of mental illness, surgical interventions and other medical treatments as preconditions. In addition, administrative burdens and additional requirements, such as a period of "life experience" in the gender of choice, make recognition procedures generally cumbersome. Furthermore, a large number of European countries have no provisions on gender recognition at all, making it impossible for transgender people to change the name and gender marker on personal identity documents and public registers.

The United Nations High Commissioner for Human Rights has recognized that judicial procedures may create severe barriers to accessing legal gender recognition of trans people, by unnecessarily prolonging the process and creating additional financial requirements, along with intrusion into persons individual rights and privacy, such as when a judge is asked to determine the validity of a person's gender identity, as it was the case in the Russian Federation, until January 22, 2018 (Transgender Legal Defense Project, 2018).[7] In February 2017, the High Commissioner outlined recommendations in regards to legal gender recognition of trans and gender diverse people (UN, 2018, p. 13), highlighting it should:
1. Be based on self-determination of the applicant.
2. Be a simple administrative process.
3. Not require applicants to undergo abusive requirements, such as medical certification, surgeries, treatments, sterilization, or divorce.
4. Acknowledge and recognize non-binary identities, such as gender identities that are neither "man" nor "woman".
5. Ensure that minors have access to recognition of their gender identity.

However, often, in reality, the countries that do legally recognize the gender identities of trans and gender diverse people, set abusive requirement for such recognition, such as: forced sterilization; medical procedures related to transition, including surgeries and hormone replacement therapy (HRT); diagnosis of a mental health disorder, forced divorce, and age restrictions. As pointed out by the *Special Rapporteur on torture and other cruel, inhuman or degrading treatment or punishment* (UN, 2018, p. 10), these requirements present severe human rights violations. The Special Rapporteur found that these practices violate the rights to physical integrity and self-determination of individuals, and are rooted in discrimination on the basis of sexual orientation and gender identity, which amount to ill-treatment or torture (ibid.). Together with the United Nations, regional human rights experts have pointed out that forced gender recognition related procedures can lead to life-long and severe mental and physical pain and suffering, and can violate the right to be free from torture and other cruel, inhuman or degrading treatment or punishment (OHCHR, 2016b). The World Health Organization, an authority for health within the United Nations system, has also highlighted that sterilization requirements violate human dignity, respect for bodily integrity and self-determination and can perpetuate and cause discrimination against transgender and intersex persons (WHO, 2014).

In April 2017, the European Court of Human Rights ruled that requiring sterilization for legal gender recognition violates human rights law, specifically the principles of bodily autonomy and self-determination. All Council of Europe Member States were called to bring relevant procedures in line with this legal principle (TGEU, 2017c), yet, fourteen countries in Europe still require sterilization in legal gender recognition (TGEU, 2018b).

The UN Independent Expert on protection against violence and discrimination based on sexual orientation and gender identity acknowledged that there are many medical traditions across the world and national implementation of classification of diseases (UN, 2018, p. 4), but that 70 percent of psychiatrists around the world use the tenth revision of the International Classification of Diseases (ICD), by the World Health Organization (Reed et al., 2011). The tenth revision of ICD included trans categories in the chapter on mental and behavioral disorders (UN, 2018, p. 4), which was often used as a justification by the countries on why the diagnosis of mental health disorder is a condition for legal gender recognition.

However, in the newest online version of the International Classification of Diseases, ICD-11, that the World Health Organization released on June 18, 2018, trans identities were removed from the mental health disorders chapter. A new chapter was added to ICD named "Conditions related to sexual health" and it includes a new diagnosis of "Gender incongruence of adolescence and adulthood", while the category of "transsexualism" was removed (WHO, 2019a). The new diagnosis does not reinforce the notion of gender defined in binary terms and does not impose gender stereotypes (UN, 2018, p. 5). This reform was welcomed not only by the trans people themselves, and national and international LGBTQI, trans-specific, and human rights organizations, different civil society organizations and groups, and relevant stakeholders, but also by the UN and regional human rights experts. The Special Rapporteur on the right of everyone to the enjoyment of the highest attainable standard of physical and mental health stated that "mental health diagnoses have been misused to pathologize identities and other diversities" and that "the pathologization of lesbian, gay, bisexual, transgender and intersex persons reduces their identities to diseases, which compounds stigma and discrimination" (The United Nations Human Rights Council (UNHRC), 2017, para. 48). During the 72nd World Health Assembly (WHA), which took place in Geneva, Switzerland, from 20–28 May 2019, the World Health Organization (WHO) officially adopted the International Classification of Diseases 11th Revision (ICD-11), which will come into effect on 1 January 2022 (WHO, 2019b). Now it is up to governments to adapt their national medical classifications and laws in accordance with this change.

This historic event for trans and gender diverse people, was welcomed globally (ILGA World, 2019) by LGBTQI organizations, which announced the continuation of the work on depathologization of trans identities (ibid.). This important change made to the ICD-11 and approved by the WHA, will still give access to gender-affirming health care for people of trans identities who need it, while ending a long history of medical and psychological pathologization of trans identities, through: so-called "conversion therapies", forced medicalization, forced hospitalization, and forced sterilization for trans and gender diverse people (TGEU, 2018a). The new diagnosis of gender incongruence will provide access to gender-affirming health care for trans people who seek gender-affirming medical treatment, or some sort of bodily change, to align their body with their gender identity. For other trans people who do not wish to do so, there is no reason to assign a diagnosis (UN, 2018, p. 5).

Future activists' efforts will be focused on replacing the term "gender incongruence" with a non-pathologizing and non-stigmatizing term; removing the category Gender Incongruence of Childhood (GIC); and ensuring access to support systems with health coverage for trans and gender diverse children (ILGA World, 2019).

The decision of WHA regarding the ICD-11 is aligned with the Yogyakarta principles[8] (2007), specifically principles number 17 and 18 and the Yogyakarta principles Plus 10 (2017), related to SOGIESC (adopted to complement the Yogyakarta principles 2007).

Yogyakarta principle no. 17 clearly states that:

> Everyone has the right to the highest attainable standard of physical and mental health, without discrimination on the basis of sexual orientation or gender identity. Sexual and reproductive health is a fundamental aspect of this right. (The Yogyakarta Principles, 2007, p. 22)

Furthermore, Principle No. 18 indicates that:

> No person may be forced to undergo any form of medical or psychological treatment, procedure, testing, or be confined to a medical facility, based on sexual orientation or gender identity. Notwithstanding any classifications to the contrary, a person's sexual orientation and gender identity are not, in and of themselves, medical conditions and are not to be treated, cured or suppressed. (The Yogyakarta principles, 2007, p. 23)

Yogyakarta principles Plus 10 (2017), from No. 30–38 highlight various LGBTQI peoples' specific rights. For the purpose of this discussion, the following rights are especially important:
– No. 30: a right to state protection from violence, discrimination, and other harm, whether by government officials or by any individual or group;
– No. 31: a right to legal recognition (to obtain identity documents, including birth certificates and to change gendered information in such documents);
– No. 32: a right to bodily and mental integrity, autonomy and self-determination, including the right to be free from torture and cruel, inhuman and degrading treatment or punishment on the basis of sexual orientation, gender identity, gender expression, and sex characteristics. This principle highlights that: "No one shall be subjected to invasive or irreversible medical procedures that modify sex characteristics without their free, prior and informed consent, unless necessary to avoid serious, urgent and irreparable harm to the concerned person" (p. 10).
– No. 33: a right to be free from criminalization and any form of sanction arising directly or indirectly from that person's actual or perceived sexual orientation, gender identity, gender expression or sex characteristics.

Furthermore, the International Covenant on Economic, Social and Cultural Rights, Adopted by the United Nations General Assembly in, 1966 (UN, 1966), highlights in Article 12 that the States parties recognize the right of everyone to the enjoyment of the highest attainable standard of physical and mental health. Another important international document related to physical health and bodily autonomy and integrity, is Intersex Resolution adopted by the Parliamentary Assembly of the Council of Europe (Council of Europe, 2017), which acknowledges intersex people's rights to bodily autonomy and physical integrity, and states that intersex people should be protected from the harm done by the medical system, and "corrective" surgeries on intersex children should be prohibited, as well as "sterilization and other treatments practiced on intersex children without their informed consent" (Council of Europe, 2017, p. 2).

It is important to note that, although intersex issues, as already explained in Chapter 1, are not the same as trans issues, nevertheless, a person can be (as Sebastian – one of the participants of my research), both intersex and trans. This participant suffered from forced medical interventions several times. First, when they were a child and were diagnosed as intersex, they were subjected to surgeries without their consent, knowledge or even a memory, as it happened at a young age, with the aim for doctors to assign a gender to them, most probably with the consent of their parents who had no knowledge on intersex issues or rights of intersex children, and whose only source of information was the opinion of a doctor.[9] Afterward, during adolescence, when coming out as trans, Sebastian had to undergo compulsory medical interventions again, to have their gender identity legally recognized, in addition to having to be diagnosed with mental health disorder (called back then a gender identity disorder) for the same purpose. Both experiences clearly represent overt violations of Sebastian's human rights.

Regardless of all presented data and existing reports of UN Independent experts and UN agencies; regardless of advocacy efforts of international human rights organizations, and specifically LGBTQI and trans-specific organizations; international declarations, charters, covenants, treaties, and documents, shockingly still 34 countries in Europe require a mental health diagnosis before adapting identity documents, including countries which are generally known for their respect of human rights, such as Sweden, the United Kingdom, and the Netherlands (TGEU, 2018b). Fourteen countries in Europe, as already highlighted, require sterilization in legal gender recognition (ibid.). Furthermore, these abusive requirements for legal gender recognition persist regardless of the above mentioned adopted Resolution 2048 *Discrimination against transgender people in Europe* (Council of Europe, 2015). The Parliamentary Assembly of the Council of Europe called its Member States to abolish compulsory medical treatments and a mental health diagnosis, as requirements to legal gender recognition. It was also recommended that national classifications of diseases be amended to ensure stigma-free access to necessary medical treatment for those trans people who need it while making clear that trans people, including children, are not labeled as mentally ill (Council of Europe, 2015).

The UN Independent Expert on protection against violence and discrimination based on sexual orientation and gender identity acknowledged that eradicating the pathologization of gender diversity from everyday life will be a long and difficult process and calls for proactive measures for enabling that change (UN, 2018, p. 5).

To conclude, the pathologization of gender diversity and trans identities has had a deep impact on legislation, jurisprudence, and public policy, in all regions of the world, impacting the collective conscience, and therefore resulting in epistemic injustice, human rights violations, and social injustice towards trans and gender non-conforming people. It has impacted education laws, policies, action plans, formal education curricula, and knowledge of the teachers and educational staff, across the globe, on gender and sexual diversity. International LGBTQI Youth and Student Organization (IGLYO) published in the 2018 LGBTQI Inclusive Education Index and Report (IGLYO, 2018).[10] The Report gathered data on LGBTQI inclusive education laws, policies, practices, and educational provision at a national level in Council of Europe Member States; ranked countries on the basis of several indicators related to LGBTQI inclusion, and provided an overview of each country based on a range of indicators, which will be elaborated further in this chapter. The report showed that out of the 49 countries reviewed, LGBTQI inclusion within education in most European countries is still lacking. There are only four countries that provide most of the LGBTQI inclusive measures (Malta, the Netherlands, Norway, and Sweden). The report stressed the need for: mandatory teacher training on LGBTQI awareness, compulsory formal education curricula which is inclusive of LGBTQI people, and national data monitoring and collection on bullying in education based on SOGIESC, with data segregated by grounds of discrimination (sexual orientation, gender identity and expression and variations in sex characteristics).

It is clear that erasure of LGBTQI, and specifically trans issues from formal education or, a stereotypical portrayal of trans issues and in a pathologizing way, is a result of the legal and policy approaches based on pathologization or erasure of trans issues. Pathologization of trans identities has been systemically, systematically, and historically reinforcing social stigmatization and discrimination, epistemic injustice, specifically testimonial injustice, testimonial erasure and quieting of trans people, as well as the erasure of trans epistemology in education. In the field of adult education and social justice education theory, practice and research, including in the subfield of adult education for social change, trans voices, voices of trans scholars and trans-related research is gaining momentum only in the last decade. Therefore, social justice activism has to penetrate all four domains of power: hegemonic, structural, disciplinary, and interpersonal domain, to enact progressive social change and initiate reparative justice towards trans and gender non-conforming people.

## 4 Legal Gender Recognition: Examples of Good Practice

Now that we understand the impact of legal and policy frameworks and pathologization of trans peoples' identities, bodies and psyches on the real, every day life of trans and gender non-conforming (TGNC) people; the impact of erasure of their lived realities, we can better understand the impact of human rights, social and epistemic injustice on the (in)visibility of trans epistemologies in education, including adult education for social change and social justice education theory, provision, and research. We might ask ourselves "what are the ways to move forward to make progressive social changes and initiate reparative justice[11] towards TGNC people?". This section will provide examples of legal and policy good practice needed for the development of trans inclusive and affirming national educational laws, action plans, policies (including school policies), which could support the curriculum and educational provision changes in this regard.

Ten countries around the world have adopted a model of legal gender recognition based on self-determination: Argentina in 2012; Denmark in 2014; Colombia, Ireland, and Malta in 2015; Norway in 2016; Belgium in 2017; and Austria, Brazil, and Pakistan in 2018. Among these, Belgium and Denmark imposed a waiting period of several months (UN, 2018, p. 16). Some countries ensured the depathologization of trans persons in the healthcare system and access to appropriate treatment, specifically Argentina, Denmark, and Malta. Argentina adopted the National Mental Health Law in 2010, which prohibited diagnosing trans people with a mental health disorder (UN, 2018, p. 15). In 2016, Malta depathologized sexual orientation, gender identity, and gender expression through legislation while ensuring (by the law) access to trans-specific, stigma-free, health care for trans adults and minors (Gender Identity, Gender Expression, and Sex Characteristics Act, 2015).[12] The Parliament of Denmark decided to remove trans categories from the section on mental and behavioral disorders of the Danish health administration system in 2016 (UN, 2018, p. 15). Furthermore, in 2013, at the request of the Government of Hungary, Hungarian Psychiatry and Psychotherapy Section and Council of the Professional College for Health stated that, what was called transsexualism, is not a mental health disorder (ibid.). In 2010, France removed the same diagnosis from the list of long-term psychiatric conditions, and before all of them, in 2009 Sweden had removed different diagnostic codes related to trans identities from the Swedish version of the tenth revision of the International Classification of Diseases (ibid.). In 2018, the Parliament of Sweden has decided to pay compensation to trans people who were coercively sterilized between 1972 and 2013, because it was a requirement for legal gender recognition. Between 600 and 700 people are eligible for the compensation of €22,500 (ibid., p. 17). That makes Sweden the first country in the world to compensate trans people for the severe human rights violation of coerced sterilizations.

Gender identity was included in the constitution and protected from discrimination in the Plurinational State of Bolivia, Fiji, and Malta (UN, 2018, p. 16).

A simple administrative procedure based on self-determination is put into practice for name and gender marker change in official documents and through the civil registry, without any court hearings and judge's approval of a person's gender identity, in Argentina, Austria, Belgium, Denmark, Ireland, Malta and Norway (ibid.). That means that, for example, trans students in these countries can easily have their own name and gender marker recognized in certificates and documents, which allows them to enroll in/attend formal and non-formal education with less stress, as well as to be referred in their own gender and by their chosen name by peers and teachers.

Unfortunately, the United Kingdom of Great Britain and Northern Ireland, and Uruguay have adopted legislation that enables the change of name and gender marker in official documents without judicial approval, but with a condition that trans persons demonstrate a history of gender dysphoria (ibid.). This pressure to prove their gender identity to medical and mental health professionals, and justify that they are really who they say they are (a trans person), along with the consequences of that requirement on a trans person's self-image, attitude and relationship towards healthcare and mental health professionals, is a topic that several participants in my research highlighted (Ugla, Aiden, Sebastian). Although Uruguay has adopted legislation enabling the change of name and gender marker in official documents without judicial approval (a step forward), but with a condition that trans persons demonstrate a history of gender dysphoria (which is problematic, as explained above in this chapter), it has put in place several programs and policies which build on the legal gender identity recognition law. Because the law recognizes that trans people face various obstacles to exercising their human rights, such as administrative procedures and economic obstacles, Uruguay has designed a specific program, linked to access to social security programs and employment opportunities, to support trans people in navigating the law (UN, 2018, p. 20). Therefore, this example shows how social programs aimed towards reparative justice can be developed on the basis of changed legislation, which has an epistemic, and educational value.

In 2018, the Supreme Court of Chile ruled that trans persons can change their name and gender marker on State registries without any hormonal treatment or required surgery to prove their gender identity. In 2016, the Constitutional Court of Peru changed the traditional definition of sex used in the legislation, acknowledging that gender is "within the social, cultural and interpersonal realities" that the person experiences (UN, 2018, p. 18). In 2017, the Constitutional Court of Colombia recognized "the right of trans persons to align their name with their gender identity in identification documents" (ibid.).

Another important issue is the legal gender recognition of non-binary genders/third gender, which is done in: Australia, New Zealand, some States in the United States of America (such as California), Bangladesh, India, Nepal, Pakistan, Malta, Canada, and Iceland. Unfortunately, implementation measures have been inconsistent in some of these countries. In India, for example, evidence of gender-affirming surgeries is required so that a person can have their gender legally recognized on their passport. In Nepal, as a result of the third gender recognition in the Constitution in 2007, the Supreme Court recognized a third gender based on self-determination and without medical requirements (ibid., p. 17), which is a progressive move. Unfortunately, in Nepal, this refers only to the third gender, while there are no options for trans women or trans men to be recognized as female in the first case, or male in the second (ibid.). In Australia, the gender marker can be changed to F (female), M (male), or X (indeterminate/intersex/unspecified) on passports, and in government records, but a statement from a medical practitioner or a psychologist is required, in both cases (ibid.).

Furthermore, in New Zealand, all persons can choose to have their gender in their passport marked as male (M), female (F) or as a third (X) category, based only on self-determined identity (UN, 2018, p. 21). This practice applies as well to children under the age of 18, although only with the support of a parent, legal guardian or a registered counselor or another health professional (ibid.). Since 2017, the option of choosing "X" gender marker based on self-identification is available in Malta, on all official documents. In Canada, that option is available since 2017, on all official documents, as well as in certain states of the United States of America: since 2018, in California (ILGA, 2017, p. 4). In Iceland, the Gender Identity Law, or Gender Autonomy Act, was adopted by the Icelandic Parliament in June 2019 (Iceland Review, 2019). It affirms legal gender recognition based on informed consent model, including of people who identify as gender non-binary: a third gender option -- X is available in passports (ibid.).

Moreover, another important issue for trans youth and students are age restrictions for legal gender recognition. Eight countries in Europe that have no age restrictions for gender recognition are Croatia, Germany, Malta, Austria, Azerbaijan, Switzerland, Estonia, and the Republic of Moldova (UN, 2018,

p. 17). In Norway, Belgium, the Netherlands and Ireland, children aged 16 years and over can obtain gender recognition. Norway allows minors aged between 6 and 16 years to apply for gender recognition with a parent or guardian (UN, 2018, p. 17). This is an important issue for trans youth and students because it doesn't impose them additional barriers to living in their true gender during schooling, which is directly related to their psychological well-being, and therefore school attendance and achievement (UNESCO, 2016b; Jones et al., 2016; GLSEN, 2016). More detailed information about legal gender recognition of children and youth can be obtained from the report of the UN Independent Expert on protection against violence and discrimination based on sexual orientation and gender identity (UN, 2018, p. 11).

Furthermore, research shows that trans people face bullying, harassment, and exclusion, in schools worldwide, which increases the risk of drop out from school (UNESCO, 2016a, 2016b; Jones et al., 2016; GLSEN, 2016; WHO, 2015a). UNESCO stated that a comprehensive education approach is needed to prevent and address homophobic, biphobic, transphobic and interphobic bullying (UNESCO, 2016a). This includes the implementation of (1) LGBTQI affirming national policies and/or action plans, (2) LGBTQI inclusive curricula and learning materials, (3) training for educational staff on LGBTQI issues, (4) support for queer students and families, (5) partnerships with civil society organizations and (6) monitoring of discrimination based on SOGIESC and evaluating the executed measures.

LGBTQI Inclusive Education Report (IGLYO, 2018), which gathered data on LGBTQI inclusive laws, policies, and practices at a national level in Council of Europe Member States, showed, as mentioned, that out of the 49 countries reviewed, LGBTQI inclusion within education in the most European countries is still lacking, and there are only four countries that provide the most of LGBTQI inclusive measures in education (Malta, the Netherlands, Norway, and Sweden). The indicators which served as a basis for comparison and ranking of the countries are: existing LGBTQI affirming education policies, teacher training, and national curricula being inclusive of LGBTQI issues; existence of anti-discrimination-law applicable to education which prohibits discrimination based on SOGIESC; the existence of gender recognition procedures; monitoring of transphobic, homophobic and interphobic violence and bullying in formal education and reporting on it; existence of support systems for LGBTQI students, and availability of information for LGBTQI students; existence of partnerships between the government, education sector, civil society organizations on LGBTQI inclusive education, and commitment of the government to international cooperation on the topic.

According to the Report (IGLYO, 2018) eleven countries in Europe, haven't implemented any LGBTQI inclusive measures at the time the research was conducted (Macedonia, Poland, Russia, Ukraine, Belarus, Armenia, Turkey, Azerbaijan, Latvia, Monaco, and San Marino). The Report highlighted (in accordance with UNESCO recommendations (2016a)) the need for: mandatory teacher training on LGBTQI awareness, compulsory formal education curricula which is inclusive of LGBTQI people, and national data monitoring on bullying in education based on SOGIESC with data segregated by grounds of discrimination (sexual orientation, gender identity and expression, and variations in sex characteristics).

## 5  LGBTQI Affirming Education Laws, Policies and Practices

According to the ILGA Europe Rainbow Map (ILGA Europe, 2019a), a tool developed to compare European countries when it comes to laws, policies, and practices that protect and/or affect LGBTIQ people in Europe today, Malta is the best ranking country in Europe with 90% (on a scale from 0–100[13]) in front of countries which have a long history of protection of LGBTIQ human rights such as Belgium(73%), Luxemburg (70%), Finland (69%), Denmark (68%), and Norway (68%).[14] Moreover, IGLYO's Inclusive Education Report (IGLYO, 2018) showed that the best ranked countries when it comes to implementation of LGBTQI inclusive measures in education and related to education, are: Sweden (89.5%), Norway (85.5%), the Netherlands (85%) and Malta (80%). The following paragraph will present the Maltese example of how changing laws and policies to ensure the protection of human rights of LGBTQI and specifically, trans people, can go hand in hand with policy changes in the field of education, end especially the development of trans-affirming educational policies. An example of the practical improvements that the Netherland has made in the last couple of years will also be presented, as well as the good situation both on the policy and the practical level in Norway, when it comes to LGBTQI affirming education.

### 5.1  *Malta: Laws and Policy Examples of Good Practice*
What made Malta the best ranked European country when it comes to legal protection of LGBTIQ rights, is the fast advancement in the development of LGBTIQ inclusive and affirming laws and policies.

According to ILGA Europe Rainbow Map (ILGA Europe, 2019a), and ILGA Europe Annual Review (ILGA Europe, 2019b), in 2018 Malta continued with the progress made in the field of affirming LGBTIQ people's rights, made in the previous years. To sum up data presented above in this chapter on Malta, the Gender Identity, Gender Expression, and Sex Characteristics Act (2015) protects individuals' physical integrity, bodily autonomy, and self-determination, meaning that legal gender recognition is based on self-determination, free from pathologization of mental health. Sexual orientation, gender identity, and gender expression are all depathologized by the law, while gender identity is included as protected grounds from discrimination in the constitution. There are no age restrictions for legal gender recognition. Furthermore, an option of choosing "X" gender marker based on self-identification is available in Malta on all official documents. Marriage equality was achieved in 2017, through an amendment of the Maltese marriage law, allowing marriage to people of the same gender, which is important because in many countries trans people are required to divorce and are denied their parenthood rights, after the medical transition. Moreover, Malta became the first country in Europe to outlaw 'conversion therapy', introducing fines and prison sentences for those who offer these harmful practices (The Affirmation of Sexual Orientation, Gender Identity, and Gender Expression Act, 2016).[15]

The advancements made in 2018 are the following: the police added to their reporting system the category of hate crime in the drop-down menu list of possible crimes; the government launched Malta's second "LGBTIQ Equality Strategy and Action Plan", for the period of 2018–2022; Malta's first Gender Wellbeing Clinic was opened, providing state-funded trans healthcare services delivered by a multi-disciplinary team; MPs voted in favor of the Embryo Protection (Amendment) Act, which gives the couples of the same gender and single women in Malta the access to in vitro fertilization (IVF) treatment for the first time domestically (ILGA Europe, 2019b, p. 66).

As for trans-specific policies, since 2016, after additional amendments to the Gender Identity, Gender Expression and Sex Characteristics Act (2015), transgender prisoners can be housed according to their lived gender, which is of vital importance for the reduction of exposure to the risk of violence. A policy on trans, intersex and gender-variant inmates (Ministry for Home Affairs and National Security, 2016) was launched in 2016, to affirm that transgender inmates have to be treated fairly and without discrimination or harassment, with ensured access to gender recognition procedures while in custody. Trans people are allowed to use the prison's shower and changing facilities according to their lived gender.

Maltese legal and policy changes became an example of good practice on an international level, and the catalyst for several other educational legal and policy changes. The second "LGBTIQ Equality Strategy and Action Plan", launched in 2018, for the period of 2018–2022, aims to mainstream Maltese legislative and policy changes into daily life and service provision (ILGA Europe, 2019b). In June 2018, the government of Malta established a SOGIESC Unit within the Human Rights and Integration Directorate (HRID), which is responsible for the day-to-day implementation of this Strategy and Action Plan (ibid.).

An example of good practice in the area of education policy is *Trans, Gender Variant and Intersex Students in Schools* (Ministry for Education and Employment, 2015), which affirms, along with a comprehensive gender recognition law (Gender Identity, Gender Expression and Sex Characteristics Act, 2015), that schools should provide a safe environment for trans, gender diverse and intersex students. This comprehensive education policy identified several issues faced by trans, gender diverse and intersex students, such as: sex and gender stereotypes in education, cultural expectations, lack of well-being due to discrimination, bullying and other unfair treatment; exclusion from sports and other gendered activities; unease with gendered uniforms, toilets and other gendered spaces (when a person is expected to wear uniform and attend gendered spaces which don't align with their self-identified gender identity); decreased attention during school time and failure to learn due to lack of safety in school and lack of support services; minority stress and social isolation, and absenteeism due to lack of safety in schools. In relation to those, the Policy identified the needs of trans students: privacy and confidentiality; persons to advocate for their wellbeing and rights: parents, teachers, psychologist, social worker, counselor, etc.; adequate facilities; inclusive policies and regulations; support from school and wider community; possibility of amendments of gendered characteristics in documentation of child's file; counseling when identity affirmation is proving difficult; access to information (p. 12). This policy focuses on how to address the issues faced by trans, gender variant and intersex students in schools and how to accommodate their needs.

One of the important and internationally recognized and praised recommendations developed by this Policy is the use of gender-neutral pronouns for a more inclusive language: "for a more inclusive policy, the use of 'they' shall be used for all genders even when referring to a single individual" (p. 4). In this book, and in my social justice education work, I always use "they" as a singular pronoun,[16] as explained in Chapter 1.

Furthermore, this Policy represents an example of good practice because it adopts a whole school approach philosophy, which refers to a "strategic collective and collaborative action by parents, students, educators, and administrators, to improve students' learning behavior, well-being and the conditions that support these" (ibid., p. 5).

The *Trans, Gender Variant and Intersex Students in Schools* Policy is developed within the context of the Framework for the Education Strategy of Malta 2014–2024 (Ministry for Education and Employment, 2014b) and the values promoted through the Respect for All Framework (Ministry for Education and Employment, 2014c). The accompanying strategy documents outline the steps schools need to take to determine how the policy's provisions should be implemented uniformly in all schools (IGLYO, 2018, p. 137).

Moreover, one year prior to launching the *Trans, Gender Variant and Intersex Students in Schools Policy*, the Ministry for Education and Employment of Malta published a policy to *Address Bullying Behaviour in Schools* (Ministry for education and employment, 2014a), which as well reflects a whole school approach philosophy. This policy is inclusive of gender identity and gender expression and has a section on homophobic and transphobic bullying.

When it comes to educational curricula, the mentioned Maltese National Framework of Education, *Respect for All Framework* (Ministry for Education and Employment, 2014c), specifies knowledge and competencies that learners should obtain in each school year. According to the guidelines outlined in this Framework, most of the content in various subjects should be inclusive of LGBTQI people and their lived realities. However, practice shows otherwise as local NGOs report (IGLYO, 2018, p. 138). The implementation of these guidelines depends on the willingness of individual teachers and schools, and is often considered to be the responsibility of Personal, Social and Career Education (PSCD), religion teachers, and student support service professionals, such as guidance teachers and counselors (IGLYO, 2018, p. 138). Up to this day, to my knowledge, Malta has not implemented a cross-curricular approach to LGBTQI affirming education, in practice.

However, regardless of the good trans-affirming policies and laws, awareness of the general population on LGBTIQ struggle and rights, and specifically trans and gender non-conforming students' needs, experiences and lived realities, including the knowledge on this topic of professionals such as teachers, is another and separate topic.

With respect to teacher training on LGBTQI issues, local civil society organizations such as MGRM have been involved in providing teacher training specifically in relation to the Trans, Gender Variant, and Intersex Students in School policy (ibid.). Since October 2016, with the creation of the Master's program in Teaching and Learning at the University of Malta,[17] the formal teacher training includes social and cultural diversity as one of the themes, which includes some, but not sufficient LGBTQI content (ibid.). The extent to which it provides Master students with the knowledge and skills to effectively address LGBTIQ issues in the school environment, is questionable (IGLYO, 2018, p. 138).

When it comes to supporting systems for trans students, according to the LGBTQI Inclusive Education Report (IGLYO, 2018) the MGRM's Rainbow

Support Service[18] receives referrals from schools regarding trans students. This service includes delivery of info-sessions to students, a youth group for LGBTIQ persons aged between 15 and 25, psychological support, a social work service, and legal counseling service. Rainbow Support Service also provides workshops and training for schools and professionals providing social welfare services (IGLYO, 2018, p. 139).

The Maltese example is widely considered as an example of good practice when it comes to the protection of LGBTQI people's rights and specifically trans peoples' rights, in education. That is possible because there is political will to create legal and policy changes. However, as we can see from the information presented in LGBTQI Inclusive Education Report (2018), the situation on the ground, in regards to teachers' training on LGBTQI issues, awareness of the general population on LGBTQI rights and issues, and the lack of cross-curricular approach to LGBTQI affirming formal education, still represent areas for improvement for Malta. Fortunately, the Maltese government cooperates closely with the local civil society organizations in the field of education, and provides funding to NGOs (especially MGRM) for delivering teacher training, lessons for students (as part of diversity initiatives, or personal and social education classes), and support for learners or education resources (IGLYO, 2018).

### 5.2   *The Netherlands: Improving the Practice*

In 2012, the parliament of Netherlands made a decision that respectful education about sexual diversity should be compulsory in all schools, by adding this topic to the Core Goals of Education, especially referring to primary education and the first years of secondary education (IGLYO, 2018, p. 149). These Core Goals outline minimum requirements and guidelines for education, as well as the level of skills and knowledge that students should obtain at the end of each level (ibid.). The guideline points out that schools must provide information about sexual and gender diversity (variations in sex characteristics are not mentioned). After the Inspectorate of Education conducted monitoring in 2016 of how sexual diversity was being taught, the Parliament ruled in 2017 that schools which do not deliver sexual diversity education will be sanctioned, therefore making this learning mandatory in vocational secondary education (IGLYO, 2018, p. 149).

According to the report (ibid.), in regards to teacher training on LGBTQI issues, in the Dutch educational system sector organizations for teacher training set their own standards and develop curricula, but they are obliged to follow a national "knowledge base" when developing their own programs. The Dutch Ministry supported a project for teacher training on social safety, including bullying, sexual and gender diversity, conducted by the School and Safety Foundation together with the sector organizations. As a result of this project, the "knowledge base" was adapted in 2018 to include sexual diversity. Therefore, starting from the next school year (2019), sexual diversity will be included in different parts of the teacher training programs, but from the IGLYO LGBTQI Inclusive Education Report (ibid.) it remains unclear if the knowledge base includes gender diversity as well, or not. Civil society organizations also provide specific lessons on this issue, especially COC Netherlands and EduDivers, (ibid.). Unfortunately, still teacher training on LGBTQI awareness is not mandatory, although all teacher training schools are obliged to use the "knowledge-base" to develop their programs.

The Netherlands is famous for its school support systems for LGBTQI students. The Safety at Schools Action Plan affirms that schools should provide support for students who have experienced bullying or harassment. The government supports some civil society organizations (COC Netherlands, Movisie, Jong&Out) in developing networks of peer support, providing information for learners, and publishing information on that matter (IGLYO, 2018, p. 150).

The key element of the Dutch LGBT policy are the Gender and Sexuality Alliances (GSA). GSAs aim to improve the social acceptance of gender and sexual diversity to ensure LGBTQI students' sense of safety at school. The Dutch LGBT policy has a GSA on Education, which promotes partnerships between LGBT and mainstream organizations. Therefore GSAs through their cooperation, tend to mainstream LGBT issues and reach people and organizations which would not otherwise be reached (IGLYO, 2018, p. 151). Dutch GSAs set an example of good practice for other countries in Europe, such as Spain, where so-called Alliances for Diversity are established in secondary schools in Malaga, Madrid, Galicia, and Barcelona during a pilot project of the organization It Gets Better España (It Gets Better España, n.d.).

In regards to information and guidelines sharing, the School & Safety Foundation, a Dutch center of expertise for a safe social learning environment, which is a partner with the Dutch Ministry of Education, Culture and Science, together with the three education councils for primary, secondary, and vocational education, has developed the website Gay & Schools,[19] which provides guidelines and information on how to improve LGBTQI inclusion in education. The website includes lesson plans, help kits for students, and other learning materials (IGLYO, 2018, p. 151).

The Government of the Netherlands is well known for its partnerships with the civil society sector both nationally and internationally. The Ministry of Education, Culture and Science established concrete measures to create an

LGBT-friendly environment in schools through funding various projects and organizations, such as COC Netherlands, Theater AanZ, Edu Divers, LCC Projecten or School & Veiligheid (IGLYO, 2018, p. 151). As for international cooperation with the civil society sector, the Dutch government provides financial support to European LGBTQI NGOs, such as IGLYO, ILGA Europe and Transgender Europe, and to local LGBTI organizations in countries where LGBTI people are at risk, through Dutch embassies worldwide. It actively contributes to international organizations such as UNESCO, the OECD, and UNICEF and contributes to strengthening networks such as the European Focal Points Network and European Rainbow Cities (IGLYO, 2018, p. 151).

### 5.3   Norway: An Example of Good Practice

According to IGLYO's LGBTQI Inclusive Education Report (IGLYO, 2018, p. 153) in January 2018, a new comprehensive Equality and Anti-Discrimination Act, applicable within education, came into force. It replaced the Gender Equality Act, the Ethnic Discrimination Act, the Discrimination and Accessibility Act, and the Sexual Orientation Anti-Discrimination Act. The new law addressed discrimination based on SOGIESC, aiming toward the protection of people on these grounds. When it comes to policies related to education, the government has adopted in 2008 *the Action Plan for Improving the Quality of Life among LGBT people*. In June 2016, the government launched *Safety, Diversity, Openness – The Norwegian Government's action plan against discrimination based on sexual orientation, gender identity and gender expression (2017–2020)*, a cross-ministerial LGBTI action plan (Norwegian Ministry of Children and Equality, 2017). For the first time in Norway, an action plan outlined the specific measures concerning intersex persons in Norway. The plan dedicated special attention to safe social and public spaces, improving the quality of life among vulnerable groups, and equal access to public services, specifying several measures related to education. Public consultation for a bill on zero tolerance for all forms of harassment, bullying, violence, and discrimination, is one of these measures, and the bill prohibits all forms of discrimination based on SOGIESC. It acknowledges that LGBTI children and youth may experience challenges in school, leisure activities, health services, and child and family counseling. According to the action plan (ibid.), all services must be grounded in a basic knowledge on sexual orientation, gender identity, and gender expression, having specialists who provide services with a specific focus on the challenges faced by LGBTI people (IGLYO, 2018, p. 153).

In relation to education curricula, the above mentioned Action Plan for Improving the Quality of Life among LGBT people (2008), affirmed that sexual orientation and gender identity must be addressed in the school curriculum. The new *Action Plan Plan Safety, Diversity, Openness* (Norwegian Ministry of Children and Equality, 2017) pays special attention to the provision of an inclusive and safe psychosocial environment in schools for LGBTI children and youth. However, according to IGLYO's LGBTQI Inclusive Education Report (2018, p. 154), the implementation in practice is criticized by LGBTQI organizations, whose opinion is that sexual orientation is included in curricula in selective ways in textbooks related to sex education. They have pointed out that Norwegian textbooks portray people who are not heterosexual as the Other. A norm-critical approach which portrays gender identities and sexualities as a spectrum, rather than binary opposites of the "usual" and the "other", is in my opinion, what we social justice educators working on LGBTQI issues from a critical perspective, are persistent about.

When it comes to teacher training on LGBTQI issues, the first Action Plan (for Improving the Quality of Life among LGBT people, from 2008), set the standard for the teacher training at university level, by explicitly mentioning equal opportunities and gender issues as part of the training. University students aiming to become teachers were exposed to the concept of families with parents of the same gender, and terminology around LGBTQI issues has changed along with the new teaching material on sexual relationships (IGLYO, 2018, p. 154).

In regards to legal gender recognition, from the adoption of the Legal Gender Amendment Act in 2016, legal gender recognition is based on a person's self-determination without medical treatments, sterilization, mental health disorder diagnosis, as requirements. Legal gender recognition procedure is available to persons who are over 16 years old, while children between 6 and 16 years old have to provide the permission of their parent(s) or legal guardians (ibid.).

Unlike many other European countries, Norway has a national monitoring system of bullying and violence in education: the Student Survey ("Elevundersøkelsen"), and the Ungdata-survey[20] which is a cross-national data collection scheme at the municipal level (ibid.). These surveys cover different aspects of lives of youth and it have optional questions on the topic of bullying and harassment in relation to sexual orientation (IGLYO, 2018, p. 155).

When it comes to support systems for LGBTQI youth and students, according to IGLYO's LGBTQI Inclusive Education Report (2017, p. 155), the Norwegian Department of Children, Youth, and Family Affairs provides online support for young people through a website.[21] In schools, school nurses are available to all students, but their level of knowledge on LGBTQI youth issues varies between the schools (ibid.). Moreover, helplines and chat services are available throughout the country. Finally, Skeiv Ungdom, an umbrella LGBTQI youth organization which was funded by the government (which is rare in Europe), offers the helpline called Ungdomstelefonen[22] providing information and answers to questions on sexuality and gender identity through phone, chat or messages.

The Norwegian government provides financial support to LGBTQI civil society organizations working in the field of education, which is more an exception of the rule than a reality in many European countries. Civil society organizations, funded by the government, provide guidance for the education sector on how to address bullying and harassment toward LGBTQI students in education, and provide information for LGBTQI students. The Norwegian Directorate for Children, Youth and Family Affairs developed a website with specific information for LGBTI youth.[23] Even more, within the school project Restart[24] members of Skeiv Ungdom meet students to explore and challenge norms on gender and sexuality, and talk about sexual orientation, gender identity, and gender expression, in the form of lectures, discussions, and exercises (IGLYO, 2018, p. 155).

An example of good practice in the area of teacher training on LGBTQI issues is the project Rosa kompetanse (Pink competency). The project is delivered by the Norwegian organization for gender and sexual diversity (FRI) and financed by the Department of Education and the Department of Health. It focuses on courses relevant to the school setting, facilitated by the people with a background in school settings. Courses focus on gender identity, sexual orientation and different types of families, and on norms around sexuality and gender. Within the project, the courses have been delivered for teachers and pre-service teachers, since 2011. The project is delivered in cooperation with Skeiv Ungdom, in a way that in some schools Pink competency delivers courses to teachers, while Skeiv Ungdom educators work with the students (IGLYO, 2018, p. 156).

Norway has committed to international cooperation in the field of LGBTQI inclusive education by signing *UNESCO's Call for Action by Ministers – Inclusive and equitable education for all learners in an environment free from discrimination and violence* (UNESCO, 2016a) and is a member of the European Governmental LGBTI Focal Points Network.

## 6    Conclusion

To conclude, education is a field which is deeply impacted by the public policy, legislation, and jurisprudence, and if they are abusive or neglectful of trans and gender diverse people's rights and realities, that epistemic, social and human rights injustice will be reflected in education as well. These injustices can be perpetuated in education in a spectrum of ways, from a complete erasure, to pathologization of trans peoples' identities and lived realities, to the stereotypical, prejudicial and generalized portrayal of gender and sexual diversity in textbooks and curricula, where gender diverse people are seen as "the other". On the other side, education is not just a field in which public laws and policies get reflected, education is a field that can initiate changes on all levels, from local, regional to national and international; school, community, policy, and legal levels, especially adult education for social change and social justice education, both formal and non-formal. The progressive, critical, adult education for social change and social justice education have a potential to challenge dominant power structures which determine knowledge production and which determine who's lived realities, histories, and epistemologies are reflected in formal education. This critical education has the power to create a deep impact on public policy, legislation, and education provision, and to initiate changes in the collective consciousness, through questioning dominant power structures and social norms which exclude people, by awareness-raising of the general population on trans people's existence, rights, and issues. A critical approach to education is needed so that the changes in the curricula and the training of teachers in trans and LGBTQI affirming approach to education can be made. Changes in education, at all levels, and in educational theory, practice and research are needed as much as the changes by the means of education, so that trans and gender diverse people can grow:

1. in school environments that are inclusive, safe and free from harassment and discrimination for all members of the school community, students and adults, regardless of sexual orientation, gender identity, gender expression, sex characteristics, and
2. in school climates in which LGBTQI students, and trans students specifically, can live as their true selves, thriving, and reaching their fullest potentials, which enable their successful learning development, mental health, and well-being.

I hope this chapter has provided social justice activists and human rights defenders and educators, but also educators working in formal education settings, ideas on the ways to open a dialogue with and assert pressure on their governments, including local governments where that is realistically possible. I also hope this chapter was useful to social justice educators working towards progressive social change, to reflect on how (non)existing national laws and policies related to trans people directly impact educational laws and policies, formal education provision and the knowledge of teachers on LGBTQI (but specifically trans) issues. While initiating conversations on this topic, educators can refer to the *Guidelines for Inclusive Education*, developed by IGLYO and OBESSU, which outline the minimum standards that should be met to ensure education is safe, inclusive and supportive of all LGBTQI learners (IGLYO & OBESSU, 2014). This publication affirms that students throughout Europe should have access to comprehensive human rights, sexuality, and relationship education. Furthermore, it affirms that formal education curricula and accompanying materials and text-books should include LGBQTI perspectives, and that anti-bullying policies should be developed and implemented so the students have access to information and support they need to be able to thrive and participate in education fully. Finally, I hope that the examples of LGBTQI affirming educational laws, policies and provision in Malta, Norway and the Netherlands have raised relevant questions for the readers and have given birth to ideas of possible projects, actions, and collaborations that can be established, so that formal and non-formal education provision becomes more reflective of the lives and realities of LGBTQI people.

**Notes**

1 Acronym that refers to Sexual Orientation, Gender Identity, and Gender Expression and Sex Characteristics.
2 According to TGEU Trans Rights Europe Index (TGEU, 2018b), in Europe only Belgium, Malta, Slovenia and Sweden recognize parenhood rights of trans people, through existing legal measures.
3 Serbia, to this day, has not adopted a gender recognition law, leaving trans people without legal options. Until January 2019, the administrative procedures in Serbia required a trans person to undergo sterilization and set of surgeries; to be diagnosed with a mental health disorder, and to be on hormone replacement therapy, in order to be eligible to change gender marker and social security number in their official documents. After changes to the Law on Registry Books, which came into force on January 2019, a trans person who is taking hormone replacement therapy, and has been visiting a psychiatrist for at least a year, can apply to change their gender marker and social security number in their documents, without surgeries as a requirement. This means that, a trans person has to provide a written recommendation of a psychiatrist showing the diagnosis of gender identity disorder, considered a mental health disorder in Serbia. Prior to the mentioned legislative change, all trans people in Serbia were required to obtain two recommendation letters from psychiatrists, whom they needed to visit for at least a year or two, to prove that person is indeed transgender and is diagnosed with, so-called gender identity disorder,

to be able to access required surgeries. Surgical requirement was available only after a person obtains another certificate, from the endocrinologist, stating that a person has been on hormone replacement therapy for at least a year. These procedures have been leaving trans people in a legal vacuum for decades, hindering their educational and employment opportunities for years (Gayecho, 2019).

4 "Sex work means that adult sex workers of all genders who are engaging in commercial sex have consented to do so (that is, are choosing voluntarily to do so), making it distinct from trafficking" (TGEU, 2016b, p. 3).

5 Such as International LGBTQI Youth and Student Organization (IGLYO), ILGA (International Lesbian, Gay, Bisexual, Trans and Intersex Association) Europe and ILGA World, Transgender Europe (TGEU), United Nations (UN), Global Action for Trans Equality (GATE), Council of Europe (CoE), World Health Organization (WHO), the Office of the United Nations High Commissioner for Human Rights (OHCHR), and others.

6 Convention on the Elimination of All Forms of Discrimination against Women, art. 15; Convention on the Rights of the Child, art. 8; Convention on the Rights of Persons with Disabilities, art. 12; American Convention on Human Rights, art. 3; and African Charter on Human and Peoples' Rights, art. 5 (UN, 2018, p. 8).

7 The Ministry of Health of the Russian Federation issued on January 22, 2018, a decree on the standards and procedure issuing a "gender reassignment certificate", which speeds up and simplifies the gender recognition procedure, allowing it to be settled out of court (TLDP, 2018c, p. 4).

8 Yogyakarta principles are documents about human rights related to sexual orientation and gender identity, created in November 2006, as the outcome of an international meeting of human rights groups in Yogyakarta, Indonesia. Ten Principles were added in 2017, to include gender expression and sex characteristics.

9 IGYLO together with partner organizations OII Europe and EPA, published a guide for parents of intersex children (IGLYO, OII Europe, & EPA, 2018).

10 All updates to the Report can be obtained from http://www.education-index.org/

11 Reparative justice refers to political practices of reparation towards individuals and groups who have been misstreated and oppressed in various ways, whether by moral/etical wrongding done to them, by wrongdoing of authorities who failed to provide justice towards them, or through political and/or social oppression. The concept of reparative justice includes the reparative possibilities and responsibilities that institutions such as universities, churches, governments, corporations can do to make amends for the wrong doing both in symbolic and material ways (Walker, 2010).

12 Act No. LVI amended in 2016.

13 Information about the criteria based on which the ranking of countries, expressed in percentages, was made can be found here: https://rainbow-europe.org/

## LEGAL AND POLICY FRAMEWORK 125

14  Ibid.
15  Bill no. 167: The Affirmation of Sexual Orientation, Gender Identity and Gender Expression Act bans conversion practices offered and/or performed by both professionals and individuals against variations of sexual orientation, gender identity and/or gender expression, particularly on vulnerable persons. This Bill also prohibits the pathologization of any sexual orientation, gender identity and/or gender expression. More information can be obtained from https://goo.gl/DlHa1G
16  For example, instead of saying: "As he stated, his family attitudes have changed ...", I would say: "As they stated, their family attitudes have changed ..." referring to a single individual, using *They* as a singular pronoun.
17  https://www.um.edu.mt/educ/mtl
18  http://maltagayrights.org/the-rainbow-support-service/
19  www.gayandschool.nl
20  www.ungdata.no/English
21  www.ung. no
22  https://ungdomstelefonen.no
23  https://www.ung.no/Homofil/
24  https://skeivungdom.no/prosjekter/restart/

CHAPTER 5

# Issues in Trans Community Organizing and Activism

## 1   History of Transgender Community Organizing

This book can be understood as a contribution to the reparation of epistemic injustice that trans people face and have historically been subjected to, therefore as a step towards reparative justice. I intended to briefly present the history of trans community organizing and activism in the European context in this chapter, knowing from my international activist and social justice education experience that there is a lack of visibility of the efforts and social justice work of TGNC activists and a lack of representation of trans activists in positions of power, influence, and agency, even within LGBTQI movements. I also know that trans activism requires hours, days, nights, months and years of unpaid work, to increase the visibility of the issues trans people face in their daily lives, and to advocate for social, political and legislative changes. I know that trans activism faces a shortage in funding opportunities, which will be elaborated later in this chapter, because of the invisibility/lack of recognition of the importance and the urgency of trans issues among donors and funders, which further pushes trans activists in poverty and lack of recognition of the historic work they are doing.

I intended to briefly present the history of trans community organizing and activism in the European context, but when I started looking for written resources in English language on the topic, looking for academic articles, books, papers; reports of civil society organizations, human rights organizations, LGBTQI and specifically trans organizations (operating on the national and international levels, including articles on their websites), I found almost nothing. The situation is not much different when looking for resources on the history of trans activism worldwide. This lack of visibility of trans issues, trans activism, and trans history in media and in academic writing is a reflection of systemic erasure of trans issues and epistemologies from all spheres of life (education, legislation, etc.). When reflecting on the history of queer movement it is important to ask ourselves the critical questions: "Whose history gets remembered and written? Whose history is forgotten and why?" However, I was delighted to come across Hodžić et al.'s (2016) chapter, entitled "The (in)visible

T: Trans activism in Croatia (2004–2014)". Apart from that, resources available in English language on the history of trans activism in Europe and globally, are scarce. This is why I have decided to provide an example of how trans history gets erased, rather than trying to present a brief summary of the historical development of trans activism in Europe. I chose to provide an example of the erasure of trans history from the event that has a historical significance and meaning for the LGBTQI communities worldwide: the 1969 Stonewall uprising, which happened in New York, USA.

### 1.1   Trans Erasure from the Stonewall Uprising

Often, when reading about the history of LGBTQI movements and LGBTQI social justice activism, it is framed as the history of "gay liberation", the history of gay movements for "gay rights". It is important to remember that 50 years ago, when the Stonewall uprising happened, the language around queer issues and identities was less diverse than it is today. Gay liberation was a common phrase used to refer to the fight for LGBTQI people's rights and terms such as transgender, gender non-conforming and intersex, were not used. Instead, the term transvestite or transsexual was commonly used to refer to trans and gender non-conforming people. Throughout time, as the visibility of heterogeneous queer communities was rising, the terminology has expanded to reflect people's lived realities and identities. That happened as people in queer communities started to own the terms for their own identities, whereas transsexual and transvestite were labels assigned to trans and gender non-conforming community by everyone else (including cisgender members of the LGB community). This is why the LGBT acronym has grown into LGBTQI or LGBTQIA2S,[1] depending on the context. Instead of the term transvestite used in the 1950s, today we use a term trans or transgender as an umbrella term for people whose self-identified gender identity does not align with the sex assigned to them at birth.

Reducing the heterogeneous communities of lesbian women, gay men, bisexual people, queer, transgender, gender non-conforming and intersex people to the umbrella phrase of "the gay movement" is an act of erasure of the diversity within queer communities. The "gay movement" umbrella phase indicates that the norm represented in the community (in the context of patriarchal societies), is a white, able-bodied, cisgender, gay man. The omnipresent whitewashed, patriarchal version of the history around the Stonewall uprising is no exception. That is why whenever I refer to the LGBTQI community in this book, I either use the acronym LGBTQI, or I use the term queer, as an umbrella term.

LGBTQI people have been historically subjected to systemic oppression, stigmatization, criminalization, and pathologization of their identities and lived realities, which becomes evident if we look at the social and political context and chronology of the events around the Stonewall uprising, the uprising which happened as a reaction to treating queer people as second-class citizens.

According to the article *Stonewall Riots* published on the History channel website (2018), just 50 years ago, being gay was illegal in New York City. It was considered a crime to engage in same-sex relationships. The police would arrest anyone perceived to be gay, and the New York criminal statute allowed the police to take into custody people who were wearing less than three "gender appropriate" pieces of clothing (History, 2018). According to the documentary film *American Experience: Stonewall Uprising* (PBS, 2019), if a person was identified/perceived as gay, their personal information, such as name and address, would be published in the local newspaper. As William Eskridge, a Professor of Law discussed in this film, social perception of the queer community was shaped by the intense and prevalent stigma. Queer people were considered to be "sexual psychopaths" and could be hospitalized on that basis and subjected to sterilization and/or lobotomies. He added that people who were known to be gay were at the risk of unemployment: they could be fired by the federal government, school boards, couldn't have a license to practice law, or couldn't be a licensed doctor, for example (ibid.). In some circumstances, queer people (who were often rejected by friends and family) would move to bigger cities like New York, and socialize around gay bars and clubs, such as those in the Greenwich Village neighborhood of Manhattan, where they could openly express themselves (History, 2018). However, that didn't mean that gay bars and clubs were a safe haven for queer people, because the New York State Liquor Authority would close or penalize clubs thought to be serving alcohol to those who were openly queer or perceived to be queer (History, 2018). Gathering of queer people was considered a disruption of the public order. Any "gay like behavior", such as holding hands, kissing, or dancing with a person of the same perceived gender, was enough to raise suspicion that the person was engaging in a criminal behavior. The police harassment in gay bars was frequent and often brutal. Many gay bars at the time didn't have a liquor license, as the New York State Liquor Authority refused to provide licenses to bars that served queers. This allowed the police to enter gay bars and clubs and look for liquor or people perceived as queer (USA Today, 2019). This situation was a fertile ground for the mafia business, as the mafia saw profit in providing alcohol for ostracized queer customers of the gay bars. In the '60s the Genovese crime family controlled most of the Greenwich Village gay bars, including the Stonewall Inn they bought, renovated, and converted into a covert gay bar (History, 2018). The Stonewall Inn became a famous queer pub, gathering transgender sex workers, gay men, including gay men of color, drag queens who were not welcome in other gay bars and clubs (which is an overt example of sexism, racism, and misogyny from within the LGBTQI community), and homeless queer youth and adults, who lived and worked on the streets of New York City. According to the History channel article (History, 2018), Stonewall Inn was one of the rare gay bars that still allowed dancing. All of this happened only 50 years ago. The Genovese mafia family would blackmail the club's wealthy patrons, who wanted to keep their sexual behavior a secret, while bribing New York City's Sixth Police Precinct to ignore the activities happening in the club (History, 2018). Police raids in gay clubs and bars were a common occurrence, but bribed police officers would sometimes let the bar management know prior to the raid that the police was on the way, so that alcohol could be hidden, and all activities which could be considered "problematic" or criminal could stop. However, on the morning of June 28, 1969, the New York City Police raided Stonewall In without prior notice, found alcohol at the bar, arrested thirteen people, and detained the club's patrons, employees, and visitors for violating the dress code (wearing less than three "gender appropriate" pieces of clothing). History channel (ibid.) reported that female police officers would take drag queens and "cross-dressed people" to the bathroom to check their gender, by checking their genitalia. However, rather than disappearing from the event, the enraged members of the queer community stayed outside of the bar, and neighborhood residents started gathering together with bar patrons, employees of the bar, and the usual guests: homeless queer youth, drag queens, transgender women of color, and trans sex workers. According to the History channel article (ibid.), the gathered crowd became enraged after a police officer hit a lesbian woman forcing her to enter a police van, and started throwing bottles, cobblestones, and pennies at the police. As the queer community gathered around the Stonewall Inn on Christopher Street fought back, it led to six days of protests and violent clashes with the police outside of the bar and in nearby Christopher Park. The Stonewall uprising became a catalyst for the community organizing, community building and LGBTQI movement building in the United States, that led to the development of the organizations such as the Human Rights Campaign, GLAAD (formerly Gay and Lesbian Alliance Against Defamation), and PFLAG (formerly Parents, Families and Friends of Lesbians and Gays). In 1970, New York and Los Angeles held the first versions of today's Pride march, called Christopher Street Liberation Days (Whose Streets Our Streets, 2019). June became known as the Pride month worldwide, and a symbol of the queer community's fight for their human rights.

Interestingly enough, the article *Stonewall Riots* published on the History channel website (2018), as well as many other articles on the topic that can be found on the Internet and in the academic literature, did not mention the role of transgender persons in Stonewall uprising, while in reality trans women of color, including Latinx and African American trans women, many who were also sex workers, were present and had an instrumental role in the Uprising. According to Equality Archive's article "Transgender women of color at Stonewall" (n.d.) and USA Today's article "Marsha P. Johnson: Transgender hero of Stonewall riots finally gets her due" (USA Today, 2019), the history of Stonewall revolution became white-washed, because transgender women of color led the fight and yet are left uncredited. In particular, Marsha P. Johnson, who was an African American trans woman and Sylvia Rivera, a Puerto Rican trans woman (both known as drag queens, whose sex assigned at birth was male, but who self-identified as women), were influential figures in the Stonewall uprising. Both women lived in New York City, and experienced homelessness, sexism, racism, homophobia, and transphobia, while struggling for safety, and to provide food and shelter (Equality Archive, n.d.). According to the Equality Archive article (ibid.), they were the first ones who fought back against the police harassment at the Stonewall Inn, but according to USA Today (2019) article, and the account of the Michael Boucai, Associate Professor of Law at the University at Buffalo School of Law, who studies LGBTQ rights and history, Marsha P. Johnson also climbed a lamppost and threw a heavy object at a police car window. Nevertheless, both Marsha P. Johnson and Sylvia Rivera are crucial figures in the development of trans and more broadly LGBTQI activism and community organizing in the United States. A year after the Stonewall Uprising, Marsha P. Johnson co-founded together with Sylvia Rivera a trans-youth organization STAR (was initially an acronym for Street Transvestite Action Revolutionaries), which provided homeless queer and trans youth food and housing, according to USA Today (2019). Together with other trans women who were STAR members – Bubbles Rose Marie, Andorra, Bebe Scarpi, Bambi L'Amour, and Miss Pixie, they fought for gender liberation within the movement (Equality Archive, n.d.). Regardless of their contribution to the queer movement, they struggled with homelessness throughout their lives, as well as incarceration (often as a result of their homelessness and/or gender identities and sexual orientation), along with the rejection of the white, cisgender, gays and lesbians, because both were socially and politically situated on the margins even within the queer movement, due to their multiple, intersecting minority identities. Some cisgender lesbian feminists, like Jean O'Leary, who started speaking out about misogyny and sexism within queer movement, saw transgender women like Sylvia Rivera as a threat to their movement, even calling Sylvia a "man in women's clothing" at the Christopher Street Liberation Day Parade in 1973 (Whose Streets Our Streets, 2019). In her famous speech at the same event, and as a response to transphobia within the queer movement reflected in Jean O'Leary's speech, along with negative reactions of the audience to Sylvia's presence on the stage, Sylvia Rivera called out privileged white, cisgender members of the movement (ibid.). Sylvia was at the time working with STAR to support homeless trans youth and queer people who were in jail. As the YouTube video titled "Sylvia Rivera 1973: Y'all better quiet down" (YouTube, 2019) of her speech at the Christopher Street Liberation Day Parade in 1973, and its transcript (Archive, 1973) showed, she said:

> Y'all better quiet down! I've been trying to get up here all day for your gay brothers and your gay sisters in jail that write me every motherfucking week and ask for your help and you all don't do a goddamn thing for them.
>
> Have you ever been beaten up and raped and jailed? Now think about it. They've been beaten up and raped after they've had to spend much of their money in jail to get their hormones, and try to get their sex changes. The women have tried to fight for their sex changes or to become women. On the women's liberation and they write 'STAR', not to the women's groups, they do not write women, they do not write men, they write 'STAR' because we're trying to do something for them.
>
> I have been to jail. I have been raped. And beaten. Many times! By men, heterosexual men that do not belong in the homosexual shelter. But, do you do anything for me? No. You tell me to go and hide my tail between my legs. I will not put up with this shit. I have been beaten. I have had my nose broken. I have been thrown in jail. I have lost my job. I have lost my apartment for gay liberation and you all treat me this way? What the fuck's wrong with you all? Think about that!
>
> The people are trying to do something for all of us, and not men and women that belong to a white middle class white club. And that's what you all belong to!

Nowadays, an organization named after her, Sylvia Rivera Law Project is working on intersectional queer issues, acknowledging the right to self-determination of one's gender identity is connected to racial, economic and social justice. The organization works on issues of systemic racism and poverty that trans and gender non-conforming queer people are exposed to, especially those who are subjected to multiple levels of discrimination. According to the organization's website, the organization focuses on raising the visibility of the political voices of low-income queer people and queer people of color who are transgender, intersex, or gender non-conforming, and improving the access to respectful and affirming social, health, and legal services for queer communities (Sylvia Rivera Law Project, 2019).

Due to the transphobic white-washing of the history of LGBTQI community organizing and movement building, and perception of LGBTQI people as a homogenous whole, represented by white, cisgender, gay men and cisgender lesbian women, another heroine and an inspirational, trans activist, Marsha P. Johnson was unacknowledged until her death in 1992. More acknowledgments of her life, activism, and contribution to the fight for queer human rights have been made in the last decade. In 2017, Netflix released a documentary *The Death and Life of Marsha P. Johnson,* that accounts to her life, activism, contribution to trans and moreover LGBTQ activism, and her suspicious death, which is officially considered a suicide, but is considered by the members of the queer community to be a possible homicide, as the film shows (YouTube, 2019). One of the rare mainstream media which have recognized the role of Marsha P. Johnson in the Stonewall uprising and trans movement building, while not leaving out one specific aspect of her life – that she was a sex worker, is the New York Times. Activists who are sex workers are not often portrayed in the mainstream media, or if they are, the sex work part of their lives gets ignored or erased. This is related to widely spread anti-sex work sentiments and social stigma towards sex workers. However, on March 8, 2018, on International Women's Day, the New York Times started a feature in its Obituaries section named Overlooked. It focuses on the aknowledgment of remarkable women who have been ignored by male editors of that section since 1851. The feature states that "Since 1851, obituaries in The New York Times have been dominated by white men. Now, we're adding the stories of other remarkable people" (Chan, 2018). In 2018, this feature published an article titled "1945–1992 Marsha P. Johnson, A transgender pioneer and activist who was a fixture of Greenwich Village street life" (Chan, 2018). The article acknowledged Marsha's role in the Stonewall Uprising, queer movement building, trans activism, and community organizing. It acknowledged her identities of an activist, a sex worker (the word prostitute was used in the article), drag performer, a homeless transgender woman, a person of color, a person who struggled with mental health, and someone who was a prominent figure in AIDS activism, trans activism, and homeless queer youth activism.

I argue that erasure of trans women (especially trans women of color who were sex workers), from the Stonewall Uprising history, and the lack of visibility of their presence and the importance of the historic role they played in LGBTIQI and specifically trans activism, community organizing, and movement building, is a result of the fact that their multiple identities were outside of what was considered to be the norm. Marsha was a woman, a trans woman, a drag queen, a trans woman of color, a trans woman of color and a sex worker, and a homeless person for the most of her life (Chan, 2018). Therefore, what made her and her fellow trans comrades invisible and erased from the history of trans and LGBTQI activism, are interlocking systems of power (such as patriarchy, misogyny, sexism, homophobia, transphobia, racism, classism; sex work and HIV and AIDS-related social stigma), that determine knowledge production. These systems of power and hegemony determine whose history is remembered and written, and whose history is forgotten and erased. From the perspective of an epistemic injustice that trans social justice activists and educators have suffered, specifically hermeneutical injustice (Fricker, 2007), the problem with the absence of trans epistemologies in the public discourse is rooted in the refusal of knowledge creators of dominant identities to allow the visibility to people of minority identities. Therefore, minority groups' interpretations of the world, the knowledge production coming from the lived realities of those who are marginally situated, as trans and gender non-conforming people are, especially of multiple minority identities, remain invisible. Acknowledging their contribution to the history of trans and, more broadly, LGBTQI activism, community organizing, and queer movement building, is a crucial step towards reparative justice and is of epistemic value for adult education for social change and social justice education. These activists were social justice educators although they might not have used those terms to describe themselves, but the contribution of their life-long work on progressive social change, is unquestionable. I deeply believe they deserve the acknowledgment in adult education for social change and social justice education discourses. The visibility of trans epistemologies in social justice education and adult education for social change is a conditio sine qua non for working towards reparative justice.

## 2  Summary of the Issues Trans People Face in Their Daily Life

As elaborated in Chapter 4, trans people can face a myriad of challenging issues in their daily lives, starting from not having their gender identity adequately recognized by law. When a trans person's name and gender marker on their official documents (birth certificate reflected in identification card, passport, driving license and health records) do not match a person's gender identity and expression, they are at risk of exclusion from school and the labor market. Moreover, they face restrictions in access to social services, health-care, housing and not being able to cross borders during emergencies, such as natural disasters or humanitarian crises.

The lack of accessible legal gender recognition procedures hinders not just employment and educational opportunities for trans people (heightening their vulnerability to poverty and social exclusion), but also exposes them to discrimination in everyday life. Exclusion and bullying in education, directly impacts a trans person's mental health and well-being, which is elaborated in Chapter 3. Several studies conducted in Western Europe and the United States show that the unemployment rate of trans people is several times higher than that of the general population (FRA, 2014; Movement Advancement Project and Center for American Progress, 2015; Whittle et al., 2007). A 2015 survey conducted in the US showed that the unemployment rate among trans people was three times higher than the unemployment rate in the cisgender US population at the time; for transgender people of color, it was four times higher (Rankin et al., 2016). Discrimination in employment and denial or lack of access to trans-affirming healthcare based on informed consent, and lack of access to housing and social security, put trans people at disadvantage, and may push them into sex work,[2] which is in many European countries criminalized (GATE et al., 2017a, p. 9). Laws and policies that focus on sex workers and anti-sex work sentiments joined with transphobia, expose trans sex workers to an increased risk of verbal and physical attacks and threats from the general public, gangs, and the police (ibid.). The previously mentioned Netflix film the *Death and Life of Marsha P. Johnson* portrays a relationship that trans people, especially those who are sex workers, have historically had with the police. Even to this day, law enforcement often uses public order laws and policies to harass people who are sex workers or perceived to be sex workers (GATE et al., 2017a, p. 9). That doesn't mean, however, that all trans people engage in sex work or that there are no trans people who are privileged, and of a higher socio-economic status and educational attainment level, but it does mean that transphobia is a systemic issue and is systemically and systematically perpetuated in many European countries. This perpetuation happens overtly through pathologization of trans people's identities and lived realities, or covertly through legal, policy and systemic erasure of trans issues from all spheres of life (education, employment, healthcare, etc.). Because of discriminatory law enforcement practices, economic exclusion, and the criminalization of sex work, trans sex workers are more likely to end up in prison where they are exposed to violence and assault (ibid.), especially if placed in cells according to their sex assigned at birth and not their gender identity or expression. As a "preventive measure" trans prisoners can be put in solitary cells for months, which is equal to torture and/or ill-treatment (ibid.). As already elaborated in chapter 4, Section 5.1, Malta represents an example of good practice when it comes to trans specific laws and policies, including those related to trans prisoners (a Policy on trans, intersex and gender-variant inmates, Ministry for Home Affairs and National Security, 2016). Trans people are harassed and abused in various gender-segregated facilities, such as in public restrooms, homeless shelters, school locker rooms and restrooms (GATE et al., 2017a, p. 9). In the United States, especially after Trump's inauguration, there is an increased public attention on "bathroom bills" which seek to restrict access of trans people to gendered public facilities, such as restrooms and locker rooms. These transphobic and discriminatory bills force trans people to use facilities based on their sex assigned at birth rather than their gender identity, which exposes them to violence and harassment (most often from cisgender males). As justification of these bills it is often said that cisgender women might not feel safe if a transgender woman or someone pretending to be a transgender woman (often referring to a cisgender male sexual predator), shares locker rooms or restrooms with them, which is an overt example of transphobia (not seeing trans women as women, but rather as men, and even more, as predatory men).[3] Trans people are held to a higher ethical standard than the general population, all the time: from asking them to provide proofs from mental health professionals certifying they are who they say they are (a trans person), when asking for legal gender recognition, to questioning if they should use the restroom which corresponds to their self-identified gender identity. In public debates and discourses, trans people have to prove themselves not to be the sexual predators, sexual abusers, or harassers, similarly to queer people being held to a higher ethical standard than cisgender, heterosexual people in public discussions on marriage equality. Cisgender people of the so-called "opposite sex" are entitled to a right to marry and form a family, but queer people of the same gender have to justify and prove in public discussions, that they are not child abusers, and that children who would be adopted by parents of the same gender, would not be abused by them. Meanwhile, cisgender, heterosexual partners are not automatically assumed to be child abusers and sexual predators. This is an example of how pathologization and social stigmatization of the "Other" are directly related to access to social services, opportunities, and resources in society that people of marginally situated identities have.

These challenges are magnified for trans people of multiple minority identities who experience the intersections of marginalization based on race, ethnicity, nationality, class/socio-economic status, caste, disability status, HIV status, mental health status, age, or because they are sex workers, incarcerated, migrants, etc.

When it comes to education, research shows that trans people face bullying, harassment, and exclusion in schools worldwide, which increases their risk of dropping out of school (UNESCO, 2016a, 2016b; Jones et al., 2016; GLSEN, 2016; WHO, 2015a). A study in New Zealand showed that trans secondary school students were nearly five times more likely to be bullied on a weekly basis than their cisgender peers (Clark et al., 2014). The survey carried out by the European Union Agency for Fundamental Rights (FRA, 2014) found that a quarter of trans respondents who attended school/university themselves or had a child/children in school/at university, felt personally discriminated against by school or university personnel in the 12 months preceding the survey, but when looking at trans students only, the number rose to 29% (FRA, 2014, p. 21).

According to the Trans Murder Monitoring Project (TMM) which systematically monitors, collects and analyzes reports of homicides of trans and gender-diverse people worldwide (TvT Research Project, 2018), more than 2,982 trans and gender-diverse people in 72 countries were killed between January 2008 and September 2018, while 271 were killed in 2018, which is an increase compared to previous years (ibid.). It is important to note that the data collected show only cases which have been reported, and there is no data and no estimates available for unreported cases. Only those which can be found on the Internet and are reported murders by the local activists and TMT partner organizations are counted. The majority of the murders occurred in Brazil, Mexico, the United States, and Colombia (ibid.). According to the Transgender Europe publication *The vicious circle of violence: Trans and gender-diverse people, migration, and sex work*, in the United States, the victims are predominantly trans women of color and/or Native American trans women (TGEU, 2017a, p. 18). Research (Stotzer, 2008) shows that hate crimes toward transgender and gender non-conforming people are especially violent and that transgender victims are targeted for violence for more complex reasons than the gender variance alone. Of those whose profession was known, 62 percent of murdered persons were sex workers (TGEU, 2017a, p. 18). In Europe, according to TMM data, Turkey has reported 51 trans women, the majority being sex workers, murdered in the last ten years (TvT Research Project, 2018, p. 2). In addition, most (55%) of the murdered transgender migrants in Europe come from Brazil (TGEU, 2017a, p. 18). In Italy, 16 of the 22 murdered trans migrants were from Brazil, and of those Brazilian trans migrants, 12 (or 75%) were sex workers (ibid.). TMM project shows that transphobic hate crimes are especially violent, with the most prevalent causes of death in homicides of trans and gender-diverse people being: shot, stabbed, beaten, strangled/hanged, stoned, asphyxiated/smoke inhalation/suffocated, decapitated/dismembered, burned, throat cut, tortured, and run-over by a car (TvT Research Project, 2018). The UN Special Rapporteur on Violence against Women highlighted that activists working in this field are targeted because they "do not conform to stereotypes of gender sexuality and/or identity, thus becoming victims of homophobic crimes" (UN Human Rights Council, 2012, p. 18).

Despite the evidence of the presence and violent nature of transphobic hate crimes, many countries around the world do not monitor the murders of trans and gender diverse people, and most countries lack anti-discrimination laws that prohibit discrimination based on gender identity and gender expression (GATE et al., 2017a, p. 10). Many of the crimes go unreported as the survivors don't trust in the law enforcement to adequately process the cases and or/protect them from further harassment and traumatization, or are not counted as trans-phobic crimes because the victim is misgendered in reporting (not seen as a trans person, but according to the person's sex assigned at birth).

Furthermore, as the research shows, minority stress, social stigma, and pathologization that trans people often face in their daily lives, has deeply harmful impacts on their mental health and wellbeing, as well as their physical well-being (Reisner et al., 2016; McNeil et al., 2012; European Parliament, 2016).

It is widely acknowledged in the research that trans and gender variant people experience higher suicide rates, suicide ideation, depression, and anxiety than the general population (Marshall et al., 2015; Haas et al., 2014; Bockting et al., 2013; Cochran, 2001; Effrig et al., 2011; Clements-Nolle et al., 2006; Marshall et al., 2015; Haas et al., 2014) and worse overall mental health (Bockting et al., 2013) especially those who wish to, but are unable to access, gender affirming surgeries and/or hormone replacement therapy to be able to live in their self-defined gender (Heylens, 2013; Colton Meier et al., 2011; Yadegarfard et al., 2014).

Furthermore, reports of international organizations and bodies show that trans people are at significantly higher risk of acquiring HIV infection because of their exposure to violence, criminalization, discrimination, and social exclusion (WHO, 2015; UNAIDS, 2014; Winter et al., 2012). Trans women are up to 49 times more likely to acquire HIV than other persons (UNAIDS, 2014). More research on HIV acquisition among trans people, access to trans-affirming health care based on informed consent, and allocating funding for HIV prevention and interventions among trans people, are matters of urgency, which is recognized both by the activists on the ground (as I know from my work experience internationally), and by international organizations (GATE et al., 2017a).

## 3 Current Issues in Trans Community Organizing and Activism

The issues presented in the above paragraph are well-known to trans and gender non-conforming activists and social justice educators working on trans issues, both from their personal life and activist work experience. That is not to say that all trans people have personally faced every issue presented above, but rather that these issues are common knowledge in trans activism and education for social change regarding the lives of trans people.

When it comes to the issues that trans social justice educators and activists face in their daily work and activism, there is a comprehensive report published on that topic, named *The State of Trans Organizing* (GATE et al., 2017a). In 2016, Global Action for Trans Equality (GATE), American Jewish World Service (AJWS) and the Astraea Lesbian Foundation for Justice (Astraea) conducted two surveys: one on intersex activist groups (GATE et al., 2017b) and the other on trans activist groups and their organizing (GATE et al., 2017a). The *State of Trans Organizing* report (GATE et al., 2017a) was developed on the basis of the data coming from the second survey of 455 autonomous trans activist groups and trans programs of larger organizations from across the world and continents, that work primarily on trans issues or with trans people. The report provides an overview of the organizational and funding needs, experiences of trans activist groups and issues they face in their daily work.

According to the *State of Trans Organizing* report (GATE et al., 2017a), trans groups all over the world are doing critical social justice work to address the human rights violations faced by trans communities, but with notably limited resources. In 2016, more than half (55.8%) of trans groups responding to the survey had annual budgets of less than US$10,000, which means that trans activist work is done with very low budgets. The largest proportion of trans activist groups that had budgets smaller than US$10,000 in 2016 were in Europe (72.1%) and the Caribbean, Central America and South America (69.7%), according to the report (ibid., p. 6). A majority of trans activist groups were autonomous (85%), which means they are led by trans people and focused specifically on trans issues (ibid.), compared to just over half (55%) in 2013, as reported from the previous survey (GATE & AJWS, 2013).[4] More than two-thirds (68.2%) of trans groups in 2016 had most or all trans people making financial decisions, compared to about two in five trans groups in 2013 (GATE et al., 2017a, p. 6).

The issue of representation in positions of power, influence, agency, and decision-making is an extremely important issue in trans activism and social justice work. Throughout my international LGBTQI youth activist work, I have noticed that there is a common practice in the European queer youth work, and European youth work in general, which I call youth-washing. When an organization claims to be a youth-lead, it means that young people have to be in decision-making roles, and that includes first and foremost, taking the lead, not merely participating, in setting the organization's strategic and financial priorities, making financial and strategic decisions, being spokespeople, and being the predominant members of the decision-making bodies of the organization. The same applies to trans-specific organizations, or programs of larger LGBTQI organizations working on trans people's human rights.

From my experience of working with numerous queer youth organizations from different countries, I noticed a pattern in the internal organizational functioning of queer youth organizations. Young people are predominantly in the role of spokespeople, being "the face" of the organization, or are members of a so-called decision-making body such as the Executive Board. But if that body in practice and in reality doesn't make strategic and financial decisions, or is a cover-up for those who really make the strategic and financial decisions (often employed white, cisgender men, or cisgender heterosexual women, who are not queer youth, but are in the position of power and decision making), then the organization in question is not a youth lead organization and is not necessarily serving the interests of youth, in my opinion. It is often serving the interests of those in the position of the real decision-making power, even if/when, they do the work that can serve the youth (which they have to do to be able to continue receiving funding for youth-related projects). I believe these organizations should be called youth-washing organizations. A youth-washing organization can have youth membership, but it is not a youth lead organization, or necessarily representative of youth's needs and interests. The same can apply to organizations working on the advancement of human rights of trans people, especially if they are trans-specific organizations, but also if they are general LGBTQI or human rights organizations, having trans programs and projects. If they want to be representative of the realities and needs of trans people, then trans people should be in positions of power and decision making, which is the first step towards reparative justice and raising the visibility of trans existence, lived realities, and trans epistemologies. If trans people are not in decision-making positions and roles and don't have that power and agency in programs and projects concerning trans issues, then my question is not "why is representation so important?", but rather "why are trans people not represented in positions of power?" Critical perspective applied to the internal organizational functioning requires asking uncomfortable questions, such as: Whose history in our LGBTQI movement gets remembered and whose history gets erased and why? Who is present (representatives of which part of the queer community) at the decision-making table when important organizational decisions are being made and who is absent and why? If there are not trans activists qualified for the role of trans organization's Executive Director, or Community Engagement Officer, or Program Officer of trans specific programs, why is that so? Do trans activists have the same access to capacity building opportunities within the queer movement and within the organization in question as their cisgender colleagues, which would allow them to develop necessary skills for decision making roles, or these opportunities are given to cisgender gay men and cisgender lesbian women? If yes, why is that so? Do trans activists feel empowered enough or deserving enough to take on leadership roles? If not, why? What role do social stigmatization and mental health pathologization play into a person's self-image and belief in their own capacities and competencies? What type of capacity building opportunities do trans activists need to be able to feel confident about applying for decision-making positions? Are they related to financial management, strategic management, communication skills, leadership skills, or are there some specific capacity building areas trans activists need, such as trauma healing, anti-oppressive work on internalized and embodied oppression?[5] Do trans people of multiple minority identities, such as sex workers, people of minority ethnic backgrounds, trans people of color, trans immigrants and refugees, and trans people of lower socio-economic status, those living with HIV, trans people struggling with mental health, and trans people living with disabilities, feel welcomed and represented in and by the trans specific organization in question, and in which ways does the organization serve their needs? Whose needs does the organization serve and why? Asking these questions, often perceived as uncomfortable, is a prerequisite for intersectionally oriented activism and social justice education work based on the "Nothing for us without us" principle. Without asking these questions and investing time, energy and resources in critical self-reflection and reflection of internal organizational functioning and organization's work, there is an increased risk of trans erasure, tokenism, and trans-washing within the organization and wider LGBTQI movement.

I argue there are four preconditions needed for trans activists to challenge the power dynamics and/or lack of their representation within the organization that claims to work on trans issues. These preconditions suggest that trans activists must:

1. Know they have the right and are deserving and capable of leading an organization (and from my activist experience I would say that marginally situated youth and activists are not socialized to believe they have the right to be in positions of power, but are rather socialized to develop an imposter syndrome while in power, or associate positions of power with the abuse of power and avoid them altogether).

2. Have access to capacity building opportunities for the development of competencies needed to challenge and dismantle abusive power structures within the organizations (first and foremost financial and strategic management skills and competencies, and open and direct communication skills).
3. Be empowered enough to challenge the power structures within an organization, and resilient enough not to back down when the power structures engage in gaslighting and power play
4. Have access to the resources needed for that action, including access to an organization's internal documentation, actual financial reports, hidden agendas, and hidden decision-making processes.

For the same reasons psychological harassment, abuse, and bullying at the workplace is not easy to legally prove, I argue that severe youth-washing in queer activism, and tokenism[6] when it comes to trans issues within LGBTQI organizations are not easy to dismantle. Those in positions of power, often people of more privileged identities such as white, middle class, able-bodied, cisgender men, often cover up issues for each other. That is why the youth sector at the European level has a persistent, severe youth-washing crisis, as well as queer activism all over Europe faces tokenism when it comes to both trans and queer youth issues and rights.

Furthermore, the *State of Trans Organizing* report (GATE et al., 2017a, p. 6) shows that autonomous trans activist groups lack paid, full-time staff. That implies that trans activists are working without financial compensation and dividing their time between jobs, which is in accordance with my experience and knowledge of internal structures of LGBTQI and trans specific organizations in the European context. Trans groups that are programs of larger LGBTQI organizations are more likely to have full-time paid staff (44.4%) than autonomous trans groups. According to the report, trans activist groups are more likely to receive funding from foundations and larger NGOs as sub-grants, and they are not likely to receive government funding (ibid., p. 7). In 2016, more than two-thirds (68%) of the trans groups surveyed had external funding and nearly half (48.6%) of trans groups in high-income countries had foundation funding, compared to just under one-third (31.8%) of trans groups in low-income countries (GATE et al., 2017a, p. 7). While writing this book, I was wondering how many trans activists that I know from the European activism, would be in a position to switch from the full-time to a freelance part-time job, so that they can dedicate 50% of their working time during 6 months period to book writing. The same way there is a shortage of funding opportunities for trans activist groups, there is a shortage of available fellowship opportunities for activist writers, especially for those who are from the countries which are not members of the European Union, coming from Eastern Europe, and not being currently employed by Universities or Research Centers, as it is in my case. Additional hindering factor to availability of fellowship opportunities for socially engaged writers, is the topic they write about, as trans issues are still not visible enough in academia, in the field of education and among funders. Before I started writing this book I reached out to most of the donors and international organizations I know which fund trans-related projects and initiatives, but they responded they cannot fund individual fellowships, most probably because trans activist groups face a shortage of funding across the world. Therefore, raising the visibility of trans epistemologies in education, is a matter of privilege. Only those trans researchers and scholars working on trans related topics who are affiliated with and financed by Research Centers and institutions of higher education, are in the position to participate in knowledge production on trans issues in education.

Furthermore, when it comes to factors hindering the work of trans activist groups and organizations working on trans issues, one of the major ones is a lack of understanding among donors of the importance and urgency of trans activism. According to the same report (GATE et al., 2017a), donors often don't prioritize funding trans groups, while simultaneously they want trans groups to be better resourced to be eligible to be considered for funding. More than a third of trans groups reported receiving feedback from donors that their group is too small or lacks capacity to be considered for funding (36.7%), and the same amount of trans groups (36.1%) received feedback from donors that despite funding LGBT or LGBTI groups, they would not fund a trans-specific group (ibid.).

Moreover, trans groups face barriers to funding, when applying for and implementing grants. According to the report (GATE et al., 2017a, p. 6), seven in ten (70.8%) trans groups reported at least one barrier when applying for funding, such as long and complex applications, lack of grant-writing skills. The same applies when the projects are approved for funding. In that case, long delays of the initial payment are major barriers to the work of trans activists.

More than one-third (35.2%) of trans groups were not registered with their country's government in 2016, which makes them ineligible for many funding opportunities, especially government funding (GATE et al., 2017a, p. 6). Unfortunately, what makes impossible for trans groups to legally register in some European countries are so-called "anti-gay propaganda" laws, which prohibit queer community organizing. For example, Russia adopted in 2013 a federal "anti-propaganda" law, which prohibits the right of queer people to assemble, protest, and organize, making it impossible for trans organizations to legally register and receive governmental, and other funding for their projects. Laws that ban so called "gay propaganda" represent an overt governmental encouragement of social exclusion and stigmatization of LGBTQI people, who are exposed to lack of legal protection against discrimination, violence, and stigmatization (Beury & Yoursky, 2019, p. 150). Currently, Chechnya, a Russian Republic, is conducting a "gay purge" with established concentration camps for gay and bisexual men and lesbian women, where they are imprisoned, tortured, and murdered. These atrocities have not been addressed or punished by the Russian government despite the urgent calls for action by international human rights organizations and bodies, such as Amnesty International and OSCE, which report that the Russian government refuses to respond and cooperate (Amnesty International, 2019; OSCE, 2018).

As fascism across the European continent on the rise, with its prominent xenophobic, racist, islamophobic discourses, and populist rhetoric favored by the right-wing governments, progressive social actions on queer issues are often framed as "gender ideology". Especially conservative forces are invested to stop the progressive social change in the field of migration, gender equity, sexual and reproductive health and rights, SOGIESC inclusion, trade unions rights (Beury & Yoursky, 2019, p. 153). For example, in 2018 Istanbul Pride and Pride events were banned by the Turkish government fourth year in a row, which represents an overt violation of the right to assembly and association, and is often justified by the totalitarian government with the argument of safety concerns (ibid.). Queer activists are constantly being gaslighted in totalitarian contexts and portrayed as they are the cause of the "safety concerns" of the government, while in reality homophobic, transphobic and the interphobic government itself encourages discrimination and violence against queer people, especially in Turkey. Additionally, Azerbaijan's law enforcement has been conducting numerous raids on LGBTI premises and individuals, arresting the activists and queer persons, blackmailing them and even conducting forced medical examinations, under the "necessity to protect public order" (ibid., p. 152). Furthermore, LGBTI asylum seekers, especially women, are exposed to violence in European governments' facilities and refugee camps (ibid., p. 154). LGBTIQI immigrants and refugees are often exposed to double marginalization and are targeted as "the other" within populist rhetoric: as LGBTQI persons and as refugees (ibid.). As the refugee crisis in Europe continues, and there is no official data across the continent on people who seek asylum based on SOGIESC, there are no supporting procedures put in practice for their application. Queer refugees and immigrants often don't have support in making asylum claims based on SOGIESC (ibid.). Therefore, queer rights in Europe are impacted not only by the national laws and policies, but also by the refugee crisis.

When it comes to beneficiaries that trans activists work with, the *State of Trans Organizing* report (GATE et al., 2017a) highlights that trans activists work with trans people who face multiple and intersecting types of oppression, such as low-income trans people, sex workers, trans people of ethnic minority identities, and trans people living with HIV/AIDS (p. 6). According to the report, more than nine in ten (91.6%) trans groups that responded to the survey replied they did advocacy, community organizing and/or community education, while nearly eight in ten (79.2%) provided social services, peer support, individual-level advocacy, or health care to trans people (ibid., p. 7). Moreover, nearly six in ten trans groups who participated in the survey reported engagement in some form of safety or anti-violence work (59.5%). I would argue that most of these activities include non-formal and informal social justice education and adult education for social change work.

The most common activities that trans groups reported they would focus on if they had the funding, according to the report (ibid.) are: provision of trans-specific health care (36.1%), and provision of health care services to trans people other than trans-specific services (32.4%). An especially relevant finding of the survey (for those who are reading this book and identify as social justice educators and/or adult educators for social change), is that trans activists report they have a need for capacity-building for sustainable activism and prevention of burnout syndrome. This capacity building work is a form of non-formal social justice education and adult education for social change, and it requires a trans-affirming approach to be relevant for and welcoming to trans people. According to the report, almost eight in ten (79%) of trans activist groups expressed the need for training in fundraising and grant writing skills, and more than seven in ten (70%) trans activist groups reported the need for the training in budgeting and financial management skills (GATE et al., 2017a, p. 8). More than three-quarters (76.5%) of trans groups reported the need for training related to healing from trauma and preventing burnout. This is another evidence of the experienced minority stress among trans people, especially trans activists. That is not surprising when we take into account not just possibly experienced minority stress, but the low rates of full-time paid staff within autonomous trans activist groups, where activists often work without financial compensation. It is important to remember that trans groups that do not receive any external funding, including foundation funding, are both less likely to receive training or capacity building support and more likely to need it (GATE et al., 2017a, p. 8). It is also important to remember that the regions where the largest proportion of trans groups had budgets less than US$10,000 in 2016 were Europe (72.1%) and the Caribbean, Central America and South America (69.7%), according to the report (ibid., p. 6).

As a response to the witnessing the needs of the trans activists for capacity building, particularly in the field of anti-opressive education related to healing from trauma and preventing burnout, after my 2 years long mandate with IGLYO ended in December 2017, my work has mostly been focused on the development of social justice education programs in that area. I currently design and facilitate international trainings on the topic of burnout prevention and resilience building for social justice activists and educators, and on the topic of embodied social justice youth work, for youth workers working with minority social groups. These youth workers are at higher risk of burnout syndrome, accompanied by compassion fatigue, and emotional and psychological drain, especially if they are persons of minority identities themselves. The importance of an anti-oppressive education in the area of trauma healing and burnout prevention with activists who are coming from and are working with minority social groups becomes apparent when we look at the literature on activist burnout (Plyler, 2006; Rodgers, 2010; Gorski & Chen, 2015). Schaufeli and Buunk (2003) defined burnout as "a state or process of mental exhaustion" (p. 383), while Pines (1994) understood burnout as "the end result of a process in which idealistic and highly committed people lose their spirit" (p. 381).

Gorski and Chen (2015) conducted and analyzed interviews from 14 cisgender activists whose activism focused on issues of educational justice. The research was on activist burnout and its implications on movements for educational justice. The results showed that the culture of social justice movements was is incredibly unsupportive for activist sustainability, because the conversations about burnout were often devalued, and attention to self-care was often shamed. The researchers named it *the culture of martyrdom* in social justice education movements, and highlighted it negatively impacts the sustainability of activism and the health of activists, threatening the efficiency and effectiveness of educational social justice movements. They identified common symptoms of burnout among the participants of their research: deterioration of psychological and emotional well-being, deterioration of physical well-being, disillusionment and hopelessness, and withdrawing from activism.

Usually, social justice activists and educators have to find support for experiencing burnout syndrome outside of their social justice movements and organizations (ibid.). They often have to pay for that support (counseling, psychotherapy) themselves. Now, if they are already underpaid or not paid at all for their social justice work, as it is often the case with trans activists, their mental health and well-being are in stake, as well as the sustainability of their work. Burnout leads activists to temporary withdrawal from movements and organizations, as the research showed (Gorski & Chen, 2015). That is in alignment with my personal experience both working with social justice activists and doing social justice activist work myself. Therefore, it is of vital importance to provide social justice activists and educators with the support in developing self-care skills, building their resilience, and increasing their capacity to bounce back from life challenges, to minimize the effects of stress on mental-health and well-being. Resilience building requires psycho-somatic[7] and emotional work to buffer the impact of stress on the mind and body (Johnson, 2017a). It is a capacity that needs to be developed for the purpose of mental health and well-being of social justice activists and educators, and sustainable social justice activism.

Moreover, as presented above, trans activists report the need for capacity building related to trauma healing. The research has recognized that microaggressions against marginalized people are a form of trauma, and there is a body of evidence of the connection between experienced societal oppression and the experience of trauma (Johnson, 2017a, p. 65). Trauma is often wrongly understood as one life-threatening event, or developmental trauma rooted in childhood, but the research undoubtedly shows that minority stress, oppression, and microaggressions that marginally situated people face, represents a prolonged life-stressor (Johnson, 2017a, p. 65). Kira et al. (2013) understand oppression as a form of collective trauma perpetrated between social groups, which exists on a continuum from microaggressions to macroaggressions. Prolonged exposure to homophobia, transphobia, hate speech, and discrimination, all based on sexual orientation, gender identity, gender expression and variations in sex characteristics, as well as societal and systemic oppression, impact marginally situated people's mental health and well-being. Research has repeatedly shown that LGBTQI people have higher rates of suicide ideation, suicidality, depression, and anxiety than the general population (Marshall et al., 2015; Haas et al., 2014; Bockting et al., 2013; Cochran, 2001; Effrig et al., 2011; Clements-Nolle et al., 2006), as a result of exposure to prolonged oppression, as was already discussed previously in this chapter, when summarizing the issues that trans people face in their daily life, and in Chapter 3 on the experiences of trans people. I would argue that prolonged exposure to societal oppression, discrimination, and microaggressions that members of minority groups are exposed to represents a form of cultural trauma, which happens in a society where there is an unequal distribution of power and agency between social groups, resulting in their unequal visibility, and unequal legitimacy of their epistemologies. In the book *Cultural Trauma and Collective Identity,* the authors acknowledge that this cultural process is "deeply affected by power structures and by the contingent skills of reflexive social agents" (Alexander et al., 2004, p. 10).

Research on the comparison of post-traumatic stress disorder (PTSD) scores between 400 people who experienced a single traumatic event, and 400 people who experienced prolonged life-stressors, showed that individuals with prolonged life-stressors reported more PTSD symptoms, such as avoidance, hypervigilance, and arousal, than those who experienced acute traumas as a result of a single traumatic event (Mol et al., 2005). Moreover, Scott and Stradling (1994) provided various examples of PTSD symptoms in members of minority groups exposed to societal oppression, who show complete PTSD symptomatology in the absence of a single acute traumatic event.

## 4 Contribution of Social Justice Education to Trans Activism

I believe it is the ethical responsibility of us social justice educators, working with marginalized social groups towards the enactment of progressive social change, to create educational programs for activists based on anti-oppressive, critical education for social change. That way we can support them in developing knowledge, skills, and competencies on resilience building, burnout prevention, and critical self-reflection of their own privileges, positionality in society, and agency needed to initiate progressive social change. The programs (international trainings for social justice educators and activists) I have designed and facilitated on burnout prevention, resilience building and embodied social justice youth work, are based on Paulo Freire's critical pedagogy (Freire, 2000), Augusto Boal's Theatre of the Oppressed Methodology (Boal, 1993), and Jacob Levy Moreno's Psychodrama (Moreno, 1956; Blatner, 2000; Karp et al., 1998). These programs aim toward an intersectional examination of how oppressive social systems and power structures have affected us personally, by creating our points of wounding and trauma, as well as our blind-spots, and privileges. Through experiential and transformative learning based on action and drama techniques, these programs enable participants to explore how they can unlearn internalized and embodied oppression, prevent burnout, and use their privileges to enact social change acting in solidarity with other people of marginally positioned identities (which they don't necessarily share). According to Johnson (2017b), embodied social justice work is rooted in the awareness that we learn oppression through daily lived experiences of social and political life and injustices, and that we learn through our bodies, as well as through our minds, which makes our lived social experience an embodied experience (felt in the body). I believe that without this critical examination, the sustainability of social justice activism, oriented towards progressive social change, is hindered. I would agree with Johnson (ibid.) in a belief that if we do not know how we've been wounded by transphobia, homophobia, patriarchy, racism, capitalism, heteronormativity, ableism, islamophobia, and other forms of discrimination and othering, and if we don't take personal and collective steps toward trauma healing and unlearning oppression, there is a high probability we will feel overwhelmed, triggered, and reactive in our behavior, when these topics appear in our social justice work. As Johnson (ibid.) states, knowing our oppression triggers, acknowledging our privileges and blindspots, and being open to critically self-reflect and truly hear other people and acknowledge their experiences of oppression, is of crucial importance for our daily work with minority social groups and on minority issues. This is of particular value when conflicts arise in our interactions with other people whether they are allies, fellow social justice educators and activists, or other beneficiaries of our work (ibid.). This knowledge and awareness of our positionality and the impact it has on the way we feel, think, act, behave and perceive the world, is necessary for emotional self-regulation during conflicts, when we activists call each other out on our privileges and blind-spots, and when blame is being placed and/or felt when talking about minority issues, as Johnson also highlighted (2017b). If we want to transform our experience of oppression and support others to do so, and collectively challenge and change oppressive social systems, through anti-oppressive, social justice oriented adult education for social change, then we need to create educational spaces that favor the development of critical consciousness and awareness. Freire understood critical consciousness as the capacity of a person to critically reflect on their own lived experience in opresive society, and to act toward social transformation (Freire, 2000). I believe that this consciousness requires transformative learning (O'Sullivan, 2002) which engages our cognitive, and emotional, but also somatic capacities, because resilience building requires psycho-somatic and emotional work to buffer the impact of minority stress on the mind and body (Johnson, 2017a).

> Transformative learning involves experiencing a deep, structural shift in the basic premises of thought, feelings, and actions. It is a shift of consciousness that dramatically and permanently alters our way of being in the world. Such a shift involves our understanding of ourselves and our self-locations; our relationships with other humans and with the natural world; our understanding of relations of power in interlocking structures of class, race and gender; our body-awareness; our visions of alternative approaches to living; our sense of possibilities for social justice and personal joy. (O' Sullivan, 2002, p. 11)

If we want to enact deep and progressive individual and social change, we need a revision of education, education systems, vision and values, as well as collaborative efforts between marginalized communities, and progressive social movements. According to O'Sullivan (2002), we need an education which can provide integral transformative learning, with the cosmological framework (planetary consciousness), and can call upon the radical reconstruction of the dominant culture. This "critical resistance education" calls for critical examination of the hierarchical power systems, calling upon their deconstruction (ibid.).

Personally, when facilitating international trainings for social justice educators and activists, I often use action and drama techniques based on the Theatre of the Oppressed methodology developed by Augusto Boal, and on Psychodrama created by Jacob Levy Moreno, to foster a sense of empathy and solidarity among people of multiple marginalized identities who are participants of my trainings. That work is based on transformative, and experiential learning. Experiential learning models (Kolb & Kolb, 2012) acknowledge that adult learners learn about the world and themselves in an interactive, ongoing action/reflection cycle. They learn through actively creating new knowledge from their own experiences. Furthermore, the neuroscientific research on mirror neurons shows that by "trying on" the experiences of others through embodied imagination, we widen our repertoire of experience (Johnson, 2017a, p. 94). That is why experiential learning based on action and drama methodologies is transformative: learners have the possibility to reverse roles with others, perceive the situation from their perspective and their social position, and feel it through the embodied imagination. Moreover, they have the opportunity to try on behaviors and roles they might not dare to exercise in their daily life, due to societal oppression and discrimination. For example, they can be verbally and emotionally expressive; dare to confront discriminative colleagues and superiors; take up the space and share their experiences of societal oppression and stigmatization; observe the situation from the role of their "future wise self", or get into the role of an aspect of themselves, whether perceived as a strength (for example, not being afraid of conflicts) or perceived as a weakness (internalized shame, internalized homophobia, transphobia, etc.). That way the participants of these programs (social justice educators and activists), have an opportunity to become aware of the ways in which societal oppression and discrimination have shaped their embodied and internalized experiences, and witness the embodied and internalized experiences of others, and ultimately, find a way through experiential and transformative learning based on action and drama methods, to liberate themselves from it, and learn how to support others, while doing so.

It is important that we, social justice educators, are always aware that education is not politically neutral, and that as Freire believed, it can either perpetuate the oppression or challenge it, aiming to empower learners to unlearn it. In order to do that, learners need to organize together to dismantle oppressive power structures, through reflection and action (as discussed in Chapter 1). That critical education work requires us, educators, to let go of control and be open to the uncertainty of the unknown, which for many of us can be a frightening experience. Jack Mezirow, who developed a comprehensive theory of transformative learning, focused on of how adult learners derive meaning from their experiences and transform current perspectives, through becoming critically aware of how their assumptions influence the way they perceive, understand, and feel about our world. He acknowledged that change and transformation are often experienced as intensely threatening (Mezirow, 2000), and argued that educators have to become aware of the assumptions underlining their ideas and emotional responses to the need for change.

> Our values and sense of self are anchored in our frames of reference. They provide us with a sense of stability, coherence, community, and identity. Consequently, they are often emotionally charged and strongly defended. (Mezirow, 2000, p. 18)

I would agree with Mezirow and argue that if we, social justice educators, do not cultivate the capacity to be open to the uncertainty of the unknown, if we are not ready to renounce control, and experience a cognitive and emotional dissonance, a loss of a sense of safety, stability and coherence; if we don't cultivate the capacity to tolerate the frustration that goes with it, that means we are resistant to change. It is questionable if people who are afraid of change themselves, can initiate progressive social change, or support others while doing so.

Social justice educators supporting the trans movement and trans activists in their capacity building, should work on becoming more flexible, curious, brave, self-reflective and aware of their social positionality, of their privileges and triggers. They should be open and willing to change, willing to engage in uncomfortable conversations and to experience uncomfortable feelings. Furthermore, they should be willing to initiate transformative learning aiming to foster critical awareness and critical consciousness among the people they work with. Social justice educators supporting the trans movement should cultivate the capacity to hold a space for trans activists, while they are undergoing critical self-reflection on their own privileges, positionality in the society and agency they have, needed to initiate progressive social change. Finally, social justice educators working on capacity building of trans activists and organizations, should work towards developing a trans-affirming, intersectional approach to education and learning, and become ready to get questioned, challenged, and invited in a mutual, relational transformative learning.

I believe that progressive social movements, such as trans movement, and broadly LGBTQI movement; the environmental justice movement, the animal rights movement, anti-capitalist, fair trade movement, movement for economic justice; anti-racist, anti-xenophobic, anti-fascist movements; disability rights movement, refugee movements, and movements of people living with HIV or AIDS, have the power to change the power dynamics perpetuated by hegemonic globalization. This can be done through collaborative efforts and actions, working and acting in true solidarity across the communities and movements, on the local, regional, national and international level; through networking, valuing "bottom-up" approach and supporting globalization from below, coming from the oppressed who are collaborating, uniting, and challenging hegemonic globalization that has detrimental impact on the lives of humans, other species and earth's ecosystems.

### Notes

1 Acronym referring to lesbian, gay, bisexual, trans, queer and questioning, intersex, asexual and two spirit people. Two spirit is a modern term, originated in the 1990s referring to native, specifically Indigenous North-American gender non-conforming people.
2 According to Transgender Europe Sex Work Policy, adult sex workers of all genders are persons who engage in commercial sex have voluntarily, which is different from human trafficking (TGEU, 2016b, p. 3). TGEU advocates for full decriminalization of sex work which means absence of any laws and forms of legal oppression that prohibit sex work itself or associated. "Decriminalisation of sex work promotes health and human rights for sex workers by reducing police violence and abuse and increasing access to police protection and justice, safe working conditions, and health services. Removing criminal prosecution of sex work results in the recognition of sex work as work, thus benefiting the long-term social inclusion of sex workers, allowing them to report crimes to the police and seek redress and not face potential criminal and non-criminal offences" (ibid., p. 13).
3 Several countries have laws that criminalize trans people, through prohibitions of so-called "cross-dressing", "female impersonation" and, in some cases, "male impersonation", like Malaysia, where these laws are used to detain and persecute trans people, especially trans women (GATE et al., 2017, p. 9).

4 In 2012, Global Action for Trans Equality (GATE) and American Jewish World Service (AJWS) did a survey of 340 trans and intersex groups, which served as the basis of the first systematic data from activists and groups about their work, leadership, funding, obstacles in accessing funding, and capacity-building needs. The findings of this survey can be found in GATE and AJWS (2013).
5 Embodied refers to the body-mind connection felt from within the body (Johnson, 2017a).
6 Term frequently used by activists to refer to a practice in activism and social justice work where there are symbolic ways to portray inclusion, or representation, such as hiring racially and gender diverse people, or stating in grant proposals that the prospective project will include minorities and will contribute to social change aiming towards equity, while in reality the decision making stays in the hands of people of often more privileged identities, who hold social power, power of common knowledge production, and financial and strategic decision-making power within an organization in question.
7 Somatic refers to the body experienced from within (Johnson, 2017a, p. 89).

CHAPTER 6

# Recommendations

As it became evident from discussions in previous chapters and presented participants' narratives in Chapter 2, progressive social changes are needed in different domains of power: hegemonic, structural, disciplinary, and interpersonal. Changes across all levels, from legislative and policy level, to the level of implementation of trans (and more broadly LGBTQI) affirming practices in education, simultaneously with raising awareness of the general population of gender, sexual and bodily diversity, are needed. Trans-affirming legislation is needed, especially when it comes to prohibition of discrimination, violence, hate speech, and hate crimes toward trans and GNC people: discrimination in employment, and specifically when it comes to legal gender recognition based on self-determination of trans and GNC people. Without accessible legal gender recognition procedures, trans people face difficulties with accessing employment and education opportunities. Trans and GNC people should have access to accessible gender recognition procedures, so that name and gender marker change in their documents can be done without compulsory psychiatric evaluation, pathologization, and compulsory sterilization (UN, 2018).

The following sections will focus on recommendations for education provision and practice, theory and research in relation to the affirmation of trans people's existence, lives, and epistemologies.

## 1 Recommendations for Education Practice

Changes in the formal education curriculum from the kindergarten level to the higher education level are needed, so that education is trans, and more broadly LGBTQI, affirming and free of prejudices, stereotypes, and pathologization of gender, sexual and bodily diversity. Introduction of LGBTQI topics, such as gender, sexual and bodily diversity in formal education curriculum should be done based on a cross-curricular approach to education and learning (across all subject areas). A cross-curricular approach to teaching is "characterized by sensitivity towards, and synthesis of, knowledge, skills, and understandings from various subject areas" (Savage, 2011, p. 8). That approach goes beyond formal comprehensive sexuality and relationships education courses and classes. Formal comprehensive sexuality education should focus not only on learning about human anatomy, prevention of unwanted pregnancies and prevention of transmission of sexually transmitted infections, but should include relational, social, and human rights aspect to human sexuality. That is especially important if we want to prevent harassment of LGBTQI youth in education contexts, and to develop education provision that doesn't fuel and perpetuate homophobia, interphobia, and transphobia. As highlighted several times throughout this book, research and international organizations warn that trans people face bullying, harassment, and exclusion in schools worldwide, which increases the risk of drop out of school (UNESCO, 2016a, 2016b; Jones et al., 2016; GLSEN, 2016; WHO, 2015a) Therefore, formal comprehensive sexuality and relationships education should be affirming of gender identity, sexuality and bodily diversity/variations in sex characteristics, so that young people can learn about these topics in an affirming way, from a young age. That type of education provision has a significant impact on youth, especially related to developing a positive attitude towards sexuality; learning about consent, personal and interpersonal boundaries; encouraging critical thinking and critical reflection on gender roles and gender based-role stereotyping; fostering emotional and relational literacy, so that young people feel comfortable and skillful to communicate about sexuality, emotions, and relationships, as proposed by Maltese *Guidelines on Sexuality and Relationships Education* (Ministry for Education and Employment, 2013).

As recognized by the World Health Organization, and noted in the conference report *Sexuality Education – Lessons Learned and Future Developments in the WHO region* (WHO & BZgA, 2017), sexuality education is "effective life-course intervention that increases the health and well-being of children and young people" (p. 4). As I have stated during the panel discussion on gender and sexual diversity in education at the same conference, if we want schools to be safe for LGBTQI students, then we need to introduce gender, sexual, and bodily diversity to the curriculum, but also to take a norm-critical stance and challenge hetero-normativity (ibid., p. 57) and cis-normativity.[1] As the report acknowledges, while it is important to understand the context and the culture in which formal sexuality education is discussed or introduced, context and culture cannot and shall not be used as excuses for preventing young people's access to comprehensive, LGBTQI affirming, sexuality education, as that is related to young peoples' basic human rights (ibid.). Moreover, the report acknowledges that providing some lessons on LGBTQI issues can be counter-productive, and I would add that it cannot effectively challenge systemic homo-, trans- and inter-phobia, if the whole school does not address heteronormativity and cisnormativity. Both are often enhanced by the lessons within other courses outside of sexuality and relationship classes, for example, in history and geography. That is why comprehensive sexuality and relationship education is important, but it is not enough. Challenging systemic oppression towards LGBTQI people, and erasure of LGBTQI epistemologies in education, requires a whole-school approach and cross-curricular, LGBTQI affirming approach (ibid.). The whole-school approach is defined as "unified collective and collaborative action by educators, administrators, parents and students that has been strategically constituted to improve student learning behavior and well-being and the conditions that support these" (Ministry for Education and Employment, 2014c, p. 7).

In addition, changes in the textbooks are necessary to remove obsolete and discriminatory content which fuels homophobia, transphobia, and interphobia. These changes need to occur simultaneously with the training of teachers and school administration on LGBTQI issues, so that teachers can challenge stereotypes and prejudices based on sexual orientation, gender identity, gender expression, bodily diversity/sex characteristics in educational settings, knowing how to react when a student comes out to them as LGBTQI. We need support systems for trans, GNC and intersex students: school psychologists and pedagogues should be sensible and trained to tackle these issues and support queer students and their parents. Therefore, LGBTQI affirming school policies and national education policies are needed, serving as a framework for addressing and combating discrimination, hate speech and bullying of queer youth in the education environment. At least "gender identity/expression" should be added to the nondiscrimination statement of the educational policy. Minimum standards to combat homophobic and transphobic bullying in education should be implemented (IGLYO, 2014). Finally, formal education institutions can organize actions and campaigns on days such as International Day Against Homophobia and Transphobia (IDAHOT), to involve queer students, their parents, and communities to learn about and/or engage with LGBTIQ topics.

When it comes to non-formal education, especially in the field of social-justice-oriented youth work, the report of the Council of Europe seminar named "Gender Equality Matters! Understanding and integrating gender equality in intercultural youth activities of the Council of Europe and its partners" highlights the issues of gender diversity and youth work (CoE, 2016). The seminar was organized by the Youth Department of the Council of Europe with the objective of understanding and integrating gender equality in intercultural youth activities of the Council of Europe and its partners. It gathered international, national, regional and local youth organizations working directly with: gender issues, issues of disability, sexuality, migration, diaspora, and ethnicity; representatives of municipalities, state bodies, and national agencies. As it can be seen from the seminar report, Sebnem Kenis, the Gender Equality Rapporteur of the Joint Council on Youth at the time, raised significant questions about, "the intersection of gender and youth work such as the use of gender-neutral language ... and need to attentively analyze whether any aspect of youth work (application forms, energizers, toilets, etc.) reinforce traditional gender binaries and stereotypes" (ibid., p. 2). The report highlighted that many trainers working with youth also lack knowledge of gender diversity issues in youth work and training.

Furthermore, the main output of the seminar were the guidelines on integrating gender equality in intercultural youth activities of the Council of Europe and its partners. These guidelines can be useful to social justice educators who are reading this book, and who are working in the field of social justice oriented youth work, especially when it comes to organizing educational trainings, seminars, and study sessions. Highlights of the guidelines relevant to the topic of this book include the following aspects (ibid., p. 4):

– Ensure gender balance of participants, trainers, experts involved, and concrete proposals on questions to ask in applications forms.
– Equal, balanced and non-stereotypical representation of all genders in materials related to training and education activities.
– Ensuring equal participation of all genders in discussions and meetings.
– Developing explicit policies for tackling sexual harassment and gender-based violence in youth work.
– Use of gender-neutral language.
– Gender training for all those involved in education and training activities.
– Further reflect with "gender glasses" critically on the educational approaches proposed and activities.

In addition, participants of this seminar developed proposals for the Youth Department of the Council of Europe, especially related to offering training on inclusive approach to gender to those involved in youth work, as well as for staff working in two European Youth Centers of the Council of Europe (based in Budapest and Strasbourg). Updating the manuals and publications of the Council of Europe related to youth work, to include gender inclusive language and approach, was another suggestion. Participants also highlighted that application forms for educational activities should allow participants to state their gender identity outside of the gender binary, through an open line where participants can state their gender identity (ibid., p. 5).

Taking into consideration and implementing the above-mentioned recommendations and guidelines, social justice activists and educators engaged in social-justice-oriented youth work, through non-formal education, should:

1. Not reinforce gender binary and invisibility of people of diverse gender identities, since transgender and GNC activists and educators can be role models especially for LGBTQI people;

RECOMMENDATIONS                                                                157

2.  Show to participants that trainers are aware of gender diversity and that living realities of trans and broadly LGBTQI people, are welcomed in the learning space;
3.  Open up a space for learning on gender diversity and different gender related stereotypes that people of different genders might face: transgender people face specific stereotypes and transphobia which deserves to be seen and addressed in education for social justice; and
4.  Work towards reparative justice by being affirming of trans epistemologies in education.

Furthermore, especially trans, and more broadly, LGBTQI affirming adult education is important, because as previous chapters of this book showed, due to systemic oppression and erasure of trans issues from all spheres of life, professionals in different fields can perpetuate systemic oppression towards trans people, trans students, and clients. Specifically, education and training of the police, law enforcement, juridical, medical, educational, mental health professionals, and public officials on how to work on gender, sexual, bodily diversity is of paramount importance.

When it comes to teacher training, and training of educators working in formal education, it is important to provide them not only learning opportunities through trainings on LGBTQI issues, but also through publications they can use in their daily work, such as, for example, a toolkit on cross-curricular implementation of LGBTQI issues in education, which could:

1.  Give teachers the opportunity to critically reflect on their teaching practice and incorporate LGBTQI topics in their curriculum planning;
2.  Create shared vision and efforts on LGBTQI affirmation in education, amongst teachers, parents, school administrators, and students through meaningful collaborations at all levels of curriculum design;
3.  Promote students' critical thinking on LBTQI issues through teachers' interventions based on critical pedagogy, taking into account intersectionality principle; and
4.  Facilitate a whole school approach where all stakeholders assume responsibility and contribute towards an inclusive, safe and respectful learning environment.

When planning, designing, implementing and delivering adult education programs, it is important to acknowledge what will be described in the following paragraphs.

*The inclusive language* shall be used. Inclusive language is a language that "does not belittle, exclude, stereotype or trivialize people on the basis of their sexual orientation, gender identity, gender expression, sex characteristics, bodily diversity" (IGLYO, 2015, p 6). "For a more inclusive policy, the use of the pronoun *They* shall be used for all genders even when referring to a single individual" (Ministry for Education and Employment of Malta, 2015, p. 4). Pathologizing language should be strongly avoided, especially in adult education for social change, and social justice education, and it should be challenged when it happens. For example, a hermaphrodite is an outdated term, coming from pathologizing medicalized language of the 19th century used to describe intersex people. Moreover, when discussing trans issues, it is important to acknowledge that there is a difference between a person's gender, sex, and sexual orientation. The use of the term "gender" is preferred over the term "sex" because sex refers to biology and gender refers to how people identify themselves. For example, we should say "gender affirming surgery", instead of "sex reassignment surgeries".

*Inclusion and affirmation.* It is not an LGBTQI person's duty to discuss or disclose their gender identity, sexual orientation, gender expression, sex characteristics, and bodily diversity at any time, nor they should be expected to discuss their experiences all the time, or at the given occasion, without prior agreement with the person. However, application forms for educational programs should provide options for people to state their gender outside of the gender binary, *if they choose to*. That can be done by providing several gender options on the application forms, for example: man, woman, trans, and a blank like so that a person can fill in their gender identity. It is important to allow students to change their name and gender within institutional educational systems. Non-binary options for gender marker should be available on application forms (a blank space to state one's gender identity). Correct pronouns should be used: adult learners should be given the chance to state their gender pronouns through badges, registration forms, rounds of names and pronouns at the beginning of education activities, when getting to know each other. It should not be assumed that a person's gender is the same as sex assigned at birth.

Trans and gender non-conforming people should have access to restrooms, and locker rooms in accordance with their lived gender identity, so that they are not exposed to potential harassment and bullying. Educational facilities should have gender-neutral restrooms, so that trans people use them without feeling stressed or at risk of violence and harassment.

*Challenge heteronormativity and cisnormativity.* Heteronormativity, the belief that heterosexuality is the only "natural", and acceptable sexual orientation and cisnormativity, the idea that everyone identifies with the gender assigned to them at birth, should be challenged throughout adult education programs, especially those related to social justice, and social change. Examples of rainbow families can be used, and LGBTQI people's lives, realities, and experiences can be discussed after reading literature on trans and queer epistemologies.

Finally, as proposed by LGBTQI Education Index Report (IGLYO, 2018) and UNESCO (2016a), a comprehensive education approach is needed to prevent and address homophobic, biphobic, transphobic, and interphobic bullying. This includes the implementation of (1) LGBTQI affirming national policies and/or action plans, (2) LGBTQI inclusive curricula and learning materials, (3) training for educational staff on LGBTQI issues, (4) support for queer students and families, (5) partnerships with civil society organizations, and (6) monitoring of discrimination based on SOGIESC[2] and evaluating the executed measures.

## 2   Recommendations for Further Research

As presented in the previous chapters, the most apparent gap in adult education research is the lack of research on the development of the identity of activist and adult educator for social change. More specifically, there is a lack of research that examines the relationship between transgender and GNC identities on the one side, and activist and adult educator for social change identity development on the other side. Previous research, presented in Chapter 2, explored the relationship between queer and activist/leadership identity development, but none of that research was focused exclusively on trans and GNC people and their activist identity development, although trans people were included in the research samples (often in small number). Furthermore, although sometimes research samples include participants who identify as transgender, the heterogeneity of the transgender community is often not taken into account. This is important since trans and GNC people face specific resistances, invalidations, microaggressions, discrimination, violence and systemic oppression in their everyday life (as discussed in Chapter 3) and suffer epistemic injustice and exclusion of their epistemologies in education (as discussed in Chapter 4).

Moreover, a common limitation of the presented research lies in the fact that it often uses gay identity development models (D'Augelli, 1994; Coleman, 1982) which are generalized to the LGBTQI community, while these models were developed without including trans experiences, or with a narrow understanding of trans identities (Renn, 2007; Chang & Chung, 2015).

In addition, the research on transgender identity development mostly uses stage models to conceptualize that development. A common limitation of predominant research proposing developmental models of transgender identity lies in the fact that they are often based on other minority identities development models (Cross & Vandiver, 2001) which were developed without including trans experiences (Renn, 2007). However, more recent research (Katz-Wise et al., 2018) acknowledges the heterogeneity of the trans identities, by including participants of various trans identities.

Furthermore, existing transgender identity developmental models often exclude gender-non-conforming individuals, and those with non-binary gender identities (Rahilly, 2015). Another limitation is that the existing body of research often doesn't take into account the heterogeneity of trans community, from an intersectional perspective, and focuses primarily on the experiences of transgender individuals who are of White race/ethnicity (Moradi et al., 2016). More research on transgender identity development among transgender individuals of different racial and ethnic backgrounds is needed, because transgender identity development occurs not only in relation person's sense of their true Self, but also in relation to one's social sphere (Levitt & Ippolito, 2014), and different domains of power, such as hegemonic, structural, disciplinary, and interpersonal (Pratt-Clarke, 2010).

Finally, stage and phase models of development have been dominating understanding of identity development, including social identity development and identity change in adulthood. But, their generalizability to populations different from those on which they were originally based, is questioned (Rossiter, 1999). As Rossiter pointed out, developmental variations might be connected to gender, class, and cultural differences, which is not necessarily taken into account when developing these models. Rossiter highlights that universality in prevalent adult identity development theories, based on stage and phase models, reflects dominant cultural values and leads to a devaluation of alternative developmental paths.

My research presented in Chapter 2 addresses this gap by especially focusing on participants who identify as trans and GNC, taking into account their multiple identities and their, as well as mine, social positionality within the systems of power (as hegemonic, structural, disciplinary, and interpersonal). This is an important step toward reparative justice, especially in the field of academia and research in education for social change.

Taking into account findings of my research presented in Chapter 2, it would be interesting to examine the relationship between experienced minority stress and psychological distress on the one side, and the development of the identity of adult educator and activist for social change among trans and GNC people, and more broadly, queer people, on the other side. The resilience of trans and GNC activists would be another possible research topic. The data I collected for the research presented in this book, could also be used to explore the topic of resilience of trans activists, through secondary data analysis, by for example, identifying redemption sequences and using the Coding system for redemption sequences (McAdams et al., 2001). Moreover, future research would benefit from exploration of the relationship between self-care, community care within trans activist circles, and the ways in which activists manage the challenges of activist work, especially those who are marginally situated on the basis of their multiple minority identitities.

Additionally, research on potential benefits of activism (e.g., decreased internalized oppression, increased empowerment, resilience, and social support), like the one conducted by Hagen et al. (2018) is needed in relation to activist identity development and transgender identity development as mutually connected processes (Renn, 2007).

Furthermore, no studies are found which explore specifically the relationship between common types of microaggressions, as covert forms of discrimination that transgender and GNC people face, and the impact on the development of their identity of adult educator and activist for social change, for those who have decided to become social activists.

Research on this topic from an intersectional perspective is needed. Hagen et al. (2018) highlight that the existence of exclusionary practices within the queer movement and activist communities (prioritizing the experiences of White, middle-class, cisgender men, and White, lesbian, cisgender women), imply that future research on gender and queer activism of people with multiple marginalized identities is needed. Moreover, future research could explore how the meaning of community may vary for people with multiple marginalized identities, and how oppression within marginalized activist communities contributes to the struggles inherent in activist work (ibid.).

Finally, understanding multiplicity of identities for both oppressed and privileged identities (Cole, 2009), which exist within a context of connected systems and structures of power, such as laws, policies, state governments, political and economic unions, religious institutions, and media (Hankivsky, 2014), is important to take into account when exploring development of a social identity, especially among marginalized social groups.

### Notes

1 The ideas that being cisgender and heterosexual is the usual, "normal", desired way of being.
2 Sexual Orientation, Gender Identity, Gender Expression and variations in Sex Characteristics.

# References

Adebajo, S. B., Eluwa, G. I., Tocco, J. U., Ahonsi, B. A., Abiodun, L. Y., Anene, O. A., ... Kellerman, S. (2013). Estimating the number of male sex workers with the capture-recapture technique in Nigeria. *African Journal of Reproductive Health, 17* (4 Spec No), 83–89.

Adriansen, H. K. (2010). *Life-history interviews: On using a time line.* Retrieved from pure.au.dk/ws/files/55130421/life_history_interviews.pdf

Alexander, J. C., Eyerman, R., Giesen, B., Smelser, N. J., & Sztompka, P. (2004). *Cultural trauma and collective identity.* Berkeley, CA: University of California Press.

American Counseling Association (ACA). (2010). Competencies for counseling with transgender clients. *Journal of LGBT Issues in Counseling, 4*(3–4), 135–159. doi:10.1080/15538605.2010.524839

American Jewish World Service (AJWS), Astraea Lesbian Foundation for Justice (Astraea), Global Action for Trans Equality (GATE). (2017a). *The state of trans organizing: Understanding the needs and priorities of a growing but under-resourced movement* (2nd ed.). Retrieved May 2019, from https://transactivists.org/the-state-of-trans-organizing-report-2017/

American Jewish World Service (AJWS), Astraea Lesbian Foundation for Justice (Astraea), Global Action for Trans* Equality (GATE). (2017b). *The state of intersex organizing: Understanding the needs and priorities of a growing but under-resourced movement* (2nd ed.). Retrieved May 2019, from https://transactivists.org/the-state-of-intersex-organizing-report-2017/

American Psychiatric Association (APA). (2013). *Diagnostic and Statistical Manual of mental disorders: DSM-5* (5th ed.). Arlington, VA & London: American Psychiatric Association.

American Psychological Association (APA). (2017). *Affirmative counseling and psychological practice with transgender and gender nonconforming clients.* Retrieved from https://www.apa.org/pubs/books/Affirmative-Counseling-Intro-Sample.pdf

Amnesty International. (2019). *Russia: Chechen authorities resume homophobic crackdown.* Retrieved May 2019, from https://www.amnesty.org/en/latest/news/2019/01/chechnya-crackdown-renewed/

Archive. (1973). *Sylvia Rivera "Y'all better quiet down".* Retrieved May 2019, from https://archive.org/details/SylviaRiveraYallBetterQuietDown1973

Balsam, K. F., Molina, Y., Beadnell, B., Simoni, J., & Walters, K. (2011). Measuring multiple minority stress: The LGBT people of color microaggressions scale. *Cultural Diversity and Ethnic Minority Psychology, 17*(2), 163–174. http://dx.doi.org/10.1037/a0023244

Baral, S. D., Poteat, T., Strömdahl, S., Wirtz, A. L., Guadamuz, T. E., & Beyrer, C. (2013). Worldwide burden of HIV in transgender women: A systematic review and meta-analysis. *Lancet Infect Dis, 13*(3), 214–222.

Beemyn, B. G., Curtis, B., Davis, M., & Tubbs, N. J. (2005). Transgender issues on college campuses. In R. L. Sanlo (Ed.), *Gender identity and sexual orientation: Research, policy, and personal perspectives. New directions for student services* (pp. 49–60). San Francisco, CA: Jossey-Bass.

Beemyn, G., Rankin, S. (2011). *The lives of transgender people.* New York, NY: Columbia University Press.

Benson, K. E. (2013). Seeking support: Transgender client experiences with mental health services. *Journal of Feminist Family Therapy, 25*(1), 17–40. doi:10.1080/08952833.2013.755081

Berg, B. L. (2001). *Qualitative research methods for the social sciences* (4th ed.). Boston, MA: Pearson.

Bess, J. A., & Stabb, S. D. (2009). The experiences of transgendered persons in psychotherapy: Voices and recommendations. *Journal of Mental Health Counseling, 31*, 264–282. doi:10.17744/mehc.31.3.f62415468l133w50

Beury, M., Yoursky, Y. (2019). Europe – increased visibility, populist backlash and multiple divisions. *State-sponsored homophobia* (pp. 149–155). Geneva: ILGA. Retrieved May 2019, from https://ilga.org/state-sponsored-homophobia-report

Bieschke, K. J., McClanahan, M., Tozer, E., Grzegorek, J. L., & Park, J. (2000). Programmatic research on the treatment of lesbian, gay, and bisexual clients: The past, the present, and the course for the future. In R. M. Perez, K. A. DeBord, & K. J. Bieschke (Eds.), *Handbook of counseling and psychotherapy with lesbian, gay and bisexual clients* (pp. 309–335). Washington, DC: American Psychological Association.

Bilić, B., & Kajinić, S. (2016). *Intersectionality and LGBT activist politics: Multiple others in Croatia and Serbia.* London: Palgrave Macmillan.

Bilodeau, B. L. (2005). Beyond the gender binary: A case study of two transgender students at a Midwestern research university. *Journal of Gay & Lesbian Issues in Education, 3*(1), 29–44.

Bilodeau, B. L. (2009). *Genderism: Transgender students, binary systems and higher education.* Saarbrücken: VDM Verlag.

Bilodeau, B. L., & Renn, K. A. (2005). Analysis of LGBT identity development models and implications for practice. In R. L. Sanlo (Ed.), *Gender identity and sexual orientation: Research, policy, and personal perspectives. New directions for student services* (pp. 25–39). San Francisco, CA: Jossey-Bass.

Blatner, A. (2000). *Foundations of psychodrama.* New York, NY: Springer Pub. Co.

Boal, A. (1993). *Theater of the oppressed.* New York, NY: Theatre Communications Group.

# REFERENCES

Bockting, W., & Coleman, E. (2007). Developmental stages of the transgender coming out process: Toward an integrated identity. In R. Ettner, S. Monstrey, & A. E. Eyler (Eds.), *Principles of transgender medicine and surgery* (pp. 185–208). Binghamton, NY: Haworth Press.

Bockting, W. O., Miner, M. H., Swinburne Romine, R. E., Hamilton, A., & Coleman, E. (2013). Stigma, mental health, and resilience in an online sample of the US transgender population. *American Journal of Public Health, 103*(5), 943–951.

Bowers, R., Plummer, D., & Minichiello, V. (2005). Homophobia in counselling practice. *International Journal for the Advancement of Counselling, 27*(3), 471–489. doi:10.1007/s10447-005-8207-7

Braun, V., & Clarke, V. (2006). Using thematic analysis in psychology. *Qualitative Research in Psychology, 3*(2), 77–101.

Bryan, S. (2018). Types of LGBT microaggressions in counselor education programs. *Journal of LGBT Issues in Counseling, 12*(2), 119–135. doi:10.1080/15538605.2018.1455556

Chan, S. (2018). Marsha P. Johnson, a transgender pioneer and activist who was a fixture of Geenwich Village street life. *The New York Times*. Retrieved May 2019, from https://www.nytimes.com/interactive/2018/obituaries/overlooked-marsha-p-johnson.html

Chang, T., & Chung, Y. (2015). Transgender microaggressions: Complexity of the heterogeneity of transgender identities. *Journal of LGBT Issues in Counseling, 9*(3), 217–234.

Chiam, Z. (2017). International law and legal gender recognition. In Z. Chiam, S. Duffy, & M. González Gil, *Trans legal mapping report: Recognition before the law* (pp. 7–11). ILGA. Retrieved May 2019, from https://ilga.org/downloads/ILGA_Trans_Legal_Mapping_Report_2017_ENG.pdf

Clark, T. C., Lucassen, M. F. G., Bullen, P., Denny, S. J., Fleming, T. M., Robinson, E. M., & Rossen, F. V. (2014). The health and well-being of transgender high school students: Results from the New Zealand Adolescent Health Survey (Youth'12). *Journal of Adolescent Health, 55,* 93–99. Retrieved May 2019, from http://download.journals.elsevierhealth.com/pdfs/journals/1054-139X/PIIS1054139X13007532.pdf

Clements-Nolle, K., Marx, R., & Katz, M. (2006). Attempted suicide among transgender persons: The influence of gender-based discrimination and victimization. *Journal of Homosexuality, 51*(3), 53–69.

Cochran, S. D. (2001). Emerging issues in research on lesbians' and gay men's mental health: Does sexual orientation really matter? *American Psychologist, 56*(11), 931–947.

Cohen, L., Manion, L., & Morrison, K. (2011). *Research methods in education* (7th ed.). London: Routledge.

Cole, E. R. (2009). Intersectionality and research in psychology. *American Psychologist, 64*(3), 170–180. doi:10.1037/a001456

Coleman, E. (1982). Developmental stages of the coming out process. *American Behavioral Scientist, 25*(4), 469–482.

Collins, P. (2015). Intersectionality's definitional dilemmas. *Annual Review of Sociology, 41*(1), 1–20. doi:10.1146/annurev-soc-073014-112142

Collins, P. H. (2017). Intersectionality and epistemic injustice. In I. Kidd, J. Medina, & G. Pohlhaus (Eds.), *The Routledge handbook of epistemic injustice* (pp. 115–124). London & New York, NY: Routledge.

Colton Meier, S., Fitzgerald, K., Pardo, S., & Babcock, J. (2011). The effects of hormonal gender affirmation treatment on mental health in female-to-male transsexuals. *Journal of Gay & Lesbian Mental Health, 15*(3), 281–299

Combahee River Collective. (1979). A black feminist statement. *Off Our Backs, 9*(6), 6–8.

Connelly, F. M., & Clandinin, D. J. (1990). Stories of experience and narrative inquiry. *Educational Researcher, 19*(5), 2–14.

Council of Europe (CoE). (2015). *Resolution 2048 on discrimination against transgender people in Europe*. Retrieved May 2019, from http://assembly.coe.int/nw/xml/XRef/Xref-XML2HTML-EN.asp?fileid=21736

Council of Europe (CoE). (2016). *Gender equality matters! Understanding and integrating gender equality in intercultural youth activities of the council of Europe and its partners*. Retrieved May 2019, from https://rm.coe.int/16806a5f2e

Council of Europe (CoE). (2017). *Resolution 2191*. Retrieved May 2019, from https://assembly.coe.int/nw/xml/XRef/Xref-DocDetails-en.asp?FileID=24232&lang=en

Crenshaw, K. (1991). Mapping the margins: Intersectionality, identity politics, and violence against women of color. *Stanford Law Review, 43*(6), 1241–1299.

Creswell, J. W. (2012). *Qualitative inquiry and research design: Choosing among five approaches*. Thousand Oaks, CA: Sage Publications.

Cross Jr., W. E. (1971). The negro-to-black conversion experience. *Black World, 20*(9), 13–27.

Cross Jr., W. E. (1991). *Shades of black: Diversity in African-American identity*. Philadelphia, PA: Temple University Press.

Cross Jr., W. E. (1995). The psychology of nigrescence: Revising the Cross model. In J. G. Ponterotto, J. M. Casas, L. A. Suzuki, & C. M. Alexander (Eds.), *Handbook of multicultural counseling* (pp. 93–122). Thousand Oaks, CA: Sage Publications.

Cross Jr., W. E., & Vandiver, B. J. (2001). Nigrescence theory and measurement: Introducing the Cross Racial Identity Scale (CRIS). In J. G. Ponterotto, J. M. Casas, L. A. Suzuki, & C. M. Alexander (Eds.), *Handbook of multicultural counseling* (2nd ed., pp. 371–393). Thousand Oaks, CA: Sage Publications.

# REFERENCES

D'Augelli, A. R. (1994). Identity development and sexual orientation: Toward a model of lesbian, gay, and bisexual identity development. In E. J. Trickett, R. Watts, & D. Birman (Eds.), *Human diversity: Perspectives on people in context* (pp. 312–333). San Francisco, CA: Jossey-Bass.

Effrig, J. C., Bieschke, K. J., & Locke, B. D. (2011). Examining victimization and psychological distress in transgender college students. *Journal of College Counseling, 14*(2), 143–157. doi: 10.1002/j.2161-1882.2011.tb00269.x

Elder, A. B. (2016). Experiences of older transgender and gender nonconforming adults in psychotherapy: A qualitative study. *Psychology of Sexual Orientation and Gender Diversity, 3*(2), 180–186. doi:10.1037/sgd0000154

Equality Archive. (n.d). *Transgender women of color at Stonewall.* Retrieved May 2019, from https://equalityarchive.com/history/transgender-women-of-color-at-stonewall/

Erich, S., Tittsworth, J., Dykes, J., & Cabuses, C. (2008). Family relationships and their correlations with transsexual well-being. *Journal of GLBT Family Studies, 4*(4), 419–432.

European Parliament. (2016). *Report on promoting gender equality in mental health and clinical research.* Committee on Women's Rights and Gender Equality, Rapporteur: Beatriz Becerra Basterrechea. Retrieved May 2019, from http://www.europarl.europa.eu/sides/getDoc.do?type=REPORT&mode=XML&reference=A8-2016-0380&language=EN

European Union Agency for Fundamental Rights (FRA). (2014). *Being trans in the European union: Comparative analysis of EU LGBT survey data.* Retrieved May 2019, from fra.europa.eu/en/publication/2014/being-trans-eu-comparative-analysis-eu-lgbt-survey-data

Factor, R. J., & Rothblum, E. D. (2008). A study of transgender adults and their non transgender siblings on demographic characteristics, social support, and experiences of violence. *Journal of LGBT Health Research, 3*(3), 11–30.

Fisher, F., & Fisher, U. (2018). *Trans teen survival guide.* London & Philadelphia, PA: Jessica Kingsley Publishers.

Foley Center. (2009). *The life story interview.* Retrieved May 2019, from http://www.sesp.northwestern.edu/foley/instruments/interview/

Foley, G. (2007). *Dimensions of adult learning: Adult education and training in a global era.* Maidenhead: McGraw-Hill International.

Freire, P. (2000). *Pedagogy of the oppressed* (30th anniversary ed.). New York, NY: Continuum.

Fricker, M. (2007). *Epistemic injustice: Power and the ethics of knowing.* Oxford: Oxford University Press.

Gagné, P., Tewksbury, R., & McGaughey, D. (1997). Coming out and crossing over: Identity formation and proclamation in a transgender community. *Gender and Society, 11*(4), 478–508.

Gamson, J. (1997). Messages of exclusion: Gender, movements, and symbolic boundaries. *Gender and Society, 11*(2), 178–199. doi:10.1177/089124397011002003

Gayecho. (2019). *The law on registries, which allows the change of gender marker in documents, came into force.* Retrieved May 2019, from http://gayecho.com/news/stupio-na-snagu-zakon-o-maticnim-knjigama-koji-omogucava-promenu-pola-u-dokumentima/

Gender Identity, Gender Expression and Sex Characteristics Act. (2015). Retrieved May 2019, from https://goo.gl/QSxoSZ

Ghattas, D. C. (2013). *Human rights between the sexes: A preliminary study in the life of inter\*individuals* (Vol. 34). Heinrich Böll Stiftung: Publication Series on Democracy.

Glesne, C., & Peshkin, A. (1992). *Becoming qualitative researchers: An introduction.* White Plains, NY: Longman Publishing Group.

Global Action for Trans Equality (GATE) & American Jewish World Service (AJWS). (2013). *The state of trans and intersex organizing: A case for increased support for growing but under-funded movements for human rights.* Retrieved May 2019, from https://www.dreilinden.org/pdf/The%20State%20of%20Trans%20and%20Intersex%20Organizing%

GLSEN. (2016). *Educational exclusion: Drop out, push out, and school-to-prison pipeline among LGBTQ youth.* Retrieved May 2019, from https://www.glsen.org/sites/default/files/Educational%20Exclusion_Report_6-28-16_v4_WEB_READY_PDF.pdf

Gorski, C., & Chen, C. (2015). Frayed all over: The causes and consequences of activist burnout among social justice education activists. *Educational Studies, 51*(5), 385–405. http://dx.doi.org/10.1080/00131946.2015.1075989

Grant, J. M., Mottet, L. A., Tanis, J., Harrison, J., Herman, J. L., & Keisling, M. (2011). *Injustice at every turn: A report of the National Transgender Discrimination Survey.* Washington, DC: National Center for Transgender Equality and National Gay and Lesbian Task Force. Retrieved May 2019, from http://bit.do/eEoeB

Haas, A. P., Herman, J. L., &Rogers, P. L., & American Foundation for Suicide Prevention and Williams Institute, UCLA School of Law. (2014). *Suicide attempts among transgender and gender non-conforming adults.* Retrieved May 2019, from https://williamsinstitute.law.ucla.edu/wp-content/uploads/AFSP-Williams-Suicide-Report-Final.pdf

Hagen, W., Hoover, S., & Morrow, S. (2018). A grounded theory of sexual minority women and transgender individuals' social justice activism. *Journal of Homosexuality, 65*(7), 833–859. doi:10.1080/00918369.2017.1364562

Hall, K. Q. (2017). Queer epistemology and epistemic injustice. In I. Kidd, J. Medina, & G. Pohlhaus (Eds.), *The Routledge handbook of epistemic injustice* (pp. 158–166). London & New York, NY: Routledge.

## REFERENCES

Hankivsky, O. (2014). *Intersectionality 101* (p. 2). The Institute for Intersectionality Research & Policy, SFU. Retrieved from http://vawforum cwr.ca/sites/default/files/attachments/intersectionallity_101.pdf

Hatzenbuehler, M. L. (2009). How does sexual minority stigma "get under the skin?" A psychological mediation framework. *Psychological Bulletin, 135*(5), 707–730.

Heylens, G., Verroken, C., De Cock, S., T'Sjoen, G., & De Cuypere, G. (2013). Effects of different steps in gender reassignment therapy on psychopathology: A prospective study of persons with a gender identity disorder. *Journal of Sexual Medicine, 11*(1), 119–126.

Hill, D. B., & Willoughby, B. L. (2005). The development and validation of the Genderism and Transphobia Scale. *Sex Roles, 53*(7–8), 531–544. doi:10.1007/s11199-005-7140-x

History. (2018). *Stonewall Riots*. Retrieved May 2019, from https://www.history.com/topics/gay-rights/the-stonewall-riots

Hodžić, A., Poštić, J., & Kajtezović, A. (2016). The (in)visible T: Trans activism in Croatia (2004–2014). In B. Bilić & S. Kajinić (Eds.), *Intersectionality and LGBT activist politics: Multiple others in Croatia and Serbia*. London: UK: Palgrave Macmillan.

Hoff, L., & Hickling-Hudson, A. (2011). The role of International non-governmental organisations in promoting adult education for social change: A research agenda. *International Journal of Educational Development, 31*(2), 187–195. doi:10.1016/j.ijedudev.2010.03.005

hooks, b. (1981). *Ain't I a woman? Black women and feminism*. New York, NY: Routledge.

Hounsfield, V. L., Freedman, E., McNulty, A., & Bourne, C. (2007). Transgender people attending a Sydney sexual health service over a 16-year period. *Sex Health, 4*(3), 189–193.

Hunt, J. (2014). An initial study of transgender people's experiences of seeking and receiving counselling or psychotherapy in the UK. *Counselling and Psychotherapy Research, 14*(4), 288–296. doi:10.1080/14733145.2013.838597

Iceland Review. (2019). *Iceland's gender autonomy act is a step forward for trans and intersex rights*. Retrieved June 2019, from https://www.icelandreview.com/news/icelands-gender-autonomy-act-is-a-step-forward-for-trans-and-intersex-rights/

IGLYO. (2014). *Minimum standards to combat homophobic and transphobic bullying in education*. Retrieved from https://www.iglyo.com/wp-content/uploads/2015/09/Minimum-Standards.pdf

IGLYO. (2015). *Norm criticism toolkit*. Retrieved from https://www.iglyo.com/wp-content/uploads/2016/03/Norm-Toolkit-WEB.pdf

IGLYO. (2016). *No more hiding*. Retrieved May 2019, from https://www.iglyo.com/no-more-hiding/

IGLYO. (2018). *LGBTQI inclusive education report*. Retrieved May 2019, from https://www.iglyo.com/wp-content/uploads/2018/05/Education_Report_April_2018-4.pdf

IGLYO & OBESSU. (2014). *Guidelines for inclusive education: Sexual orientation, gender identity and gender expression*. Retrieved May 2019, from https://www.iglyo.com/wp-content/uploads/2015/09/2014-Inclusive-Education-Guidelines.pdf

IGLYO, OII Europe, & EPA. (2018). *Supporting your intersex child*. Retrieved May 2019, from https://www.iglyo.com/wp-content/uploads/2018/10/Supporting-Your-Intersex-Child.pdf

ILGA. (2017). *Trans legal mapping report*. Retrieved May 2019, from https://ilga.org/downloads/ILGA_Trans_Legal_Mapping_Report_2017_ENG.pdf

ILGA Europe. (2019a). *Rainbow map*. Retrieved May 2019, from https://www.ilga-europe.org/sites/default/files/Attachments/rainbowmap2019online_0_0.pdf

ILGA Europe. (2019b). *Annual review of the human rights situation of lesbian, gay, bisexual, tran and intersex people in Europe*. Retrieved May 2019, from https://www.ilga-europe.org/annualreview/2019

ILGA World. (2019). *Organizations from across the world have signed a joint statement and call to action to join with us in working together to fully dismantle pathologization*. Retrieved May 2019, from https://ilga.org/icd11-depathologizes-trans-gender-diverse-identities?fbclid=IwAR1sl2hY-_m7dW8crpAXNWeLd9YeYwyl-q3D1NqUQu-GyQRfn0gBF0ZmPwo

International Labour Organization (ILO). (2016). *Gender identity and sexual orientation: promoting rights, diversity and equality in the world of work, results of the ILO's PRIDE project*. Retrieved May 2019, from http://www.ilo.org/wcmsp5/groups/public/---dgreports/---gender/documents/briefingnote/wcms_481575.pdf

Israel, T., Gorcheva, R., Burnes, T. R., & Walther, W. A. (2008). Helpful and unhelpful therapy experiences of LGBT clients. *Psychotherapy Research, 18*(3), 294–305. doi:10.1080/10503300701506920

It Gets Better España. (n.d.). *Alianzas por la Diversidad (AxD)*. Retrieved May 2018, from http://www.itgetsbetter.es/alianzas-por-la-diversidad-axd/

James, S. E., Herman, J. L., Rankin, S., Keisling, M., Mottet, L., & Anafi, M. (2016). *The report of the 2015 U.S. Transgender Survey*. Washington, DC: National Center for Transgender Equality. Retrieved from http://www.transequality.org/sites/default/files/docs/usts/USTS%20Full%20Report%20-%20FINAL%201.6.17.pdf

Johnson, L. T. (2014). *Transgender college student activists: The intersections of identities* (Doctoral dissertation, 627). The University of Wisconsin-Milwaukee, Milwaukee, WI. Retrieved May 2019, from http://dc.uwm.edu/etd/627

Johnston, R. (2006). Adult learning for citizenship. Towards a reconstruction of the social purpose tradition. In P. Jarvis (Ed.), *From adult education to the learning society: 21 years from the international journal of lifelong education*. London: Routledge.

Johnson, R. (2017a). *Embodied social justice*. New York, NY: Routledge.

Johnson, R. (2017b). *Embodied activism*. Retrieved May 2019, from https://raejohnsonsomatic.com/2017/09/23/embodied-activism/

## REFERENCES

Joint United Nations Programme on HIV/AIDS (UNAIDS). (2014). *The gap report 2014: Transgender people.* Retrieved May 2019, from http://www.unaids.org/sites/default/files/media_asset/08_Transgenderpeople.pdf

Jones, T., Smith, E., Ward, R., Dixon, J., Hillier, L., & Mitchell, A. (2016). School experiences of transgender and gender diverse students in Australia. *Sex Education, 16*(2), 156–171. Retrieved from http://www.tandfonline.com/doi/full/10.1080/14681811.2015.1080678

Josselson, R. (2007). The ethical attitude in narrative research: Principles and practicalities. In D. J. Clandinin (Ed.), *Handbook of narrative inquiry: Mapping a methodology* (pp. 537–566). Thousand Oaks, CA: Sage Publications.

Karp, M., Holmes, P., & Bradshaw Tauvon, K. (Eds.). (1998). *The handbook of psychodrama.* London: Routledge.

Katz-Wise, S., Budge, S., Fugate, E., Flanagan, K., Touloumtzis, C., Rood, B., ... Leibowitz, S. (2017). Transactional pathways of transgender identity development in transgender and gender-nonconforming youth and caregiver perspectives from the Trans Youth Family Study. *International Journal of Transgenderism, 18*(3), 243–263. doi:10.1080/15532739.2017.1304312

Kira, I. A., Ashby, J. S., Lewandowski, L., Alawneh, A. W. N., Mohanesh, J., & Odenat, L. (2013). Advances in continuous traumatic stress theory: Traumatogenic dynamics and consequences of intergroup conflict: The Palestinian adolescents case. *Psychology, 4*(4), 396–409.

Klein, A., & Golub, S. (2016). Family rejection as a predictor of suicide attempts and substance misuse among transgender and gender nonconforming adults. *LGBT Health, 3*(3), 193–199. doi:10.1089/lgbt.2015.0111

Kolb, A. Y., & Kolb, D. A. (2012). Experiential learning theory. In N. M. Seel (Ed.), *Encyclopedia of the sciences of learning* (pp. 1215–1219). New York, NY: Springer.

Komives, S. R., Longerbeam, S. D., Owen, J. E., Mainella, F. C., & Osteen, L. (2006). A leadership identity development model: Applications from a grounded theory. *Journal of College Student Development, 47*(4), 401–418.

Komives, S. R., Lucas, N., & McMahon, T. R. (2007). *Exploring leadership: For college students who want to make a difference* (2nd ed.). San Francisco, CA: John Wiley & Sons.

Komives, S. R., Owen, J. E., Longerbeam, S. D., Mainella, F. C., & Osteen, L. (2005). Developing a leadership identity: A grounded theory. *Journal of College Student Development, 46*(6), 593–611. doi:10.1353/csd.2005.006

Kumashiro, K. (2000). Toward a theory of anti-oppressive education. *Review of Educational Research, 70*(1), 25–53.

Kuper, L. E., Nussbaum, R., & Mustanski, B. (2012). Exploring the diversity of gender and sexual orientation identities in an online sample of transgender individuals. *Journal of Sex Research, 49*(2–3), 244–254. doi:10.1080/00224499.2011.596954

Learning Outcomes Framework. (n.d.). Retrieved May 2019, from http://www.schoolslearningoutcomes.edu.mt/

Levitt, H. M., & Ippolito, M. R. (2014). Being transgender: The experience of transgender identity development. *Journal of Homosexuality, 61*(12), 1727–1758. doi:10.1080/0 0918369.2014.951262

Mack, L. (2010). The philosophical underpinnings of educational research. *Polyglossia, 19*, 5–11.

Marshall, E., Claes, L., Bouman, W., Witcomb, G., & Arcelus, J. (2015). Non-suicidal self-injury and suicidality in trans people: A systematic review of the literature. *International Review of Psychiatry, 28*(1), 58–69. doi:10.3109/09540261.2015.1073143

McAdams, D., & McLean, K. (2013). Narrative identity. *Current Directions in Psychological Science, 22*(3), 233–238. http://dx.doi.org/10.1177/0963721413475622

McAdams, D. P., Reynolds, J., Lewis, M., Patten, A. H., & Bowman, P. J. (2001). When bad things turn good and good things turn bad: Sequences of redemption and contamination in life narrative and then-relation to psychosocial adaptation in midlife adults and in students. *Personality and Social Psychology Bulletin, 27*(4), 474–485.

McCullough, R., Dispenza, F., Parker, L., Viehl, C., Chang, C., & Murphy, T. (2017). The counseling experiences of transgender and gender nonconforming clients. *Journal of Counseling & Development, 95*(4), 423–434. doi:10.1002/jcad.12157

McIntosh, P. (1999). White privilege: Unpacking the invisible knapsack. In E. Lee, D. Menkart, & M. Okazawa-Rey (Eds.), *Beyond heroes and holidays: A practical guide to K-12 anti-racist, multicultural education and staff development* (pp. 79–82). Washington, DC: Network of Educators on the Americas.

McKinney, J. (2005). On the margins: A study of the experiences of transgender college students. *Journal of Gay & Lesbian Issues in Education, 3*(1), 63–75. doi:10.1300/ J367v03n01_07

McNeil, J., Bailey, L., Ellis, S., Morton, J., & Regan, M. (2012) *Trans mental health and emotional wellbeing study*. Retrieved May 2019, from http://www.gires.org.uk/ assets/Medpro-Assets/trans_mh_study.pdf

Meyer, D. (2010). Evaluating the severity of hate-motivated violence: Intersectional differences among LGBT hate crime victims. *Sociology, 44*(5), 980–995.

Meyer, I. H. (2003). Prejudice, social stress, and mental health in lesbian, gay and bisexual populations: Conceptual issues and research evidence. *Psychological Bulletin, 129*(5), 674–697.

Meyer, M. D. E. (2004). "We're too afraid of these imaginary tensions": Student organizing in lesbian, gay, bisexual and transgender campus communities. *Communication Studies, 55*(4), 499–514.

Mezirow, J. (2000). Learning to think like an adult. Core concepts of transformation theory. In J. Mezirow & Associates (Eds.), *Learning as transformation. Critical perspectives on a theory in progress* (pp. 3–33). San Francisco, CA: Jossey-Bass.

Miles, B. M., & Huberman, A. M. (1994). *Qualitative data analysis: An expanded sourcebook*. Los Angeles, CA: Sage Publications.

Miller, K. L., Miller, S. M., & Stull, J. C. (2007). Predictors of counselor educators' cultural discriminatory behaviors. *Journal of Counseling and Development, 85*(3), 325–336. doi:10.1002/j.1556-6678.2007.tb00481.x

Ministry for Education and Employment. (2013). *Guidelines on sexuality and relationships education in Maltese Schools*. Retrieved May 2019, from https://education.gov.mt/en/resources/Documents/Policy%20Documents%20 2014/Guidelines%20on%20Sexuality%20booklet.pdf

Ministry for Education and Employment. (2014a). *Addressing bullying behaviour in schools policy*. Retrieved May 2019, from https://education.gov.mt/en/Documents/ Addressing%20Bullying%20Behaviour%20in%20Schools.pdf

Ministry for Education and Employment. (2014b). *Education strategy for Malta 2014–2024*. Retrieved May 2019, from https://education.gov.mt/en/resources/ Documents/Policy%20Documents%202014/BOOKLET%20ESM%202014-2024% 20ENG%2019-02.pdf

Ministry for Education and Employment. (2014c). *Respect for all framework*. Retrieved May 2019, from https://education.gov.mt/en/resources/News/Documents/ Respect%20For%20All%20Document.pdf

Ministry for Education and Employment. (2015). *Trans, gender variant and intersex students in schools policy*. Retrieved May 2019, from https://education.gov.mt/en/ resources/Documents/Policy%20Documents/Trans,%20Gender%20Variant%20 and%20Intersex%20Students%20in%20Schools%20Policy.pdf

Ministry for Home Affairs and National Security. (2016). *Trans, gender variant & intersex inmates policy*. Retrieved May 2019, from https://homeaffairs.gov.mt/en/media/ Policies-Documents/Pages/-Trans-Gender-Variant--Intersex-Inmates-Policy.aspx

Mol, S. L., Arntz, A., Metsemakers, J. M., Dinant, G., Vilters-Van Montfort, P. P., & Knottnerus, J. (2005). Symptoms of post-traumatic stress disorder after non-traumatic events: Evidence from an open population study. *British Journal of Psychiatry, 186*(6), 494–499.

Moradi, B., Tebbe, E. A., Brewster, M. E., Budge, S. L., Lenzen, A., Ege, E., & Flores, M. J. (2016). A content analysis of literature on trans people and issues: 2002–2012. *The Counseling Psychologist, 44*(7), 960–995.

Moreno, J. L. (1956). The dilemma of existentialism, Daseinsanalyse and the psychodrama. *International Journal of Sociometry, 1*(1), 55–63.

Morgan, S. W., & Stevens, P. E. (2012). Transgender identity development as represented by a group of transgendered adults. *Issues in Mental Health Nursing, 33*(5), 301–308.

Morrow, S. L., & Smith, M. L. (2000). Qualitative research for counseling psychology. In S. D. Brown & R. W. Lent (Eds.), *Handbook of counseling psychology* (pp. 199–230). New York, NY: John Wiley & Sons.

Movement Advancement Project and Center for American Progress (MAPCAP). (2015). *Paying an unfair price: The financial penalty for being transgender in*

*America*. Retrieved May 2019, from http://www.lgbtmap.org/file/paying-an-unfair-price-transgender.pdf

Nadal, K. L., Davidoff, K. C., Davis, L. S., & Wong, Y. (2014). Emotional, behavioral, and cognitive reactions to microaggressions: Transgender perspectives. *Psychology of Sexual Orientation and Gender Diversity, 1*(1), 72–81.

Nadal, K., Issa, M., Leon, J., Meterko, V., Wideman, M., & Wong, Y. (2011). Sexual orientation microaggressions: "Death by a Thousand Cuts" for lesbian, gay, and bisexual youth. *Journal of LGBT Youth, 8*(3), 234–259.

Nadal, K. L., Rivera, D. P., & Corpus, M. J. H. (2010). Sexual orientation and transgender microaggressions in everyday life: Experiences of lesbians, gays, bisexuals, and transgender individuals. In D. W. Sue (Ed.), *Microaggressions and marginality: Manifestation, dynamics, and impact* (pp. 217–240). New York, NY: Wiley.

Nadal, K., Skolnik, A., & Wong, Y. (2012). Interpersonal and systemic microaggressions toward transgender people: Implications for counseling. *Journal of LGBT Issues in Counseling, 6*(1), 55–82.

National Coalition of Anti-Violence Programs (NCAVP). (2016). *Lesbian, gay, bisexual, transgender, queer, and HIV-affected hate violence in 2016*. New York, NY: New York City Gay and Lesbian Anti-Violence Project, Inc. Retrieved May 2019, from https://avp.org/wp-content/uploads/2017/06/NCAVP_2016HateViolence_REPORT.pdf

Netflix. (2017). *The death and life of Marsha P. Johnson*. Retrieved May 2019, from https://www.netflix.com/title/80189623

Nishida, A. (2016). Understanding political development through an intersectionality framework: Life stories of disability activists. *Disability Studies Quarterly, 36*(2). doi:10.18061/dsq.v36i2.4449

Norwegian Ministry of Children and Equality. (2017). *Safety, diversity, openness – The Norwegian Government's action plan against discrimination based on sexual orientation, gender identity and gender expression (2017–2020)*. Retrieved May 2019, from https://www.regjeringen.no/en/dokumenter/action-plan-against-discrimination-based-on-sexual-orientation-gender-identity-and-gender-expression/id2505393/

Office of the United Nations High Commissioner for Human Rights (OHCHR). (1966). *International covenant on economic, social and cultural rights*. Retrieved May 2019, from https://www.ohchr.org/en/professionalinterest/pages/cescr.aspx

Office of the United Nations High Commissioner for Human Rights (OHCHR). (2015). *Joint UN statement on Ending violence and discrimination against lesbian, gay, bisexual, transgender and intersex people*. Retrieved May 2019, from https://www.ohchr.org/EN/Issues/Discrimination/Pages/JointLGBTIstatement.aspx

# REFERENCES

Office of the United Nations High Commissioner for Human Rights (OHCHR). (2016a). *Living free and equal.* New York, NY & Geneva. Retrieved May 2019, from https://www.ohchr.org/Documents/Publications/LivingFreeAndEqual.pdf

Office of the United Nations High Commissioner for Human Rights (OHCHR). (2016b). *Pathologization: Being lesbian, gay, bisexual and/or trans is not an illness, statement for the International Day against Homophobia, Transphobia and Biphobia.* Retrieved May 2019, from https://www.ohchr.org/EN/NewsEvents/Pages/DisplayNews.aspx?NewsID=19956&LangID=E

O'Hara, C., Dispenza, F., Brack, G., & Blood, R. A. C. (2013). The preparedness of counselors in training to work with transgender clients: A mixed methods investigation. *Journal of LGBT Issues in Counseling, 7*(3), 236-256. https://doi.org/10.1080/15538605.2013.812929

Organization for Security and Co-operation in Europe (OSCE). (2018). *OSCE rapporteur's report under the Moscow mechanism on alleged human rights violations and impunity in the Chechen Republic of the Russian Federation.* Retrieved May 2019, from https://www.osce.org/odihr/407402?download=true

O'Sullivan, Edmund (2002). The project and vision of transformative education. Integral transformative learning. In E. O'Sullivan, A. Morrel, & M. A. Connor (Eds.), *Expanding the boundaries of transformative learning.* Basingstoke & New York, NY: Palgrave.

PBS (Producer). (2019). *Stonewall uprising. American experience.* Retrieved May 2019, from http://www.pbs.org/wgbh/americanexperience/films/stonewall/

Pearce, R. (2012) Inadvertent praxis: What can "genderfolk" tell us about trans feminism? *MP: An Online Feminist Journal, 3*(4), 87–129.

Pines, A. (1994). Burnout in political activism: An existential perspective. *Journal of Health and Human Resources Administration, 164*, 381–394.

Plyler, J. (2006). How to keep on keeping on: Sustaining ourselves in community organizing and social justice struggles. *Upping the Ante, 3*, 123–134.

Pohlhaus, Jr., G. (2012). Relational knowing and epistemic injustice: Toward a theory of willful hermeneutical ignorance. *Hypatia: Journal of Feminist Philosophy, 27*(4), 715–735.

Prasad, P. (2005). *Crafting qualitative research: Working in the postpositivist traditions.* New York, NY: M. E. Sharpe.

Pratt-Clarke, M. (2010). *Critical race, feminism, and education.* New York, NY: Palgrave Macmillan.

Pulice-Farrow, L., Brown, T. D., & Galupo, M. P. (2017a). Transgender microaggressions in the context of romantic relationships. *Psychology of Sexual Orientation and Gender Diversity, 4*(3), 362–373.

Pulice-Farrow, L., Clements, Z. A., & Galupo, M. P. (2017b). Patterns of transgender microaggressions in friendship: The role of gender identity. *Psychology & Sexuality, 8*(3), 189–207.

Rachlin, K. (2002). Transgender individuals' experiences of psychotherapy. *International Journal of Transgenderism, 6*(1).

Rahilly, E. (2015). The gender binary meets the gender-variant child: Parents' negotiations with childhood gender variance. *Gender and Society, 29*(3), 338–361. doi:10.1177/0891243214563069

Rankin, S. R. (2003). *Campus climate for gay, lesbian, bisexual, and transgender people: A national perspective.* New York, NY: The National Gay and Lesbian Task Force Policy Institute. Retrieved May 2019, from https://www.whoi.edu/cms/files/CampusClimate_23425.pdf

Rankin, S. R. (2005). Campus climates for sexual minorities. In R. L. Sanlo (Ed.), *Gender identity and sexual orientation: Research, policy, and personal perspectives. New directions for student services* (pp. 17–23). San Francisco, CA: Jossey-Bass.

Reed, G. M., Correia, J. M., Esparza, P., Saxena, S., & Maj, M (2011). The WPA-WHO global survey of psychiatrists' attitudes towards mental disorders classification. *World Psychiatry, 10*(2), 118–131.

Reicher, S. (2004). The context of social identity: Domination, resistance, and change. *Political Psychology, 25*(6), 921–945.

Reisner, S. L., Poteat, T., Keatley, J., Cabral, M., Mothopeng, T., Dunham, E., ... Baral, S. D. (2016). Global health burden and needs of transgender populations: A review. *The Lancet, 388*(10042), 412–436. Retrieved May 2019, from http://www.thelancet.com/journals/lancet/article/PIIS0140-6736(16)00684-X/abstract

Renn, K. A. (2007). LGBT student leaders and queer activists: Identities of lesbian, gay, bisexual, transgender, and queer-identified college student leaders and activists. *Journal of College Student Development, 48*(3), 311–330.

Renn, K. A., & Bilodeau, B. L. (2005a). Leadership identity development among lesbian, gay, bisexual and transgender student leaders. *NASPA Journal, 42*(3), 342–367.

Renn, K. A., & Bilodeau, B. L. (2005b). Queer student leaders: An exploratory case study of identity development and LGBT student involvement at a Midwestern research university. *Journal of Gay and Lesbian Issues in Education, 2*(4), 49–71.

Renn, K. A., & Ozaki, C. K. (2005). *Student leaders in identity-based campus contexts.* Paper presented at a meeting of the Association for the Study of Higher Education, Philadelphia, PA.

Riessman, C. K. (1993). *Narrative analysis.* Newbury Park, CA: Sage Publications.

Riggs, D. W., Taylor, N., Signal, T., Fraser, H., & Donovan, C. (2018). People of diverse genders and/or sexualities and their animal companions: Experience of family violence in a bi-national sample. *Journal of Family Issues, 39*(18).

Rodgers, K. (2010). "Anger is why we're all here": Mobilizing and managing emotions in a professional activist organization. *Social Movement Studies, 9*(3), 273–291.

Rossiter, M. (1999). A narrative approach to development: Implications for adult education. *Adult Education Quarterly, 50*(1), 56–71. http://dx.doi.org/10.1177/07417139922086911

Saldaña, J. (2009). *The coding manual for qualitative researchers*. Thousand Oaks, CA, Sage Publications.

Savage, J. (2011). *Cross-curricular teaching and learning in the secondary school* (1st ed., p. 8). New York, NY: Routledge.

Schaufeli, W., & Buunk, B. (2002). Burnout: An overview of 25 years of research and theorizing. In M. Schabracq, J. Winnubst, & C. Cooper (Eds.), *The handbook of work and health psychology* (pp. 383–425). Hoboken, NJ: Wiley.

Scott, M. J., & Stradling, S. G. (1994). Post-traumatic stress disorder without the trauma. *British Journal of Clinical Psychology, 33*(3), 71–74.

Serano, J. (2007). *Whipping girl: A transsexual woman on sexism and the scapegoating of femininity*. Emeryville, CA: Seal Press.

Shelton, K., & Delgado-Romero, E. A. (2011). Sexual orientation microaggressions: The experience of lesbian, gay, bisexual, and queer clients in psychotherapy. *Journal of Counseling Psychology, 58*, 210–221. doi:10.1037/a0022251

Shipherd, J. C., Green, K. E., & Abramovitz, S. (2010). Transgender clients: Identifying and minimizing barriers to mental health treatment. *Journal of Gay & Lesbian Mental Health, 14*(2), 94–108. doi:10.1080/19359701003622875

Smith, J., Breakwell, G., & Wright, D. (2012). *Research methods in psychology*. London: Sage.

Smith, W. A., Allen, W. R., & Danley, L. L. (2007). "Assume the position ... you fit the description": Psychosocial experiences and racial battle fatigue among African American male college students. *American Behavioral Scientist, 51*(4), 551–578.

Sperber, J., Landers, S., & Lawrence, S. (2005). Access to health care for transgendered persons: Results of a needs assessment in Boston. *International Journal of Transgenderism, 8*(2–3), 75–91. doi:10.1300/J485v08n02_08

Stone, A. (2009). More than adding a T: American lesbian and gay activists' attitudes toward transgender inclusion. *Sexualities, 12*(3), 334–354. doi:10.1177/1363460709103894

Stotzer, R. L. (2008). Gender identity and hate crimes: Violence against transgender people in Los Angeles county. *Sexuality Research & Social Policy: A Journal of the NSRC, 5*(1), 43–52.

Sue, D. W., Capodilupo, C. M., Torino, G. C., Bucceri, J. M., Holder, A., Nadal, K. L., & Esquilin, M. (2007). Racial microaggressions in everyday life: Implications for clinical practice. *American Psychologist, 62*(4), 271–286. doi:10.1037/0003066X.62.4.271

Sullivan, N. (2006). *A critical introduction to queer theory.* Edinburgh: Edinburgh University Press.

Sylvia Rivera Law Project. (2019). Retrieved May 2019 from https://srlp.org/

The Affirmation of Sexual Orientation, Gender Identity and Gender Expression Act. (2016). Retrieved May 2019, from https://goo.gl/DlHa1G

Theoharis, G. (2007). Social justice educational leaders and resistance: Toward a theory of social justice leadership. *Educational Administration Quarterly, 43*(2), 221–258. https://doi.org/10.1177/0013161X06293717

Transgender Europe (TGEU). (2016a). *Legal gender recognition in Europe* (2nd version). Retrieved from http://tgeu.org/wp-content/uploads/2017/02/Toolkit16LR.pdf

Transgender Europe (TGEU). (2016b). *Sex work policy.* Retrieved May 2019, from https://tgeu.org/wp-content/uploads/2016/11/TGEU_SexWorkPolicy_en.pdf

Transgender Europe (TGEU). (2017a). *The vicious circle of violence: Trans and gender-diverse people, migration, and sex work* (TvT Publication Series, Vol. 16). Retrieved May 2019, from https://transrespect.org/wp-content/uploads/2018/01/TvT-PS-Vol16-2017.pdf

Transgender Europe (TGEU). (2017b). *Overdiagnosed but underserved: Trans healthcare in Georgia, Poland, Serbia, Spain, and Sweden: Trans health survey.* Retrieved from http://tgeu.org/wp-content/uploads/2017/10/Overdiagnosed_Underserved-TransHealthSurvey.pdf

Transgender Europe (TGEU). (2017c). *Human rights victory! European court of human rights ends forced sterilisation.* Retrieved from http://tgeu.org/echr_end-sterilisation/

Transgender Europe (TGEU). (2018a). *World Health Organisation moves to end classifying trans identities as mental illness.* Retrieved May 2019, from http://tgeu.org/world-health-organisation-moves-to-end-classifying-trans-identities-as-mental-illness/

Transgender Europe (TGEU). (2018b). *Trans rights Europe map & index 2018.* Retrieved May 2019, from https://tgeu.org/trans-rights-map-2018/

Transgender Legal Defense Project. (2018). *Transgender people in Russian society: Research 2016–2017.* Retrieved May 2019, from http://bit.do/eSaoe

TvT Research Project. (2018). *Trans murder monitoring results: TMM update 2018.* Retrieved May 2019, from https://transrespect.org/wp-content/uploads/2018/11/TvT_TMM_TDoR2018_Tables_EN.pdf

United Nations (UN). (1966). *The international covenant on civil and political rights.* Retrieved May 2019, from https://treaties.un.org/doc/publication/unts/volume%20999/volume-999-i-14668-english.pdf

United Nations (UN). (2015). *Universal declaration of human rights.* Retrieved May 2019, from https://www.un.org/en/udhrbook/pdf/udhr_booklet_en_web.pdf

United Nations (UN). (2018). *Protection against violence and discrimination based on sexual orientation and gender identity.* A/73/152. Retrieved May 2019, from https://www.un.org/en/ga/search/view_doc.asp?symbol=A/73/152

## REFERENCES

United Nations Educational, Scientific and Cultural Organization (UNESCO). (2016a). *Call for action by ministers – Inclusive and equitable education for all learners in an environment free from discrimination and violence*. Retrieved May 2019, from https://unesdoc.unesco.org/ark:/48223/pf0000246247

United Nations Educational, Scientific and Cultural Organization (UNESCO). (2016b). *Out in the open: Education sector responses to violence based on sexual orientation and gender identity/expression*. Retrieved May 2019, from http://unesdoc.unesco.org/images/0024/002447/244756e.pdf

United Nations Human Rights Council (UNHRC). (2012). *Report of the Special Rapporteur on violence against women, its causes and consequences, Rashida Manjoo*. A/HRC/20/16. Retrieved May 2019, from http://www.ohchr.org/documents/issues/women/a.hrc.20.16_en.pdf

United Nations Human Rights Council (UNHRC). (2017). *Report of the Special Rapporteur on the right of everyone to the enjoyment of the highest attainable standard of physical and mental health*. Retrieved May 2019, from https://documents-dds-ny.un.org/doc/UNDOC/GEN/G17/076/04/PDF/G1707604.pdf?OpenElement

USA Today. (2019). *Marsha P. Johnson: Transgender hero of Stonewall riots finally gets her due*. Retrieved May 2019 https://www.usatoday.com/story/news/investigations/2019/03/27/black-history-marsha-johnson-and-stonewall-riots/2353538002/

Venn, C. (2006). *The postcolonial challenge: Towards alternative worlds*. London: Sage.

Von Doussa, H., Power, J., & Riggs, D. (2017). Family matters: transgender and gender diverse peoples' experience with family when they transition. *Journal of Family Studies*, 1–14. doi:10.1080/13229400.2017.1375965

Walker, M. (2010). *What is reparative justice?* Milwaukee, WI: Marquette University Press.

Whittle, S., Turner, L., & Al-Alami, M. (2007). Engendered penalties: Transgender and transsexual people's experiences of inequality and discrimination. *The Equalities Review*. Retrieved May 2019, from http://www.pfc.org.uk/pdf/EngenderedPenalties.pdf

WHO & BZgA. (2017). *Sexuality education lessons learned and future developments in the WHO region*. Retrieved May 2019, from https://www.bzga-whocc.de/fileadmin/user_upload/Dokumente/BZgA_Conference_Report_Online_fin.pdf

Whose Streets Our Streets. (2019). *Christopher St. Liberation Day, 1973*. Retrieved May, 2019, from https://whosestreetsourstreets.org/washington-square-park/

Wilchins, R., Lombardi, E., Priesing, D., & Malouf, D. (1997). *The first national survey on trans violence*. New York, NY: Gender Public Advocacy Coalition.

Winter, S. (2012). *Lost in transition: Transgender people, rights and HIV vulnerability in the Asia-Pacific region*. Thailand: UNDP Asia Pacific Regional Center. Retrieved May 2019, from http://www.undp.org/content/dam/undp/library/hivaids/Lost%20in%20translation.pdf

World Health Organization (WHO). (2014). *Eliminating forced, coercive and otherwise involuntary sterilization: An interagency statement.* Retrieved May 2019, from https://apps.who.int/iris/bitstream/handle/10665/112848/9789241507325_eng.pdf?sequence=1&isAllowed=y

World Health Organization (WHO). (2015a). *Technical brief: HIV and young transgender people.* Retrieved May 2019, from http://www.unaids.org/sites/default/files/media_asset/2015_young_transgender_en.pdf

World Health Organization (WHO). (2015b). *Transgender people and HIV* (Policy brief). Retrieved May 2019, from http://apps.who.int/iris/bitstream/10665/179517/1/WHO_HIV_2015.17_eng.pdf?ua=1&ua=1

World Health Organization (WHO). (2019a). *ICD-11 for mortality and morbidity statistics, version 04/2019.* Retrieved May 2019, from https://icd.who.int/browse11/l-m/en#/http%3a%2f%2fid.who.int%2ficd%2fentity%2f411470068

World Health Organization (WHO). (2019b). World Health Assembly update, 25 May 2019. Retrieved May 2019, from https://www.who.int/news-room/detail/25-05-2019-world-health-assembly-update

Yadegarfard, M., Meinhold-Bergmann, M.E., & Ho, R. (2014). Family rejection, social isolation, and loneliness as predictors of negative health outcomes (depression, suicidal ideation, and sexual risk behavior) among Thai male-to-female transgender adolescents. *Journal of LGBT Youth, 11*(4), 347–363.

Yogyakarta Principles. (2007). Retrieved May 2019 from http://data.unaids.org/pub/manual/2007/070517_yogyakarta_principles_en.pdf

Yogyakarta Principles Plus 10. (2017). Retrieved May 2019 from http://yogyakartaprinciples.org/principles-en/yp10/

YouTube. (2019). *Sylvia Rivera 1973: Y'all better quiet down.* Retrieved May 2019, from https://www.youtube.com/watch?v=DRAQ9AX8F2A

Zamani-Gallaher, E., & Choudhuri, D. (2016). Tracing LGBTQ community college students' experiences. *New Directions for Community Colleges, 2016*(174), 47–63. http://dx.doi.org/10.1002/cc.20202

Printed in the United States
By Bookmasters